JAMAICA
BETRAYED

JAMAICA BETRAYED

Institutional Failure in a Caribbean Setting

Locksley I Lindo

ARAWAK
publications
KINGSTON, JAMAICA

A r a w a k publications
17 Kensington Crescent
Kingston 5

ISBN 976 8189 17 7

06 05 04 03 02   5 4 3 2 1

NATIONAL LIBRARY OF JAMAICA CATALOGUING IN PUBLICATION DATA

Lindo, Locksley
        Jamaica betrayed : institutional failure in a Caribbean setting

p. ;   cm.
Bibliography : p.   . – Includes index

ISBN 976 8189 17 7

1.   Jamaica – Politics and government – 1962 -
2.   Jamaica – Social conditions – 1962 - I. Title

972.9206 - dc.20

Credits:

cover concept: Julie Coulton
cover photographs: Ray Chen
Cover and book design: Errol Stennett

Set in Galliard 10.5/13 x 24
Printed in Jamaica by Pear Tree Press

The author dedicates this work to his grandchildren Jeana, Frances, Marisa, Katya, Leslie and another not yet born and to all the children of Jamaica. They deserve a better future.

Contents

Preface / ix
Acknowledgments / xii
List of Abbreviations / xiii

INTRODUCTION / 1

CHAPTER ONE:
CONTEMPORARY JAMAICA: THE SYMPTOMS / 17
I: Institutions / 17
II: Failure of Economic Development Initiatives / 28

CHAPTER TWO:
NATIONAL AIMS AND OBJECTIVES / 39
I: Emerging National Society / 39
II: National Aims and Objectives / 42
III: The Ordinary People of Jamaica / 46
IV: Aspects of Social Structure / 54

CHAPTER THREE:
TOOLS FOR ACHIEVEMENT / 60
I: Available Institutions / 60
II: Political Parties / 63
III: The Political Culture / 68
IV: Power Distribution / 76
V: Sectors of the Economy / 77

CHAPTER FOUR:
OUTCOMES AND CONSEQUENCES / 86
I: Economic Results / 86
II: Image and Appearance / 99
III: The System of Justice / 104

CHAPTER FIVE:
PERCEPTIONS, ATTITUDES AND VALUES / 111
I: Systems Theory / 113
II: Cultural Influences / 116
III: Norms, Standards and Expected Behaviour / 124

CHAPTER SIX:
THE INSTITUTIONALIZATION OF POVERTY *or*
THE INCOME-LESS SOCIETY: OVERVIEW, HISTORY
AND DEFINITIONS / 138
I. Symptoms and Effects / 140
II: Sources and Causes / 149
III: Breaking the Cycle of Poverty / 152
IV: The Creation of Wealth / 157

CHAPTER SEVEN:
ADMINISTRATIVE IMPACT TODAY / 167
I: National Development / 168
II: Entrepreneurship and Private Sector Theory / 176
III: The Constitution and House of Representatives / 184

CHAPTER EIGHT:
CREATING THE NEW POLITICAL CULTURE / 196
I: Aims and Objectives / 196
II: The Obstacles: the Character of the Parties / 206
III: : The Team and its Leadership / 208
IV: Psychological and Behavioural Realities / 215
V: Organization, Strategies and Tactics / 220

References / 228
Index / 238

Preface

The major theme of this work is the almost complete failure of all Jamaican institutions in the 1990s, which has created a state of social and economic chaos. The collapse was most spectacular in the financial sector, but many other organizations and institutions did not fare much better. The work also discusses the inability to function of many of Jamaica's organizations and institutions, including the system of justice and law, the constitution, the economy and the public and the private sectors. These can be traced to a single source, the political culture and value system which has evolved over the past sixty years or so in Jamaica. This political culture has caused deformities in every single institution in the country, including the major political parties. The behaviour of the political parties, in turn, has reinforced the political culture. The means has become the end. The democratic power of the People has been displaced by the oligarchic power of the Party.

The Introduction to the work sets the philosophical background as the working of a medieval morality play between *Power* and *People*. Chapter one, entitled "Contemporary Jamaica: the Symptoms", describes the state of the institutions of the country. The themes include the form and substance of political regimes, the role of leadership and the notion of accountability in the face of overwhelming power. The topic of governance in the light of the Constitution, and its failure to guarantee the rights and freedoms of the people, are touched on in this chapter. Two sections on the socialization process engendered by the political culture and its impact on the failure of the economy bring this chapter to a close.

Chapter two, "National Aims and Objectives", demonstrates the choices that were available to our founding fathers as to the type of society they wanted Jamaica to be. The chapter shows how short-term considerations and invalid assumptions about the nature of the majority of the Jamaican people led to a policy of welfare and handouts for the poor and privileges and patronage for the rich, which is still present as government policy some 60 years after. This deliberate turning away from the ideas and ideals of Marcus Garvey represents a betrayal of the hopes and aspirations of the Jamaican people and accounts for the title of the book.

Chapters three ("Tools for Achievement") and four ("Outcomes and Consequences") depict the consequences of the interaction of the wrong aims and objectives with the wrong tools. The tools devised and introduced post 1938 included the two major political parties, the trade unions, the 1944 Constitution (followed, in due course, by the Independence Constitution) and the political culture which justified the practices of these institutions. How sensitive an issue any criticism of the political culture might be, can be attested to by the fact that Roger Mais was prosecuted and jailed for publishing an opinion that the 1944 Constitution was designed to maintain the colonial system.

Chapter five, "Perception, Attitudes and Values", shows how the experience of the Jamaican people over these 60 years has acculturated them into a unique blend of attitudes and values. The very people whose behaviour in the past has contributed to the formation of the attitudes and values deplore these attitudes. Subjecting the same people to another set of more positive experiences, over a roughly similar time period, can only change them.

Chapter six, "The Institutionalization of Poverty or the Income-less Society", describes the result of the welfare and handout policy that has been the major feature of the political culture over the past 60 years, even during the golden years of the 1950s and 1960s. More efforts have been made at poverty alleviation than at wealth creation. Charity and handouts, especially at election time, have greatly contributed to leading the ordinary people away from the habits and opportunities for the creation and distribution of wealth. This chapter also examines the nature of economic growth as distinct from that of economic development and concludes that welfare and handouts can never break the cycle of poverty.

Chapter seven, "Administrative Impact Today", examines the effects of the political culture on national development, the private sector, creativity and entrepreneurship and economic development. The chapter generally considers the question of the nature of the private sector and the other institutions set up to undertake the development process. It also considers how the political culture influences the culture of organizations in general and makes the government's administrative arm, the civil service, quite ineffective for the task. It takes a critical look at how the Constitution and Parliament have evolved under that culture.

The last chapter, "Creating the New Political Culture", handles the themes of reform, renewal and regeneration in different ways and examines the feasibility of certain interventions into the current culture. The revolution must be one of changes in attitudes, values and behaviour. It sums up what needs to be done by introducing a completely new paradigm and a way of thinking which has been fatally absent from the Caribbean ever since colonial times. The chapter introduces some simple strategies which, if followed, should be the key to genuine political reform and have a lasting effect on the fortunes of the country.

The basis for this book is some one thousand citations from newspaper reports, letters, editorials and articles collected mainly between February and September 1988. Virtually all the relevant opinions and views of a small sample of literate citizens who are also lucky to have their work published in the newspapers have been examined. Contributions from professional and part time reporters and correspondents have supplemented these sources. The second source is the usual scholarly references from periodicals, magazines and books. Unfortunately, much of the work which should be of interest to the ordinary citizen remains buried in the pages of books in libraries and has no impact on public debate.

The author considers this book to be his personal interpretation of events he has lived through for more than 60 years. It does not claim objectivity and detachment in its approach. While taking every care not to misrepresent any verifiable facts, he perfectly understands and accepts the risks attendant upon departing from the orthodox analytical framework and thinking 'outside the box'. Any errors and fallacies that remain must therefore be charged to his account.

Throughout the endnotes, the numbers after the name refer to the alphabetically ordered list of books and articles appended at page 239 below. For example, Lee Kuan Yew, *The Singapore Story: Memoirs of Lee Kuan Yew*. Singapore: Times Editions, 1998, is simply referred to as Lee Kuan Yew, 66.

Locksley I Lindo
March 2002

Acknowledgments

The author would like to acknowledge the help of his numerous friends and colleagues who discussed many of the preceding ideas with him, sometimes very passionately, and read parts of the arguments as they developed. While they did no formal evaluation of the complete text, they nevertheless saved him from gratuitous errors of fact and argument, which, if not removed, would have rendered this volume less than useful.

In particular he would like to acknowledge the help and encouragement of Professor Sir Roy Augier, Donny Miller, Wilberne Persaud, Byron Noble, Diaram Ramjeesingh, Noel Cowell, Patrick Stephens, Gordon Shirley, Alvin Wint, Ann Crick, Hilary Hickling, Wolfgang Grassl and Hilton McDavid, among the author's University colleagues, provided insights and challenging criticisms on occasion. He must thank Miss Julia Tan, Dr Lee Kum Tat and Mr Leong Sze Hian, Honorary Consul of Jamaica in Singapore for their insights into Singaporean life, and Dr Earl Carr, Jamaican Ambassador to Japan, for facilitating the interviews in Singapore. Thanks are due to the University of the West Indies for granting him a Sabbatical year in 1998/99 to enable him to start the writing phase of the project.

On the home front he would like to record his gratitude to his wife Pauline who endured many discussions and rehearsals of arguments even at the most inappropriate of times. He would also like to acknowledge the help of his daughter Julie, who provided the original concept for the cover design, and his sons Terence and Derek, who encouraged the project and undertook some of the promotion and marketing.

To the publisher, Pansy Benn of Arawak publications and the anonymous reader, now revealed to be his former student, Wes Van Riel, who saw the possibilities in an earlier, rambling version of the work, he records his gratitude. The reader's initial critique led to a substantial reworking and reducing of the original draft to manageable proportions. If there are any defects still left, they must be charged to the author's account.

Abbreviations

ALCAN	Aluminum Company of Canada
BCG	Boston Consulting Group
CAFFE	Citizens' Action for Free and Fair Elections
CARICOM	Caribbean Community
CPA	Certified Public Accountant
Edu-Tech	Educational Technology
FINSAC	Financial Sector Adjustment Company Limited
GDP	gross domestic product
GNP	gross national product
HEART	Human Employment and Resource Training
IBM	International Business Machines
ILO	International Labour Organization
IMF	International Monetary Fund
JAMPRO	Jamaica Promotions Ltd.
JLP	Jamaica Labour Party
JMA	Jamaica Manufacturers Association
LOJ	Life of Jamaica (Insurance Company)
MP	Member of Parliament
MPM	Metropolitan Parks and Markets
NDM	National Democratic Movement
NIRs	Net International Reserves
NTA	National Training Agency
NTS	National Training Service
OAS	Organization of American States
PAHO	Pan American Health Organization
PAP	People's Action Party (Singapore)
PNP	People's National Party
PSOJ	Private Sector Organization of Jamaica
SDC	Social Development Commission
STATIN	Statistical Institute of Jamaica
TNCs	transnational corporations
UNESCO	United Nations Educational, Scientific and Cultural Organization
UNO	United Nations Organization
UTECH	University of Technology
UWI	University of the West Indies

Introduction

In the battle 'twixt People and Power
Some folks must inevitably cower
For sheer Power if rife
Leads to warfare and strife
And the standard of living gets lower

All history is the interplay of two themes and two themes only: *Power* and *People*. All other so-called themes are derived from these two. Orthodox historians mainly concerned themselves with the first theme and primarily with that aspect of *Power*, which manifested itself and was embodied in the state. Hence the preoccupation with kings and queens and a wide variety of characters who challenged, successfully or unsuccessfully, the existing institution through which the power was wielded, whether monarchy, republic, dictatorship, protectorate, feudal and ecclesiastical systems, socialism, capitalism, communism, liberal democracy or all the other institutional forms into which state power, like Proteus, can transform itself.

The other theme, *People*, was treated as a sort of backdrop against which the struggles for state power were played out, fulfilling the role, in modern theatrical parlance, of noises off, or extras. To give them credit, orthodox historians have recognized the vital role that people play in providing the means by which the *materiel* and the energy for the pursuit of the power play can be supplied.

In Japan the peasants and farmers ranked very high in the order of society, since they provided both the food and the manpower so desperately needed by the warrior (and the ruling) class. Other historians, including some in the Caribbean, are beginning to realize that the roles the people play should be brought more to the centre of the stage, since the truth, that real power is derived from the people, is something which some political ideologists have recognized in theory, but rarely put into practice. This is indeed so, since the people provide the means, willingly or unwillingly, through taxes and other impositions, such as volunteer service in a military undertaking or just working at their ordinary jobs, in creating and maintaining the wealth to pay for the play of the potentates.[1]

The tale of the interaction between *Power* and *People* may sometimes be cast in the mode of a medieval morality play in which good eventually triumphs over evil. Given the vicious depths into which power can descend on occasion, it perhaps may be more justifiably called an immorality play. One problem here is that since power can only be exercised by (some) people, it is sometimes difficult to identify, especially in the heat of the moment, which is the good and which is the evil.

Prudent historians realize this trap and normally wait for some time, a minimum of 30 to 50 years, for some of the dust to settle. Even then, they are very careful to go a little further than giving as accurate an account as they can, refraining from any general evaluation of the meaning of what has taken place and never venturing into any sort of prediction or projection of what form the next manifestation of the interplay between People and Power will take.

Nevertheless, it is an immensely fascinating tale which has captured the imagination and provided the means of living for generations of historians, political scientists, sociologists, economic historians and journalists. Each of them acts under the constraints peculiar to his individual discipline, lest he be asked to forfeit membership of the club. This writer claims freedom from any such constraint, preferring, as a scholar in the ancient classics of Latin and Greek, to follow the words of his favourite poet Horace: "*nullius addictus iurare in verba magistri.*" Perhaps it is a sign of the times that Caribbean readers in another era would have no need of a translation, though what such a sign signifies escapes this writer at the moment. Horace said, and we heartily concur, that he was not bound to swear in the words of any master. Besides, the nature of the subject does not respect the convenience of academic boundaries nor investigations confined to the narrow straits of any one academic discipline.

Some very far-seeing economists and political scientists have recognized this problem and now freely use the term *political economy* to describe, with a bit more accuracy, the process of economic growth and development, or in too many states of the Third World, the shrinkage and underdevelopment (as a process, not a condition) which are currently taking place in the region. We believe that this term is a good start, but to more accurately describe what has happened to Jamaica over the past 63 (since 1938), 57 (1944) or 39 years (1962) one needs a monstrosity like political, historical, sociological, anthropological, legal, educational or behavioural economy. The focus on politics and economics only has left far too many crucial and significant variables out of the equation. Omar Davies and Michael Witter admit as much in the opening paragraphs of their contribution to Nettleford but having expressed that, they declare that they intend to focus "on the economic process only", against the background of perceptions of change occurring in other spheres. They also express their expectation that "the other contributions in this volume will serve to clarify the ideas left obscure in this essay, to correct the errors and to sharpen the insights gained in this review of the development of the Jamaican economy."[2]

The other contributors are unlikely to do any such thing, equally specialized as they are. The reader cannot therefore judge whether the administrative requirements outlined in Jones and Mills' essay "Institutional Framework of Government" are affordable or feasible in the light of the economic limitations explored in the previous essay or whether the institutional arrangements explored in the latter essay will provide the kind of administrative support necessary to achieve the economic aims and objectives of the previous essay. They cannot determine whether the component parts, assembled together, can work and be effective. The inability of any single decision maker to integrate all these insights, especially in the light of a hidden agenda, belonging to one more powerful than himself, may explain a large proportion of the failures of institutions which have led to the present chaos in the Jamaican society.

The problems of Jamaica cannot be explained merely in terms of politics and economics. In fact, it might be fair to say that *the most pressing of Jamaica's economic problems do not have economic causes at all* and that solutions that apply only economic tools will be doomed to failure in the future as they have continuously failed over the past 25 years or so. Over this period the gross domestic product (GDP), generally accepted as a quick measure of economic performance, has recorded a steady decline.

The significance of the dates chosen above will be immediately apparent to most Jamaicans. I have chosen 1938 as my starting point because many of the seeds have been sown since then. Nineteen forty-four marks the first time we had a parliament chosen by universal adult suffrage (many will now spell it 'sufferage', with some justification) and in 1962 our fate was squarely placed in our own hands with the achievement of independence. Although many persons may believe otherwise, we can no longer blame anybody, whether the IMF, World Bank, the gnomes of Zurich or New Kingston, the oppressive USA or the terms of international trade, for our progress or, rather, lack of it. William Shakespeare made one of his characters say, "The fault, dear Brutus, lies not in our stars, but in ourselves, that we are underlings." Our problems lie not in the fact that the world has assigned us the role of hewers of wood and drawers of water, but in our meek acceptance of that role.[3]

The determination on the part of the founding leadership of Singapore to refuse a menial role in the international division of wealth is not an economic cause, but it has worked miracles in their part of the world. Singapore's version of this miracle has come about largely because one man, Lee Kuan Yew, doggedly, some might say pig-headedly, refused to accept this prescribed role, especially when it was forced on him by the Tunku Abdul Rahman of Malaysia. One theory, to which I subscribe, is that this rejection was the second most important motive for the phenomenal growth of Singapore: Lee had to demonstrate conclusively to the Malays that Singapore could prosper all by herself. The conventional wisdom of the time insisted that federations were the key to survival and progress for small nations: hence the establishment (and subsequent collapse) of federations all over the post-British colonial world.[4]

On the other hand, generations of economic and general historians have documented ad nauseam, the wrongs perpetrated on the Third World. These historians include Eric Williams, Walter Rodney, Tom Barry et al., Carl Stone, Michael Manley and others. This constant iteration acts as a sort of brainwashing in which the lesson, *you are black, you cannot succeed, don't even bother to try* is driven home by example and precept. Politicians, citizens and commentators of all stripe drive in the lesson daily. To counter this negative and pessimistic view, the *Gleaner*, in desperation, has resorted to the artifice of having a special column, or more presumptuously, a whole page in which it hopes to print good things about Jamaica.

In the final analysis, the sole responsibility for the progress of any man or nation must rest on the action taken by that man or nation. In other words, the fortunes of a nation are determined more by the response of the inhabitants of the country than by the environmental economic conditions prevailing in the world. One might call it the *internal response theory*, since it will be referred to many times in the course of this volume. Adverse world conditions cannot be used as an excuse for non-performance, since this is generally the normal condition in the drama played out between power and people.

This book has arisen out of the conviction that, yet again, we are seeing another episode of the interplay between Power and People being acted out on the small stage called Jamaica, land we love. It would be wrong to describe it as a war, since each side desperately needs the other. A few skirmishes for a temporary advantage are about all that is likely to happen. It is in all cases a temporary condition, since overweening Power always promotes revolutions, overthrows, executions and other unpleasant consequences, like gas price protests.

At this point there is usually an accommodation, a kind of renegotiation of the terms of the agreement under which both survive. Such initiatives have been documented for us in the *Report of the Moses Committee*, the *Manley Bauxite Accord*, and the *Barbados Protocol*. Power inevitably claims that the People are demanding too much, whether wages, participation, democracy or some other perceived good. People on the other hand excoriate Power, claiming it is greedy, wicked or some other pejorative description worthy, in countries dominated by Christianity, of the lowest depths of hell.

Power generally holds most of the advantages, primarily from its command of organizations and institutions and knowledge, which it tries to keep zealously unto itself, but never completely so, since some of the People need it in order to better serve Power. Each advance and retreat is heralded by some commentator as a major advance or defeat for one side or the other. Hence the many predictions about the death of capitalism and the Western jubilation over the apparent death of socialism. Power is protean: it can indeed take many forms, sometimes making it very difficult for the observer to be sure of its identity. People do not have that facility, and remain mostly static, unchanging or slow to change. But Obika Gray has shown that People are not without some resources of their own, even if they sometimes operate in negative ways.[5]

It is slowly dawning upon Power that the major contribution to economic progress was not natural resources, but human ingenuity, innovation and creativity. In the heyday of the Industrial Revolution, the limited human ingenuity necessary was provided by power, and people made very little contribution to the process other than their muscle power. Once output and productivity were found to be linked with brain rather than brawn, Power recognized that it now had to share not just the spoils, but some of the control with the People. Power, however, still has the upper hand, because while the People can and do assert their power, mostly as single individuals (very few professionals and creative people join trade unions), Power can concentrate itself into massive corporations with enormous annual revenues far greater than most governments (to the extent that they represent People) can achieve.

The first chapter will attempt to show the present state of the game (1998-99) between People and Power on the Jamaican stage. Other chapters will follow up on this theme, in an attempt to account for the current impasse and imbalance. The final chapter will offer solutions based on the renegotiation of a new accommodation between Power and People. The best and most permanent solution is a partnership between Power and People on (almost) equal terms, such as Singapore has achieved and Barbados is trying to achieve.

At the moment in Jamaica, in spite of the apparent seizing of the upper hand by Power and its stranglehold on the fortunes of the nation for some 60 continuous years, people are responding in a manner that is creating unaccustomed fear in Power. In the aftermath of the gas price demonstrations in April 1999, government ministers, advisers, columnists and letter writers all competed with call-in and talk shows in presenting well meaning but severely limited solutions for the reasons outlined above. None of these will work on a permanent (or preferably long-term basis) unless they create a working arrangement between People and Power.

Impressions of Singapore

Singapore has stunned the world with the speed of its transformation from an ordinary British ex-colony in 1965 to its present position as a First World country, second in productivity, for the fifth year running, only to the United States of America. A mass of economic and political statistics blazons this triumph to the entire world. Along with the publicity there has been a lot of controversy about the methods used in the achievement. Many Jamaicans are convinced that this undoubted prosperity was created at great cost to the civil liberties of the people of Singapore and overwhelmingly reject it as a model. Such a concern is understandable among a people whose civil liberties have been denied through nearly two centuries of slavery and one century of colonialism.

In Jamaica, the position since 1938 (and especially the period since 1972) is by no means clear, with many citizens contending that there has been remarkable improvement and others maintaining that the system of today is no better than slavery. On the other hand, if one played a word association game with the majority of Jamaicans the automatic response to the name 'Lee Kuan Yew' would be 'dictator' and to 'Singapore' would be 'regimented'. Many economists and political scientists are convinced that the transformation was achieved mainly, if not solely, by force and coercion. Others simply ignore the part undoubtedly played by the people of Singapore in their own transformation. By ignoring these basic factors, they regard the achievement as something of a miracle, well beyond the comprehension and reach of other countries who at present occupy the position today that Singapore occupied before its independence in 1965.[6]

The example of Singapore, therefore, has failed to be a model for many a Third World country desperately seeking, on the surface at least, a way out of its economic troubles. The irony of this, with respect to the Caribbean, is that the original impulse for the programme pursued by Lee Kuan Yew and his associates was first presented to the governments of the Caribbean by future Nobel laureate Sir Arthur Lewis in the late forties, just after World War II. As we shall show elsewhere, Jamaica implemented only the first part of the model, the import substitution part, and the most dangerous and sterile part at that. Lee Kuan Yew understood the implications of the entire model and brilliantly carried it through to completion. One may, with some justification, refer to this as the Lee-Lewis model. Obviously the model has been changed beyond recognition to the casual observer.

The question must arise therefore, why did Singapore succeed so brilliantly and Jamaica fail so miserably, in implementing what was basically an identical model, with of course, some appropriate changes to match the society in which it was implemented? The crucial answer which has escaped many observers lies primarily in one phrase, the society in which it was implemented, and secondarily in the other, with some appropriate changes. A few notes about the nature of Singaporean society might clarify the issue.

At independence, the major racial and cultural groups present in the country were the Chinese, about 76 per cent, the Indians about 15 per cent, the Malays about 6 per cent with other small minorities – Indonesians, Thais and of course Europeans making up the remainder. As Lee narrates it, the major impulse for the separation of Singapore from Malaya (or better the Malaysian Federation) was the second class citizenship offered by the majority Malays in Malaysia to the people of Singapore.[7]

From the point of view of the Malayans, since the Chinese were the undisputed majority in Singapore, incorporation into Malaysia would have shifted the racial balance more in favour of the Chinese who would now become a significant minority in the entire federation. Hence the offer of second class citizenship and other disabilities as the price of admission. Lee's party, the People's Action Party (PAP) would have none of this and quietly sneaked out of the Federation with a unilateral declaration of independence before the Rhodesians (1968) capitalized the term. The Malaysians maintain that they were kicked out.

As indicated in the previous paragraph, the three major racial groups represent three great civilizations, the Hindu, the Chinese and the Malay. There is no need to find out which was older: all of them exceed 5,000 years. They were favoured with the possession of a written tradition, all based on family values including the sanctity of marriage, with no pre-marital sex and childbirth. Anecdotal evidence suggests that a girl impregnated out of wedlock was thrown out of the family and left to die for the disgrace she brought upon it.

The discipline which marks modern Singapore does not rest upon the authoritarianism of Lee Kuan Yew, as many Westerners think, but upon respect of self and elders and obedience to their wishes. When the author mentioned to his Singaporean-born informant that Jamaicans believe that Singaporeans have lost their freedom, she contemptuously enquired if they meant freedom to spit in and throw garbage in the streets, to chew gum, and to board public transport trains and buses without forming a line. Morris Cargill would undoubtedly have added "freedom to engage in slap happy reproduction". Their societies regard the choice of a marriage partner as of much too importance to be entrusted to a pair of starry-eyed lovers. Even Lee had to keep his own marriage to his beloved Choo secret for some three years, until the formal arrangements between the families were completed.

While there have been many deviations under the influence of Western cultures, the basic value systems have remained intact in all three societies, Hindu, Malay and Chinese. The Chinese, primarily, have always placed an extremely high value on learning. In ancient China, learned individuals walked miles to Peking (now Beijing) to sit the Imperial examinations. Those who passed became Mandarins, men of learning and ability, the only ones permitted to hold office in the service of the government. There was a great reverence for scholarship and learning. The system, by the way, rested solely on merit and provided a great avenue for social mobility.[8]

Anecdotes and stories often tell more about the character of a people than official surveys and precise statistics. Some Jamaican students recall Lee's visit to universities abroad attended by Singaporeans and many other ex-colonialists. Lee asked to meet his students, and generously invited students from other parts of the commonwealth to attend the meeting. He told the students of the plans he had for improving the living standards and economic performance of the country. He informed those who were studying subjects like engineering, computers, production technology, chemistry and other natural sciences to come home at the end of their courses because he would have jobs waiting for them. Those who were studying history and philosophy and the humanities were told to stay away.

Before he is condemned as a Philistine, we must say it was just a matter of priorities. He is now making amends by building an opera house, art galleries, a symphony hall and an academy of dance, in the light of the success of Singaporean artistes on the concert stages of the world. Jamaicans tend to have different priorities: one of our first structures at independence was a sports stadium, which we have great trouble finding the funds to maintain. This writer understands that the recent lunacy of constructing a new parliament building is being reconsidered.

Two more anecdotes may illustrate why externally imposed discipline, which has figured largely in the history of the Caribbean, is not considered necessary in the Asian countries. A Japanese engineer commissioned to build and launch a ship carried out the ceremony with a bottle of champagne in his right hand and a dagger in his left, to commit hara-kiri in case the ship sank and he lost face. A Singaporean minister caught in some major irregularity was not arrested, but when the news was publicized, he was expected to do the right thing. He committed suicide, thereby making some atonement for the disgrace he had brought upon the family. By contrast, our folk hero is Anancy, who generally gains his way by fraud or by taking advantage of the ignorance of his victims.

The ways in which Jamaicans and possibly other Caribbean people interpret the conditions of Singapore are no doubt influenced by their own experiences. Their impressions of Singapore are arrived at through the medium of projection, one of the side effects of the perception process. It is a fact that the PAP has been the ruling party of Singapore since 1965. Faced with the experience of Burnham in Guyana, whose long rule was the outcome of blatant fraud and manipulation of the electoral system, the manipulations of Eric Gairy in Grenada, and the activities of other assorted Caribbean politicians, including those in Jamaica, whose electoral record is not exactly spotless in spite of CAFFE and Jimmy Carter, it is easy to project similar behaviour and motive to the authorities in Singapore. Even the declaration by the United Nations organizations that, among other subjects, the electoral record of Singapore is spotlessly clean, merely evokes a shrug, seeing that our own electoral practices have been declared free and fair by assorted 'experts'.

One recent joke runs that Canadians, as a result of their unique history and geographical location had the opportunity to acquire British culture, French cuisine and American technology. Instead they have settled for American culture, British cuisine and French technology. The government and people of Singapore have made no such mistake. Secure in their recorded history and the traditions of some five millennia, they are in no hurry. The banning of chewing gum is commendable, as this writer personally finds the practice, especially the method of disposal of the remnants, exceedingly disgusting. The same sentiments support the caning of those who spray graffiti on walls and on cars.

To resume the theme of anecdotes and stories, their revelations about the national character, and the impact they have upon the behaviour of the people, it matters little whether the 'facts' of the anecdote are real or imagined. It is the *perception* of the potential actor that counts. Thus the frontier stories of the United States, stressing the themes of independence, drive and individual responsibility, the Horatio Alger rags to riches stories, the rough and ready images of the Australian outback, implausible and improbable as they may be, have considerable impact on the imagination and therefore upon the economic fortunes of the people about whom they are told. The reason is that they are told to generations of children, who even if they do not believe the tale, absorb the lesson, which is *I can do*.[9] On the contrary, casual recollection of West Indian stories by our novelists note a focus on failure and ridicule as the inevitable outcome of the efforts of Caribbean man to find a place in the sun, Vidia Naipaul being the major culprit in *The Mimic Men*, and *A House for Mr Biswas*.

Our national character and culture are replicated in our organizational culture, structures and behaviour. Another anecdote concerns my own experience as a faculty adviser to a group of health professionals in a workshop in North Carolina in 1983. At the end of four weeks, each of the four groups presented its programme to provide health care for a hypothetical developing country. One African from the Sudan gave his own minority presentation in which each official in the health organization (permanent secretaries, directors, deputies, etc.) was provided with a plethora of minor officials in his entourage under the titles of porters, drivers, doormen, etc. After having a laugh at the 'backwardness' of this fellow African, we now discover that the laugh was always on us. It was the accepted practice in that part of Africa that an appointed official makes provision for members of his family, clan or tribe by giving them petty appointments as doormen, porters, and so on. This makes a farce of any official development budget, not to mention actual performance of the duties.

Much the same thing happens in Jamaica, but the stakes are higher and the recipients do not generally settle for petty rewards. At the moment of writing there is a flap over the National Investment Bank of Jamaica, but if the past is any guide, this will join the many scandals covered up by this and previous governments.[10]

Writers on development administration who refuse to face the consequences and evaluate the impact of practices like these, are doing a disservice both to their profession and to their clients. They mislead themselves and their readers and the organizations in question simply do not perform as planned. This observation raises a number of questions which this writer hopes that he can answer in the remainder of this volume. We have successfully avoided posing and answering them for some 60 years but the continuing crisis in our economy and the rest of the state compels us to do so now. If we are to even think of following the model of Singapore, the following questions must be asked and answered:

- Is the Singapore style of development feasible in the case of Jamaica?
- If not, what sort of development is feasible?
- Are the prospects of development in Jamaica too vitiated by corruption?
- Is Jamaica, including as a matter of course the majority of the population, poor, black and underprivileged, capable of development of any sort?
- If we decide to use the promise of technology, can we build a vibrant and self-renewing technological structure on the foundation of a shattered family base?

All the questions are vital and merit close examination. The last question raises a number of issues of immediate importance. The increasing use of computer technology for the production of goods and services has not escaped the notice of many forward looking Jamaicans and the government must be credited with pushing the pace of computerization with all possible speed. My own caution, excessive perhaps, makes me impatient of the pace of the process, but I am even more concerned in the light of the reality of our educational base.

When one examines the history of wealth creation in the modern world, one may conveniently classify the process into waves: the first wave of agricultural production, the second of industrialization marked by massive assembly line operations using unskilled labour, and the present wave (the third wave, according to some) resting mainly upon the contributions of brain rather than brawn. This third (some writers identify a fourth) wave, application of technology, fits easily into the framework of a social structure dominated by strong family ties, values and tradition of hard work and attention to detail.

Other questions go even further into the core of the problem which we face in the second to last year of the second millennium. They might best be presented as another series of questions:

- Do Jamaican political leaders, opinion makers, upper, middle and working classes, or ordinary citizens want development, or are they satisfied which the current state of affairs?
- What sort of development do they want? Can one define the parameters of such development?
- Can the current political culture initiate and sustain the development process which is agreed on?
- Is it possible to get any agreement at all under the current political culture?
- If the answer to the last two questions is no, what kind of political culture must be designed, initiated and maintained to achieve the desired goals?

The first question in this section is far from rhetorical. First, one cannot assume that every Third World leader wants development for his country. Secondly, In some societies there are strong cultural taboos against making any change in the way of life which the people have lived for centuries. Thirdly, there may also be a strong vein of fatalism, that the Lord provided us with what we have and it is blasphemy or worse to desire otherwise. Some of the churches in Jamaica seem to propagate a similar belief. Finally, in many cases, the wish, if expressed at all, takes the form: *it would be nice if*, or *it would not be a bad thing if* – or some such innocuous or non-committal statement. In Caribbean countries, especially Jamaica, there is no trace of that burning desire or the passionate commitment, to the point of obsession, which energizes the true believer in development. There is also no trace of the desire or commitment to change the behaviour, not only of others, but of the self as well. A small echo of this is the behaviour of the senior executives of a company who make everyone else go to the workshop on organizational development without going themselves.

Lee Kuan Yew's *Memoirs* suggest two extremely strong motives for initiating and carrying through his plan to enrich and modernize Singapore in the teeth of all kinds of opposition, internal and external, the Japanese occupation of Singapore in World War II and the treatment of the people of Singapore by the Malaysians in the run up to independence. He almost lost his life through maltreatment and starvation during the occupation and was threatened with arrest and assassination in the pre-independence period. For his country, he realized that these circumstances could be resisted and the chances of a repetition minimized only if the country was strong and rich. Although he has achieved the latter, he did not take any chances on the former: since independence the country has boasted a strong and sophisticated military establishment.

Back to the Caribbean

The dilemma facing the Caribbean today is to explore the extent to which ancient traditional authorities and relationships can be adapted to the demands of modern practice or to which modern practices can be adapted to coexist, where necessary, with the traditional. Either process is currently incomplete, but the speed of the adaptation will determine the speed of the subsequent development.[11]

One major problem is that the modern practices are themselves changing and evolving, with the result that as soon as a workable adaptation between the traditional and the modern is made, the modern practice changes. The last pair obligingly declare on their cover: "Forget what you know about how business should work – most of it is wrong!"[12] Since so much is at stake, and the machinery of government moves so ponderously to change its practices, the habits of thought of those who are charged with modernizing the civil service, for example, constrain them to wait until the perfect model emerges, one which meets mostly political rather than rational and organizational criteria. Typically some seven to ten years elapse before the new model is implemented, by which time it is some ten years or so out of date! And the process continues.

To return briefly to the reluctant model of Singapore, the experiences of the people of Jamaica have made them complete cynics and disbelievers with respect to the effects of simple admonitions upon the behaviour that ministers of government and other officials should display. My Singaporean informant believes that ministers of government have been kept in line simply because of Lee's original warning to them, on their taking office, about the dire consequences of corruption. Such action would be treated cynically in Jamaica and elicit nothing other than incredulous and derisive laughter. Yet Mr Patterson has called repeatedly for changes in our attitudes and values. In a following chapter that theme will be more thoroughly explored. As mentioned earlier, Singapore is in a position to be selective about the external cultural influences it will permit. They have no drug problem. The Chinese are not natural users of opium: the Opium Wars leading to their loss of Hong Kong were caused by the British trying to force the use of opium upon them. The banning of drugs and the dire consequences to drug traffickers were no strain upon the Chinese.

Many Jamaicans are also cynical about the course of action embarked upon by the government and people of Barbados. They simply refuse to believe that an entire country can be mobilized into a unanimous defence of their currency, by uniting behind the government, even to the extent of enduring voluntary pay cuts where necessary.

Jamaicans and their leaders are accustomed to thinking in terms of political tribalism and divisiveness: Gordon Lewis believes that the greatest single source of distress for Jamaica is the two-party system which was set up in the 1930s and 1940s.[13] One small example: after the women's march on the Wednesday following the gas price demonstrations of April 1999, Mr Seaga publicly announced that he was concerned about the safety of his own people. Given the previous history of Jamaican politics that could be easily interpreted to mean not Jamaicans, nor the citizens of the country, including the women of other political parties who came out to show solidarity with the women since they all face the common enemy of poverty and deprivation, but only the people of his constituency. The leaders of Singapore and Barbados have and are uniting their people for development: our leaders find it profitable to divide them. For this reason and this reason alone, the development of the Jamaican people on the lines of Singapore is impossible.

If that were my last word on the subject, then there would be no point in writing this book. The first part of it will make painful reading, but if we are to make progress we have to know our enemy and thoroughly identify it. Fortunately for us, the enemy is not a person or persons, nor a political party, nor a government, but an idea, or better, a set of ideas. In identifying this set of ideas, we will be examining, as mentioned at the outset, the interaction between People and Power. At the moment, Power appears to be running havoc among us. In destroying the ideas that divide and impoverish us, we need to make some very far-reaching changes in the basic institutions which we have created in the belief that they would help rather than hurt us. Fortunately, no society need adopt wholesale the cultural norms of another, even in so noble a cause as development.

A particular difficulty among people of African descent is that the circumstances of their arrival and domicile in the Caribbean left them bereft of their traditions. They could only half-heartedly assimilate the European plantation culture, which everybody acknowledges today to be an inferior caricature of the real thing. Much of the debate today centres on whether the Afro-Jamaican should continue on that path and totally assimilate the modern Western culture, far removed as it now is from its eighteenth century caricature and still evolving continuously, or revert to a half remembered, half understood African reality, if ancient traditions can be identified and reestablished. For better or worse, modern Africa is itself overlaid with the structures and artifacts of western culture. At this distance, I for one cannot detect any hankering after the old traditions. It would be the most cruel of ironies if the Caribbean was hastening to embrace the African traditions just when the continent was busily abandoning them. In any case, its own failures to sustain the development processes make it an uncertain model for its Caribbean offspring.

My answer is that the imperatives of keeping up with the modern world are so pressing that for our economic and indeed our complete survival they in any case demand that we adopt the culture of the modern world, at least in our productive endeavours. The Asian tigers have shown that economic development is possible without sacrificing one jot of what identifies them as their own societies.

While there is a tremendous aesthetic satisfaction in enjoying the arts of Africa, its dance, its rhythms and all the other delights documented by Alleyne and Nettleford, we have to face the reality of unemployment, malnutrition, crime, violence, deprivation, shattered families, despair, hopelessness and all the evils that make modern Jamaica less than a perfect place to be.[14] We need to answer the question of just how much change is necessary for us to be assimilated into the modern world, in conditions under which we, as a country, can earn an income commensurate with our aspirations and our desired living standards. We have no choice but to do this if we are to maintain the living standards we have come to believe that we deserve. There is no need to repeat here the desiderata: a high standard of education, technology, organizations which perform, accountable government and so on, since they have already been delineated by experts.

The lessons of Singapore are based on the contribution that an educated and dedicated people can make to their own development when they are led by committed, passionate and enlightened leadership within a framework in which all the necessary discipline comes from within. We should never forget that the word *discipline* is derived from the same word as *learning*: the connotation of externally imposed direction and control is a much later addition. We need to go much further than minute examination of the trees, which is the staple of much scholarship, learning more and more about less and less, as the parody goes. Perhaps it is not even enough to examine the forest also. One has to consider the terrain and the landscape as well.

This book attempts to give the reasons for the loss to the society of the sort of experiences and good things that the *Gleaner* wishes to have stories written about, including the sort of stories that the romantics among us find pleasure in. One cannot enjoy these wonderful memories and values if one has a rotting corpse lightly buried in the front lawn. It must first be removed and the earth made fragrant and sweet again.

In 1938, 1944 and 1962 the people of Jamaica believed that these events and the movements and changes they portended would put them on fairly even terms with Power, so that they could at least renegotiate the terms of a fairer existence. They were disappointed and betrayed. Hence the title of this book.

Throughout these endnotes, the numbers after the name refer to the alphabetical list of Books and Articles appended at page 239 below, e.g. Lee Kuan Yew, 69. The page numbers, *if applicable*, are given after a comma, e.g. Nettleford, 103, p 75.

Notes

[1.] Rodney Clark, 22, p 13.

[2.] See Nettleford, 103, p 75, for the references to Davis and Witter, and p 105 to Jones and Mills.

[3.] Shakespeare, *Julius Caesar* Act 1, Scene 2.

[4.] Lee Kuan Yew, 69 and 70, p 3.

[5.] Obika Gray, 44, p 178.

[6.] John Rapley, 126, chapters 2 and 5; and Sanjaya Lall, 67, p 21. For a contrary opinion, see Henry Rowen, 133, p 147 ff.

[7.] Lee Kuan Yew, 69 and 70. See 69, p 18ff for the events leading up to the separation from Malaysia.

[8.] C. Northcote Parkinson, 114, p 98 in the essay, "The Short List or the Principles of Selection".

[9.] Horatio Alger (1832 to 1899) was a Massachusetts born American clergyman and writer on rags to riches stories, aimed especially at boys. His titles included *Ragged Dick* (1867) and *From Canal Boy to President* (1881). For a discussion on the social role played by Alger's work, see Kristol, 66, p 79–84.

[10.] Edwin Jones, 61. For similar experiences related by a former Contractor General, see Ashton Wright, 162, p 266 ff.

[11.] Edwin Jones, 62, p 22.

[12.] For texts dealing with the theme of organizational renewal, see John Naisbitt and Patricia Aburdene, 100; Thomas Peters and Robert Waterman, 119; Alvin Toffler, 156; Michael Hammer and James Champy, 45.

[13.] Gordon Lewis, 77, p 167 ff. The entire chapter is a critique of institutional failure.

[14.] Mervyn Alleyne, 2; Rex Nettleford, 101 and 104.

1

Contemporary Jamaica: The Symptoms

I: Institutions

In Jamaica a nation was made
But then our best hopes were betrayed
For somehow we got lost
Drifting much to our cost
We survive now on overseas aid

amaica in the 1990s presents a state of institutional collapse with its systems either not working or working inefficiently. There is a state of paralysis spread across the country with no area of national life exempt and no apparent solutions in sight. Since most of the symptoms appear in the economic sphere of life the tendency is to believe that the major causes, and therefore solutions, are economic in nature. The government has been declared bankrupt of ideas, the flow of energetic inputs into the system in the form of money, especially given a debt service ratio of 62 per cent of the national budget (and 113 per cent of revenue), has declined. Along with these, the normal hope, innovative ideas, euphoria and well-being have been replaced by an absence of joy, increasing desperation, a feeling of gloom and doom, and a lack of confidence in the future.

The symptoms of the problem faced may be gleaned from the daily complaints on call-in and talk shows on television and radio. The image projected is a nationwide sense of drifting, hopelessness, helplessness and near panic. Wilmot Perkins, in his daily talk shows, indulges his cynical amusement in pointing out inconsistencies, primarily in the political and social spheres, since the political rhetoric of our leaders does not match reality. In society in general, there is loss of a sense of direction, an absence of rationality, a feeling of insignificance and a perception of a lack of effect of economic measures. Short-term horizons in thinking and planning and lack of national unity are some of the other symptoms. There is a desperate search and grasping for meaning.

Happily, one or two bright spots enliven this national gloom and doom, but these exist on the periphery, and not in the mainstream, of society. The 'Road to France', the excitement and euphoria of playing in our first ever World Cup final, of scoring our first goal, of winning our first match; the current successes of the West Indies Cricket team (this was written before the tour to South Africa in 1998) and Jamaican athletes led by Merlene Ottey and Courtney Walsh, to name just a few, have considerably lightened what would have been an otherwise unrelieved gloom.

Unfortunately, this hopeful picture has been countered by the dismal performance of the supporting economy. Questions are being asked quite justifiably: Why can our economy not perform as well as our football team? Why can we not maintain the national unity we showed in the preliminaries to the World Cup? The answers appear inconclusive and the people are left bewildered. There is widespread disappointment with surrogate measures of success. Injustices in society are rampant and its reward systems prove inappropriate and dysfunctional. Performance standards have been falling. The traditional explanations that the current conditions represent the fallout of slavery and colonialism do not appear convincing, since these explanations fail to consider those countries which have successfully negotiated the post-colonial period, Singapore being the outstanding example as discussed in the introduction. It is much more likely that our present situation is the outcome of our own failings as a nation. In any case, it does not matter much where the failings originated, since the task of cleaning up the mess will fall upon our shoulders. There is nobody else around to do the job for us.

There is credible evidence to suggest that these impressions have not arisen in the heat of this writer's own scholastic imagination. In a review of the Grace, Kennedy lectures, Professor Gladstone Mills in 1997[1] noted that the current emphasis on the market economy had been accompanied by an increasing tendency to sacrifice wider community and non-material goals on the altar of self-interest and short-term economic gains. Rev. Burchell Taylor noted in 1992 that there was evidence which pointed to a wide scale of diminished moral commitment and purpose, while Leo-Rhynie in 1993 noted the consequences for family and nation of an inadequate educational system. Elsa Leo-Rhynie felt that it played a major role in perpetuating low self-esteem and was responsible for the psychological damage resulting from a syndrome of violence and a combination of conditions in a crisis of human relations. Panton, in 1994, drew a contemporary picture of widespread cynicism, pessimism and negativism among Jamaican citizens and the disenchantment with existing institutions.

Professor Mills' own contribution concerned a search for solutions in the nature of our constitution, particularly the Westminster-Whitehall heritage, its companion political system and its appurtenances such as tribal and garrison features, the breakdown of the electoral system, the emasculation of local government and the decline in the quality of the civil service.[2]

We have not been able to evaluate the *Gleaner's* initiative (and the citizens' response) in their quest for good things to write about, but the headlines seem more preoccupied with detailing what's going wrong. What is going right does not seem to be getting as much attention. We are appealing to our fellow citizens to tolerate the bad news for a little longer while we look for the reasons for the causes of our present problems and search for ways to solve them on a longer term basis. We hope to show the need for a detailed and thorough examination of our institutions as they really operate, not as they are formulated and framed. One must examine all the subsystems and relationships, both the formal and informal. The important question must always be: Do they produce the results that we as a society of citizens desire and from which we can benefit? No institution can be exempt from this examination, not the prime minister's office, nor the cabinet, nor the parliament, nor the justice system, nor the constitution. The universities, the church, the police, community, family, news media and the private sector must face their searching appraisal: nothing can be taken for granted. We must approach each institution on the lines of a zero-based budgeting exercise. Every single one of them must justify its own continued existence, in its present form, in terms of what it has done, what it is doing and what it will do in the future.

The citizens of Jamaica have realized all along that the right to engage in a meaningful discussion need not be left by default in the hands of the experts. While the experts may have a deeper insight into the significance of any particular phenomenon, the citizens have expressed in the national news media, from their own personal situation, a view which is of more immediacy than those ratified by the scholarly exertions of the experts. They have cast a spotlight upon two of the crucial arms of a democracy – the systems of justice and of elections – and have enquired into the meaning of democracy.

Thus, a diatribe against the payment of jurors has aroused the ire of the newspaper editors who reject the argument that service should be voluntary and plead a strong case for compensation for lost time at work, transportation and meals. The contrary argument is based on the traditions of the ancient regime, mostly of feudal times, which demanded free service from well-off citizens. Since then times have changed radically and jury service is demanded of every citizen, even of, and especially so, those least able to take the time off from work. Much of this imposition is aggravated by the fact that many financially able persons are exempted from jury duty.[3]

Another citizen strongly believes that the corruption of the 1997 election was so great that the wrong party won. In his eyes, democracy is threatened at every level and he resents the arrogance of the prime minister in arranging for the election before the electoral system was ready. The entire country is falling and people are being murdered and brutalized. The news media, which in democratic countries play the role of unofficial watchdog on the activities of authority, are regarded as corrupt and biased, and thus cannot play a useful role. Complaining about the injustices of society has always been the right of citizens in a democracy. In the case of Jamaica it is a staple complaint arising from the political culture which has been imposed and maintained for over 60 years.[4]

The theme of *Power* and its interaction with *People* appears in this part of the work as well. The theory of a democracy demands that Power is not alienated from People. The behaviour patterns, which surround the practices designed to promote democracy, are always of concern. Representative democracy, based on periodic voting, depends heavily upon the integrity of the system. Thus a mischievous act by an Opposition Senator who tried to masquerade as a volunteer of Citizens Action for Free and Fair Elections (CAFFE) was roundly denounced in an editorial for being either enterprising or extremely foolish. The editorial writer could not say at which level of the party the plan was developed. If it was designed perhaps to embarrass CAFFE, it did not succeed. Furthermore the problems and difficulties of the electoral system hardly rest with CAFFE. Worse than that, it demonstrates the contempt with which party officials hold the citizen. This initiative was developed and carried out in sincerity by citizens. This belittling of the citizens and their concerns reduce our parliamentary system to a farce. Whether the political activists would have exerted influence by way of affecting the outcome one way or another is not the point here, and that cannot be put forward in defence of Opposition Senator Johnson's action.[5]

Form and substance of political regimes

Earlier, we considered the question as to whether the institutions we establish are capable of performing well and whether they produce the results that we as a society of citizens desire and from which we can benefit. In any society, the government is the prime institution and perhaps we should start our examination there. One major consideration in the choice of government would be the model's prospects for enhancing social and economic growth and development and creating equal opportunities for all the citizens to develop to their full potential. It may, however, be a futile search to look for factors or features in governments which always correlate highly with social and economic growth and development or any kind of system which, more often than not, appears to be associated with these objectives. It does not seem to matter whether the form is democratic, socialist, communist, or a dictatorship of the right or left. On the other hand, stagnation is not the experience of any particular type of regime to the exclusion of any other type. It would appear that there is no correlation between the form of the regime and the presence of economic development.[6]

This simple fact has bedevilled doctrinaire advocates of both the left and the right. The evidence is overwhelming: we have had economic growth and development in Chile under dictator Pinochet's regime; in Singapore under the near dictatorship (according to many Jamaicans) of Lee Kuan Yew; in China under a socialist regime, and in the democratic states of old Europe, the USA and Japan. We need to look at other non economic and non political factors such as the disposition of the people and their leaders, their political and social culture and their willingness and ability to generate the necessary behaviours and follow the necessary economic growth and development scenarios.

The Russians used to believe that economic growth and development were possible only under their type of socialist regime The Americans had essentially the same idea, that development and growth were possible only under their type of presidential and congressional type of regime. Both nations spent massive resources to propagate their points of view: the most favourable outcome of this costly experiment was to prove to the rest of the world that the adoption of one or the other regime, as a necessary condition, was completely irrelevant. A similar, equally futile argument rages in Jamaica, where the so-called capitalism of Seaga and the JLP is engaged in a battle to the death with the so-called socialism (somewhat muted) of Patterson and the PNP, a battle that most Jamaicans are thoroughly fed up with.[7]

China is another country that challenges the orthodox belief that there is some correlation between economic growth and form of political regime. This country has virtually the same regime as Russia, but from all reports, it is enjoying a rate of economic growth such as Russia has never seen. The reason for this is that they have been able to separate political aims and objectives from economic ones, and have set up systems with separate ideologies to handle both aspects of their society. Some believe that this presents the country with a massive dilemma that they may have to deal with some day. One is more likely to find productive organizations of the type more common in the West than those called for in socialist ideology. In the economic areas the chances are high that even in the government they look more like Western than socialist organizations.

The role of leadership

Judging from the amount of interest generated by the public locally over the question of leadership, especially of the three political parties, one would be forgiven if one formed the impression that leadership is the single most important missing ingredient in the current battle of Jamaicans to keep their economy and society afloat. Litres of printer's ink have been utilized on the question of the leadership capabilities of Mr Patterson, Mr Seaga and Mr Golding. Some writers are convinced that if this question is solved, Jamaica would be up and prospering in a matter of months. These high hopes, unfortunately, may have to undergo radical revision for the truth is more complex than that, and the relationship between leadership and national success is not a direct linear one. Thus excellent leaders may lead inefficient and ineffective governments and vice versa.

Management and other literature abound with discussions about the topic of leadership and many theories have been generated about who or what makes the best leader. Without going into any of these one can agree that the main factors that must be considered are the leader, the followers and the goal. Simply speaking therefore, a leader is one who arranges and gets his followers to attain a specific goal or goals. The best way of achieving this is the subject of many a learned dissertation. We may begin by asking a simple question. Over the last 60 or so years, have Jamaican leaders, political and non-political alike, managed to arrange and get the Jamaican people to attain a specific goal or goals of economic growth and development? Most Jamaicans will agree that the answer is a resounding 'No!'

Jamaica has no doubt had its share of outstanding leaders.[8] The towering personality of Alexander Bustamante, the tremendous intellect of Norman Manley, the studious competence of Donald Sangster, the humanity of Hugh Shearer, the overwhelming charisma of Michael Manley, the thorough technicism of Edward Seaga, and the populist appeal of P.J. Patterson, have all added life and colour to the Jamaican scene. Yet one must ask: given the economic and social mess that the country has now found itself in, how did these men, collectively, create what now exists in a country that its first European visitor (Columbus) described as "the fairest isle that man has ever set eyes on"? What has gone wrong?

Other chapters will resume and discuss different aspects of this question as this volume unfolds. For the moment we would like to deal with one of the many ideas which our researchers and writers have thrown out from time to time. This is the idea that leadership is both a process and a property. As a property it is a particular characteristic of an individual. In this way, the definition focusses only on the leader and pays very little attention to his followers or his environment. The preceding paragraph attached a few such properties to individuals, perhaps neither accurately nor elegantly. These are only illustrations. The second notion of leadership as a process fits more easily within the description of leadership given above. This notion takes into account the followers and the goals. The process of taking a set of followers towards the achievement of goals becomes thus much more complex and takes into account a vast number of variables which intervene between the leader and his goal achievement.

Whereas the first notion only requires the leader to *be*, the second requires not only that the leader *does*, but also *inspires and guides his followers into their doing*, that is, to create valuable and desirable outcomes. Collectively, the above-mentioned leaders, for all their success at being, failed miserably at the task of getting their followers to do. Successful leadership, therefore, within an institution like a government or any other organization, requires many more inputs than just the qualities of the leader, however admirable they might be. This of course does not exhaust all the various theories and the curious reader is referred to the works of Fiedler, Lewin and others. The leadership behaviour required today is one which will serve the needs of the Jamaican people in the second millennium and after.[9]

Perhaps this is the appropriate time to introduce the Undisputed Leadership Theory and its past and future impact on Jamaica's economic fortunes. It is a fact that in our post-independence history the only period of expansion of the Jamaican economy took place between the late 1950s and the early 1960s. Economists are at pains to explain that this was a general period of expansion in the world economy and cite, quite correctly, the massive investments in bauxite and tourism that took place at that time. In the minds of many, this was the sole and sufficient reason for the advance. It amounts almost to heresy to suggest an alternative cause or causes. The weight of the evidence is on the side of the orthodox. They have the figures to prove it.[10]

A number of unsettled issues hover around this writer's head like so many persistent mosquitoes at 3:00 am. There is also general agreement that this bounty of investment has never been repeated on a similar scale since the 1960s. Is one to accept that no 'general expansion' of the world economy has taken place since? The World Bank figures show otherwise. Other figures also exist to show, even now, that investments are pouring into our sister Caribbean islands while we continue to languish. Why is our boat not rising with the tide? This writer's 'internal response theory' suggests that our boat is full of holes and rocks. Perhaps one answer is that in spite of Minister Robertson's manful efforts we are not quite presenting to investors the enticing picture we believe that we are portraying. Macro-economic stability is not the foremost thing that the investors need.

One may note, in passing as it were, that this massive economic growth (Norman Girvan is at pains not to call it development) occurred at a time when the leader of the governing party was being challenged for the leadership role. The Bustamante-Sangster-Shearer succession was under strong challenge by Seaga, Lightbourne and Hill and assorted others. By contrast, and coincidence according to the economists, the period of 1973 to 1999 has been marked mostly by continuous shrinkage in the Jamaican economy. This, again apparently by coincidence at a time when the leadership on both sides of the house – of the government and opposition – faced no credible challenge. These were times, in terms of my theory, of undisputed leadership. Except for a slowdown in the US economy in 1993, the Clinton years were responsible for the longest peacetime expansion in most of the world. Why should Jamaica have been excluded from this expansion? The undisputed leadership and the internal response theories provide a possible answer. Unfortunately for the orthodox, there exists a massive corpus of theory and research on the dynamics of groups and the behaviour of people within them, and how they respond to the opportunities and threats from their environment.

Having undisputed power is a heady possession for any mortal being. To be surrounded by persons who regard your every wish as their command, must give a man the feeling of being elevated to the godhead. Yet, like all good things, it comes with a price. In the case of the prime minister of a developing country like Jamaica, the price is paid by the *People*, not by *Power*. For a prime minister who genuinely wishes to improve the welfare of his people (and to be fair, all those mentioned above have expressed this desire at some time or another) the price paid is the disastrous impact of undisputed power on creativity, innovation, technological advance, realistic assessment of ideas, and all the artifacts that precede development.

In times of undisputed power and leadership, creativity suffers; competent managers and administrators are exiled from the centres of power and hangers-on and flatterers are given unlimited access to the top man. This is inevitable unless the leader is exceptionally perceptive and can see beyond the adulation. There can be no critical analysis of any design or undertaking, however absurd, hence the resolve to construct a new parliament building, now mercifully postponed, in the teeth of a massive debt and budget deficit. Fear and awe of the top man replace informed judgment and charismatic leadership becomes ascendant. As we shall show in the course of this volume, this behaviour is supported by deliberately designing accountability out of the system. Just recently one of our most prominent leaders invited wayward members of his party to *Sing a Sankey, light a candle and find their way home*. Many of his followers seem willing to accord to him the leadership by divine right.

It cannot be overemphasized that a*ny individual, male, female, black, white or rainbow coloured, elevated to the Office of the Prime Minister under our current political culture, is going to behave in that way*, with what social scientists would call 100 per cent probability. In a real way, he becomes entrapped within the system rather than being its controller. He cannot vary his behaviour, since his followers have come to expect and to demand such action from him as the price of their support. To that extent, leader and led become victims of the system which they helped to create and maintain.

It must be stressed that the behaviour of the undisputed leader does not reflect any weaknesses or defects in the personality of the individual. Citizens should not therefore attempt to look at the individual's personality for the reasons, although Mr Patterson has invited such enquiry by having his biography published.[11] The search for the appropriate leader on the basis of personality alone will not achieve the results desired by most Jamaicans. The only answer is to find a man or woman of reasonable honesty and competence and design a system around that person that he or she cannot subvert. How we have failed to do this in the past, and how we may achieve it in the future, if we really want to, is one of the themes of this work.

In accordance with the theme of leadership as a process, we may append a final illustration, which has to do with the display of arrogance and aristocratic behaviour that ministers sometimes present to citizens. In the course of the nation's business, a proposed meeting between Minister of Transport and Works Phillips and the Parish Council was aborted in spite of the presence of a 'high powered team' of ministry officials. Further proceedings had proven futile when it was discovered that the ministry team was without decision authority. In view of the expectation that the meeting would have created access to funding for projects, the members were quite annoyed with this display of high-handedness. Leaders are expected in the best of societies to be persons of infinite courtesy.

There is another, less pleasant, side to this episode. The expectation of patronage plays a very vital role in a society whose culture rests on welfare and handouts. Persons in inferior positions believe that they must reach the head of the organization to make their cases, since the subordinates are perceived (and sometimes rightly) to have no discretion. Other deleterious effects flow from this. In the absence of organizational structures and in the face of a concentration of power, the head becomes overburdened and cannot discharge his duties in the optimal manner.[12]

Single course and systems thinking

In the last subsection we made the point that the only way to make sure that the leaders we choose do not go astray and hurt our interests is to design and implement a system around such an individual. This is an appropriate time to introduce the concept of the systems approach or systems theory. The basic idea is that all of the phenomena that we sense are parts of a system, not existing entirely on their own, but having some relationship with other parts of the whole. An individual human being is such a system, since he has various parts – brain, stomach, liver, kidneys, heart and muscle – working together. If there is a serious failure in any one part of the system, the entire organism dies.

It is very easy to extend the analogy to society and the various parts of it. Government is a system but so is the individual ministry or department. We can see that each system may consist of several subsystems, going from the largest to the smallest, or starting with the smallest going up to the largest system of all, the universe. The important point is that within a particular system, every component is related to every other component in some way, and a happening in any one may have impacts upon every other one.

In the Introduction the point was made, illustrated in the essays of Davies and Witter on the one hand and Jones and Mills on the other, that much more enlightenment could be gained if both pairs of essayists did their investigations with reference to each other, since the mutual impact of the economic environment and the administrative arrangements demand that they must fit and work together. One of the disadvantages of academic specialization is that we tend to think that nature observes these artificial boundaries and we elaborate great plans for one part of a system without taking into account all aspects of that system. We call this approach *single course thinking*. We would like to propose another approach which might save us from many of the pitfalls of the former.

The very structure of a government with its many departments and ministries tends to promote the single course idea, each doing its work without much reference to another. A far more useful approach is *systems thinking*, which conceives the component parts as related in complex ways to others. The leader must function within this complex web.

When we are designing systems of the sort which constrain the leadership only to those desirable behaviours, we have to bear in mind that many factors and variables from a variety of components may have an impact upon the leader's action. In Jamaica we demand that our leaders be accountable to us. We mean, in most cases, that they must tell us how they spend our tax money and that they must not waste it in corruption. Yet every Jamaican knows that governments rarely tell us any of these things and that corruption is the norm and not the exception. In our present situation there is no way we can compel them to do so. Why we cannot, will be explored later and we will also discuss what we can do to make them tell. In the meantime, the following 1998 report will illustrate the issues and clarify some of the problems we face.

According to this report, the prime minister announced in 1998 that small and medium sized firms would have to provide jobs for those who have been laid off or made redundant. He explained that worldwide employment has been triggered more by small enterprises than large conglomerates. Some factory places were being built with more to come and that some 60,000 square feet of factory were being built in the Montego Bay Freezone to accommodate our thrust into management informatics. On the very sensitive question of his trip to France during football fever

1988, he appeared to be justifying it in rather vague terms without elaboration. Some politicians believe that they can play games by dodging questions by journalists, but when the subject is on plans to attract much needed investment to create jobs to replace those lost through redundancies and so on, the issue rises beyond a game.[13]

II. Failure of Economic Development Initiatives

Economic and social development
Must avoid geographic envelopment
For when everything's global
One exports to Cristobal
And thereby we achieve our empowerment

Economic background – myth and reality

Over the years there have been countless initiatives aimed at the economic growth and development of Jamaica. Impressive gains were recorded in the 1960s and by 1973 Jamaica was held to be a model for a developing country and it is believed that one of the reasons that Lee Kuan Yew of Singapore visited Jamaica was to see how we had achieved this growth and development. Unfortunately for Jamaica, the following eight years were years of shrinkage of the economy (described under the pseudonym of *negative growth*). It appears that one of our mistakes was to confuse economic growth with economic development. Another was to pay very little attention to the social and non-economic background of the nation for which we created such wonderful development plans.

The possible effects of non-economic and social factors upon the success of economic initiatives are also adverted to in Grassl's discussion. By remarking that the lack of production and growth is not caused by the high crime rates or disrupted families, but rather the other way around, he acknowledges the contribution made by economic growth to social goods and services:

> It seems that the causal factor that explains most social evils is an economy that has not grown in real opportunities to the mass of Jamaicans. But there is no abstract 'economy' independent of the decisions of individuals, policy makers and citizens alike. If we had to take cultural and social factors as given, why, then, are culturally similar neighbours in the Caribbean prospering, and why was Jamaica developing well until 1973?[14]

There is much support here, especially in the second part of the quotation, for my basic thesis that the economic fortunes of the country depend less on the environmental economic conditions existing at any given time, and more on the decisions of ruling individuals within the country. In assessing the contribution that each country makes to its own development, the cultural and social environment cannot be taken as givens. In our view, these factors play a crucial and decisive role in economic development, greater even than the presence of natural resources or industrial financing. If the people do not want to develop, economic factors are immaterial. Jamaican apologists go to great pains to minimize the impact of the individual policy decision, the process by which this decision is arrived at and the structures and cultures which determine the process. The conventional explanation of the growth of the 1960s rests on an abundance of capital, a circumstance not repeated. One should compare the fortunes of Singapore in the 1970s.

We have maintained that economic initiatives taken without due regard for the social and cultural environment are likely to fail, as most of those have over the last 25 years. Where they do not fail outright, they might also produce absurd results that are certainly unintended. The following citation illustrates such a situation. The writer notes the existence of a report that the government is contemplating legislation to prosecute citizens who take illegal taxis, and he is advising the government to hold off. He suggests that government first improve the transport service. This is a perennial problem for Third World countries faced with limited resources since bus services are expensive and unprofitable, if spread all over. Most public systems over the developed world are expensive for the user and heavily subsidized. If public transport is left to private initiative in Jamaica as at present, flaws will occur in the system, such as overloading, cutting out unprofitable routes, and enforcing a policy of no children and other such antisocial methods. This case illustrates quite clearly the limits to welfare and shows up the absurd results of the no wealth creation or the income-less society policy. Threats to prosecute individuals for doing what is economically rational have the appearance of scare tactics used against the very poor.[15]

Economic growth and development

It appears that economic growth and economic development are two completely different things, and that their measurement cannot be done in the same way. Growth refers to positive changes in the quantity of outputs over a period of time and is conveniently measured by changes in the value of the gross domestic product. Economic development refers to changes in the quality of the inputs and productive elements that produce the outputs.

In the context of a developing country, economic development must only mean qualitative changes in the nature of the inputs, including the use of technology in creative and innovative ways by the people who are native to and think of the country as their only home. Mere ownership of part of the assets exploited by a foreign company does not count as economic development. In Jamaica, those native persons who are appointed to run our bauxite mining and refining operations cannot be said to be part of a development process until they have mastered the arts of financing, producing and marketing aluminum products, not just raw alumina, competitively in any part of the world.

The expansion enjoyed by the financial sector in the early part of the 1990s, if genuine, represented impressive growth to many persons, including the minister of finance. To this writer, it appeared that there was little development. Much earlier, about 1993, he told members of the Rotary Club that he was unhappy with what was going on in the sector, because even with the upbeat mood then prevailing, he believed that the sector was losing sight of its mission, and was distorting the economy. Subsequent events have shown that this observation was right, although he could not have foreseen the magnitude of the debacle, helped along as it was by outright fraud and various degrees of mismanagement. Observers might have gained more insight into the reality of the situation if they had asked themselves a simple question, as he did. What was there in the Jamaican economy of the early 1990s that generated real returns in excess of 40 per cent per annum? A lot of grief may have been avoided by the answers to this question! As the German poet Schiller puts it, "Mit der Dummheit kampfen die Gotte selbst vergebens!" (Against stupidity the gods themselves struggle in vain!) One might also compare the phenomenon of the partner schemes of the year 2001: despite popular belief, they cannot produce wealth.

Much of this is not new, but apparently it has been consistently ignored by our decision making individuals, whether government or private. George Beckford, in his *Persistent Poverty* refers to the workings of the plantation system and mentions that the welfare orientation has had the effect of inhibiting creativity, the introduction of technology and real development.[16] Industrialization by invitation had the effect of reducing Jamaicans to the status of bystanders and spectators of their country's growth, but contributed nothing to their own personal development.

The welfare orientation has been an essential part of our political culture. In the late 1990s there was some dislocation of the economies of the Far East, somewhat similar to what has happened to us. It is more than likely that those countries that have taken longer to recover from their financial difficulties are those whose economies had merely grown, but have not developed. On the one hand, the developed economies of Hong Kong, Singapore and Japan have shrugged off their difficulties as a mere glitch or blip in the pattern of stability, while on the other, Indonesia is struggling to come to terms with the IMF.

Economic development would mean that a significant proportion of the population had developed expertise to the point where their natural creativity and spontaneity could be channelled into productive or even export oriented enterprises. This is what has happened in Singapore as a result of the massive investment in education, especially of the technological variety. Just how far we have lagged behind is illustrated in the following comment by Mark Wignall. He duly praises the small man's guile and wit, even if he has to forgive them for some bad logic. He cites examples of the "explosive qualities of that logic" among craft vendors in Ocho Rios.[17]

Beckford's analysis of the deep structural reasons for the persistent poverty of the Jamaican people has already been alluded to. To these we may add the ignorance of the vendors of the nuances of the market place and their reliance on power and patronage, rather than on the quality and merit of their goods. This attitude and behaviour reflects part of their conditioning by the political culture. They may even believe that things are to be had for the taking.[18]

It has become fashionable to devise indices to measure both concrete and abstract quantities, especially when the desire is to make comparisons between and across countries. This desire is partly driven by the wishes of governments to make a point to their citizens of just how well they are catering to their needs. In this case it provides a useful service by showing governments just how well they measure up and may lead to improvement on their performance. This is the good side. On the other hand, the information may be used just to enter the international bragging stakes, as if countries should be ranked like football clubs in the playing season! Whatever the motive, many readers would like to know just how Jamaica stacks up on the survey of living standards. The *1998 Annual Quality of Life Index*, ranks the country in seven main categories, namely:

Cost of Living (least expensive)	74	(New York 100, Tokyo 167)
Culture and Recreation	47	
Economy	29	(Haiti 26)
Freedom	75	
Infrastructure	20	
Health	63	
Safety and risk	70	(Barbados, Bahamas 100)

These figures are for Jamaica only, higher figures meaning better scores, except in the cost of living category. We have reproduced a few others for comparison, to make it quite clear just where we stand. These results are a tribute to the welfare orientation of the past 60 years. A number of questions arise, however. Given the extremely low scores in the 'sustaining categories' of economy and infrastructure, just how long can the others maintain their position? What has been the trend over the past years? The 'least expensive' category, from the point of rich countries, depends upon earning money in a rich country and spending it in a poor one. Foreign diplomats assigned to Jamaica, who get paid in US dollars or the equivalent, would benefit from these rankings. The Jamaican people, who both have to earn Jamaican dollars and spend them here, would not rank the country in this way. The most expensive countries, Japan, Sweden, Norway and Denmark, also have per capita GDPs that are some of the highest in the world. High incomes and high costs of living tend to go together. Perhaps other figures should be compared on a misery index, compiled by the residents of the country. Better figures give some aid and comfort to the apologists for the various governments.[19]

Aspects of economic growth

This section attempts to interpret economic growth not so much in terms of figures, but in terms of what it means to the lives of the people who live in this country. The standard measurements of growth such as GDP and per capita GDP cannot really describe the economic situation in the country in terms of how these are experienced by the people. Many other aspects need to be considered before one can make any accurate assessment of the meaning of the figures in human terms. The first issue concerns the figures themselves, whether they measure what they are supposed to measure and their degree of accuracy. Thus Cargill gets the feeling that the prime minister, the minister of finance and the governor of the Bank of Jamaica are living in a world different from ours. They exude unjustified optimism and always see improvements coming, in their insistence that the economy is on the right track. Many of these results can only stem from creative bookkeeping. This refusal to face reality further strengthens our notion that governments of Jamaica have a vested interest in the institutionalization of poverty.[20]

The same theme surfaces in a letter from Earl Taylor who believes that some massaging of the economic performance figures is taking place. He reckons that the figures are out of touch with reality, recognizing that "professionalism and ethics" these days are "fast disappearing values in our society". Accountability and truthfulness are designed out of the system. Manipulation of symbols is the only option left for the governments to take.[21]

There can be no justification for the cynical manipulation of the economic growth figures, which many citizens suspect the government to be involved in. Far more devastating from the point of view of economic development is its impact on the behaviour of citizens including their investment behaviour. A June 1998 *Observer* editorial calls the attention of government to recent Stone polls showing that 92 per cent of businessmen have no confidence in the projected growth figures announced by the prime minister, the Ministry of Finance and the governor of the Bank of Jamaica. They are also concerned with the quality of the supporting infrastructure and the unpredictable labour environment.[22]

In the same way that economic initiatives founder because of an inadequate infrastructure, so do the figures on that performance. Questions arise here of the impact of the political culture and all the other consequences of the flaws in the current culture. As demonstrated in almost every election since 1944, political fortune does not depend upon performance. Unfortunately, these complaints about the relevance and accuracy of figures have absolutely no impact upon the subsequent behaviour of the political directorate. They seem to have built-in mechanisms to insulate themselves from the expressed concerns of citizens.

The views expressed by the official opposition do not seem to have much impact either upon the political behaviour of the ruling regime. In 1998, Audley Shaw believed that government would soon be seeking help from the IMF. He noted that persons were getting bailouts while nothing had gone into production.[23] The emotional impact of borrowing through the IMF and admitting it publicly were too much for the PNP, since it would remind the public of the failed Michael Manley era.

Continuing our discussion of the meaning in life terms of economic growth or in this case, the lack of it, we may refer to an article by Mark Wignall. He is concerned that the nation's people shun the national budget debate to attend to finding the next meal, securing money for school fees, rent or mortgage, transportation. He accuses the government of talking over the heads of the people, and adding insult to injury by their self-congratulations. He supplies much anecdotal evidence of the realities of economic survival for the small people.[24]

This is an incisive comment on what we have achieved after 36 years of independence and any careful observer of this period should not be surprised by any of it. It must surely annoy Jamaicans to have their country compared unfavourably to any country, least of all Barbados. This writer has been told in private conversation that Barbadians make sure they are home to listen to a Budget presentation, which they then discuss among themselves. The major interest in this comparison between the two experiences is their potential effects upon the nation building exercise. Since one of my major theses is the suggestion that successive Jamaican governments have given a low priority to the creation of wealth perhaps the governments of Jamaica really wanted this effect and it is not unintended at all.

This book was partially inspired by a puzzling phenomenon. The record is replete with dozens of economic plans and programmes, in the form of five-year plans and other designations. All of these have been presented at some time or other to ruling governments. If they or a goodly portion of them had been all implemented, the chances are that we would not be in the current economically foundering boat. It would seem that the main cause of our economic backwardness has been our failure to implement workable and feasible economic plans. Leading economist Owen Jefferson, former deputy governor of the Bank of Jamaica, appears to agree with this assessment. The country's failure to develop and sustain a correct mix of macroeconomic policies is one of the major obstacles to sustained economic growth. He maintains that the right mix would have produced a climate encouraging high domestic savings and the investment of those savings in productive activities, etc. He admits that macroeconomic stability by itself would not have guaranteed economic growth citing social conditions as an important element.[25]

Very few economists like to admit that factors outside the reach of their discipline can have a major impact on factors within, so we owe our thanks to Dr Jefferson for this candid admission. Our country's failure to develop this mix may well be traced to the absence of appropriate institutions that can carry out the necessary programme. The absence of a supporting social and cultural base may have also been responsible for the failure. We should also be grateful to him for his admission that the major responsibility for the failure of these policies was ours instead of world economic conditions, which seem to be the whipping post beloved by most other commentators.

My internal response theory states quite unequivocally that the economic fortunes of a country depend not so much on the external environmental conditions as on the response of the people and their decision makers to these conditions. In this context one can compare the overall response of Michael Manley of Jamaica and Lee Kuan Yew of Singapore to identical economic conditions in the 1970s. This response is further modified by the outlook, ideology, personality and so on of the decision makers, as it has in the cases mentioned.

The textbook characterization (almost a caricature) of the 'profit maximizing entrepreneur' puts undue emphasis on economic rationality as the major or sole consideration for an economic decision. Jefferson's report, though extremely useful and informative is full of 'loaded' terms, in the sense that they are based on assumptions that may not be all valid for Jamaican society. The important question of the extent to which social conditions interfere with the economic conditions is not sufficiently explored.

To bring this section to a close, I would like to briefly discuss one of the effects or outcomes of economic growth. For Bowen, the 1998 reports are a mixture of good news/bad news. The recent sales foray into Caribbean markets by JAMPRO nets $18m in sales. (It is not stated whether these were US or Jamaican dollars.) These results derive from the efforts of a 19-member team. The bad news is that the "national trade balance remains out of whack". The deficit at March 1998 stood at US$1.7b. Exports were at half the value of imports. There had been a fall in raw material imports, a very good indicator of declining manufacturing activity. "A concerted national effort needs to be made to bring exports up to a more valuable level, as well as to keep imports from rising any higher."[26]

It is part of our national tragedy that this effort will not be made. First, it is not in the mission of the political culture; secondly, there is no drive to make the nation wealthy. A massive imbalance exists between effort and reward when a 19-member team is needed to generate $18m in sales. This is a very inefficient use of resources and the results are insignificant in terms of national needs. On the other hand, growing imports are an indicator of the welfare-handout-comfort syndrome in action.

Poverty, unemployment and welfare

In Jamaica the government and other well-wishers believe that they can supply dignity and self-confidence to a people who are basically unemployed or underemployed. We have seen above that many of the official government figures are not trusted by a significant number of citizens. The unemployment figures tend to understate the real situation. I believe that they count as unemployed only those persons who are actively seeking employment in any given week. Those citizens who have never sought employment or who have been frustrated into ceasing to seek employment because they rate their chances of landing a job as nil conveniently fall out of the statistics.

Dignity and self-confidence flow to individuals from an acceptable occupational identity. Mary Richardson defines occupational identity as being concerned with the choice of an adult role, with the individual's feelings for the future and the perceived value of his present course to what he hopes to become.[27] The unemployed (and the unemployables) would not be able to claim the benefits of an occupational identity. It can be shown that occupation is one of the determinants of social ranking.

As usual one may begin this section with a look at some of the figures with respect to employment and unemployment, bearing in mind the caveats mentioned above. According to one report, the October 1997 unemployment figures showed a slight decline from 1996 figures. One should bear in mind that these point to point comparisons do not reveal the story between the points. They are generally good-looking figures. Whether they have been massaged as is sometimes alleged, this writer cannot say. Whether the measurements selected of employment and unemployment are appropriate to our setting is of much greater import.[28]

The second report is more detailed and attempts to link illiteracy with unemployment. "More than 160,000 persons aged 17 to 24 are neither employed, in school, nor undergoing training, primarily because they lack literacy and numeracy skills", according to Social Development Commission (SDC) chairman Rev. Garnet Roper. The 1996 figure of 160,000 increased by 15 per cent (184,000) with 40,000 added in the month of June only. The figure continues to grow by 5 per cent each year.[28]

One quick comment is that the fuller figures of the second report throw considerable doubt upon the accuracy of the first. The chronic unemployment figures and their link with illiteracy may be taken as a fallout of the absence of a plan for the majority of the people in the formulation of national aims and objectives. Illiteracy increases the potential for high unemployment and a high crime rate, although the prime minister denies the connection between economic progress and social flaws.

The next two observations try to interpret these unemployment figures in terms of what they mean to those members of the society who fall into that category. Wignall admits to a few bright spots, including a bright Common Entrance student, a candidate who gained 10 'O' levels at Kingston College with high marks, and the Spelling Bee triumphs; but these are exceptions to the general rule. More typical of the society are 'the young unemployed desperados' of Rema, Waterhouse, August Town or Seaview Gardens. He believes that officialdom engages in a game of deception and self-deception. There is a tendency among members of the society to accept the official stories, instead of finding out the truth, the life and values of the ghetto and the struggle for literal survival.[30] His report paints a graphic picture of the reality of our society of which many citizens are unaware. An important question is how much can the few 'good' stories compensate for the 'bad' realities. For their own purposes, governments insist on looking on the situation with rose-coloured glasses and their well paid apologists ride along with them.

The final citation regarding poverty, unemployment and welfare is a letter from James Robertson who notes that: "Academic success at secondary or tertiary level no longer provides confidence or assurance for young Jamaicans in their pursuit of gainful employment." No connection is perceived between hard work and job acquisition – not even in farming, stifled by a policy that assures the primacy of imports over local production. There is a need for post school training for better employment prospects. Programmes like HEART/NTA and NTS are good, but limited. Robertson continues: "The government has created an atmosphere of panic in the minds of prospective investors and has caused many established ones to pack and leave." Severing the link between work and reward is one of the outgrowths of a culture based on privilege and patronage, accounting for designations of Jamaicans as lazy and unmotivated. This explains why many initiatives do not work.[31]

Notes

1. Gladstone E Mills, 93, p 3 ff.
2. The same theme is further elaborated in Mills and Robertson, 95, pp 311 – 343.
3. "Rethink this one Justice Wolfe" (editorial), *Sunday Observer* (29 March 1998), p 10.
4. Isaac Hughes, "Where Is Jamaica Heading?" (letter), *Daily Observer* (30 March 1998), p 8.
5. Winston Witter, "Much Ado About Nothing" (article), *Sunday Observer* (29 March 1998), p 10. See also, Senator Johnson's "Strange Act" (editorial), *Sunday Observer* (29 March 1998), p 10.

6. Ian Boxill, "Democracy and Development" (article), *Daily Gleaner* (Thursday 21 July 1998), p A4.

7. Carl Stone, 145, Intro, p vi ff. See also David Panton, 111, p 151 ff.

8. For a personal view of Caribbean leaders, see Theodore Sealy, 137.

9. Kurt Lewin, 74; and Fred Fiedler, 35.

10. Owen Jefferson, 57.

11. Arnold Bertram, 9.

12. Phillips "Keep Councillors Waiting" (report), *Daily Observer* (Thursday 16 April 1998), p 4.

13. "Small, Medium Sized Firms To Provide Jobs – PM" (report), *Daily Gleaner* (Wednesday 1 July 1998).

14. Wolfgang Grassl, "A Passion for Economics" (article), *Daily Gleaner* (Wednesday 4 March 1998), p D1.

15. Clifton Segree, "Prosecuted for Taking a $20 taxi?" (report) *Daily Gleaner* (21 March 1998), p B6.

16. George Beckford, 6, p. 53 ff.

17. Mark Wignall, "Bulls and Oversized Phalluses" (article), *Daily Observer* (Monday 20 July 1998), p 7.

18. Obika Gray, 44, p 169 ff.

19. Desmond Henry, "How We Measure Up World Wide" (article), *Daily Gleaner* (Saturday 4 April 1998), p A4.

20. Morris Cargill, "Fantasy Land" (article), *Daily Gleaner* (23 July 1998) p A4.

21. Earle Taylor, "Jamaica's Poor Economic Performance" (letter), *Daily Gleaner* (Saturday 4 April 1998), p A5.

22. "A Lack of Confidence" (editorial), *Daily Observer* (Wednesday 22 July 1998), p 8.

23. "Jamaica's Economy in Crisis", (report) *Daily Gleaner* (Tuesday 3 March 1998), p B 11.

24. Mark Wignall, "We Don't Want To Taste Dirt" (article), *Daily Observer* (Thursday 16 April 1998), p 7.

25. "Report, We Missed the Boat with the Policies – Jefferson" (article), *Daily Observer* (Thursday 16 April 1998) p 30.

26. Calvin Bowen, "More Exports – a National Challenge" (article), *Daily Gleaner* (Wednesday 10 June 1998), p A4.

27. Mary Richardson, 128, p 10.

28. "Jamaican Unemployment Figures Show Slight Decline" (report), *Daily Gleaner* (Saturday 4 April 1998), p A11.

29. "SDC to Address Illiteracy: Thousands of Youth Not Employed" (report), *Daily Gleaner* (Friday 17 July 1998), p A2.

30. Mark Wignall, "What Next?" (article), *Daily Observer* (Thursday 30 April 1998), p 7.

31. James Robertson, "Tackling the Problem of Youth Unemployment" (letter), *Daily Observer* (Thursday 16 April 1998), p 8.

2

National Aims and Objectives

For centuries our history has run
Based on finding our place in the sun
Though we came up from slavery
Due to some people's knavery
Our current lifestyle's not much fun!

I: Emerging National Society

The pre-independence period in Jamaica, roughly 1938 to 1962, has been given much coverage by our historians and political scientists like Gordon Lewis, Ken Post, Carl Stone and many others. Most of these scholars have examined in some detail the themes of political development, tracing the process by which the government of Jamaica evolved and increased in autonomy, while passing through periods of limited, then full internal self-government, and finally to full independence. Other writers have concentrated on themes of cultural development, focussing their enquiries on the processes of building a nation and shaping a society. Others have given their attention to the themes of social development examining the processes of fostering, identifying and using talents and the building of lasting and useful institutions.

Themes of economic growth, the answer to questions like how the new nation is supposed to earn its living, are naturally the province of economists such as Owen Jefferson, Norman Girvan and George Beckford. They would also handle themes like the modernization of the production facilities and how the country would insert itself into the post-war world.[1] A basic responsibility like this is something that men of vision would consider. Themes of economic development are also the province not only of economists but also of everyone who is concerned about the future of the people. The vital question here is: how are the people going to participate in their own growth and nation building? Singapore and the developed world have proved that the best way to distribute wealth among people is to have them contribute to its creation. Unfortunately, in Jamaica, this very promising method was set aside in favour of a welfare orientation.

Marcus Garvey did not play a role in the political developments, but he influenced the social and cultural life of Jamaica with his inspirational, motivational, revolutionary ideas and charismatic personality. To him we might attribute the first sounds of the awakening.[2] Unfortunately, for myth and legend, he personally failed at economic organization. His seeds fell on stony ground as there were hostile forces that proved much too powerful for him. Gordon Lewis notes that Garvey "openly challenged the reigning false standards of racial values based on racial self-respect and organized political party". This daring vision may have been betrayed by the conservatism and pragmatism of Bustamante and Norman Manley.

Historical and social setting

Historian Gordon Lewis deals mostly with themes of political development, with some social themes thrown in. He has been given credit for an in-depth analysis of the forces that have contributed to the shaping of West Indian Society.[3] He documents such forces as were at work in Jamaica. The title of his section, borrowed by this writer, is "The Emergence of National Society, Jamaica". He notes the differences in these forces as they operated in Trinidad, Barbados, Guyana and other territories. The weakness of most comparative studies is that they minimize significant and fundamental differences and over emphasize mostly superficial similarities. Such an error is not made by Lewis. He appears essentially to support my internal response theory since the crucial factors in the development of a nation are not the externally imposed systems and structures but the internal response. Those of other islands are essentially different from that of Jamaica.

Lewis also notes the desire of leaders to become heroes in colonial garb and to maintain the Jamaican social structure which Stone describes as a pyramid mound of three separate tiers. At the top is a white, upper class, including the older rural squirearchy and the top mercantile families. Next, there is the urban middle class groups and finally the great Jamaican working class, urban and rural. Wright agrees that the top classes are considered to be socially and politically reactionary. They continue to act as junior partners of expatriate financial enterprises and remain mentally colonized.[4]

Rex Nettleford, one of our foremost commentators on the cultural scene, in his collection of the speeches of Norman Manley raises questions about how broad Manley's vision of the New Jamaica was.[5] Did it go beyond the political and constitutional framework, the social levelling and welfare orientation? How was the new nation expected to make its living and contribute to the wealth of the world? Was the new nation to be a mere continuation of the status quo, the stratified society, the society of privilege, or was it to be one of equality, not just one man one vote, but one man equal opportunity? Was the society to be based on merit and contributions and excellence? Historians may not have the answers to these questions, but they should be the basic stock in trade of nation builders.

Modern political theory supports the notion that it is the responsibility of a government to provide for the welfare of all its citizens. Colonialism was a persistent denial of this theme. The colonial governing bodies cared for the welfare of the Jamaican people only so far as it served the interests of Empire. The unanswered question in the story of the Jamaican constitution is, for whom was it designed. Echoes of this unfinished business reverberate throughout the body politic even today. Thus *Gleaner* columnist Dawn Ritch calls into question the nature of the emergent society, the roles of justice and inequity. One explanation is that they are holdovers from the colonial period and that the evolution process was still incomplete in 1998. Ritch notes that the Financial Sector Adjustment Company Ltd (FINSAC) has been called upon to make the Ernst and Young and other reports public. No action has been forthcoming. She believes that there is enough evidence to prosecute individuals for taking depositors' money and using it for their own personal benefit and making loans to themselves or related parties and entities, which were neither properly secured nor are being serviced. She charges that "unsecured loans made to political figures and their friends are being extinguished. In such a cloudy atmosphere 'Big Tief' gets away because he has the best political connections".[6] As a matter of fact, the ancient Romans were faced with the same problem, according to the censor Cato who complained that petty thieves were punished while big thieves lived in purple and gold.

This observation neatly corroborates the thesis that privilege and patronage, rather than merit, formed the basis of the Jamaican political culture. Since very little was done to prevent this in the formative years, it should be no surprise that it is continuing to happen in 2001. Strictly speaking it cannot even be considered as a holdover from slavery and colonialism. It is more likely to have been reinstated as a feature of the modern political culture, since it continues with unabated vigour. This nests within a much larger issue of the belief that government has not conceded that the public has rights, despite transparency and the draft Freedom of Information Act.

Diana McCaulay, another *Gleaner* columnist, airs another aspect of the failure to change. She demonstrates that strongman rule and class structures are as firmly entrenched as ever. She uses the saga of Patrick Terrelonge and his dispute with Cable and Wireless as her illustration. She deplores the strongman tactics leading to his arrest, since a civil dispute does not call for criminal procedures. Government appears to be on the side of the large monopolists, in spite of its professed interest in the plight of the farmers.[7]

II: National Aims and Objectives

At present our culture political
To our nation's welfare proves inimical
To our People's dismay
It is bent on decay
And it calls for reforms that are radical

Michael Manley's *Struggle in the Periphery* is, among other things, a spirited defence of Jamaica's opposition to the imperialist policies of the United States in the period 1972 to 1980 and an account of the impact of this programme on the domestic scene.[8] Manley notes the strong opposition to his domestic policies by vested interests and seems unaware of the impact his close friendship with Cuba had on how people perceived his domestic actions. He seems to have forgotten that every move of his, however logical and reasonable, is going to be interpreted in the light of that friendship and the possibility that the Jamaican government was likely to adopt a communist regime, in spite of the many assurances to the contrary. His regime was a time of mostly social legislation and change without a concomitant economic base to sustain it.

In the light of the fact that the people of Latin America suffered more than others the injustices of the Monroe Doctrine, it is interesting to note that modern Latin America has been putting economic development, rather than getting even, at the forefront of its strategies. They know that any hope they have of redressing the wrongs wrought on them over the centuries by American commercial interests can only be fulfilled if they have strong economies, able to bargain on equal terms with the same interests. Israel's success at gaining recognition and compensation owes more to its strategic location on the access routes to Arabian oil and the wealth and power of Jewish interests in the United States than to any notions of right and wrong and ethical behaviour.

Alister McIntyre provides a profile of a typical Caribbean economy in the latter part of nineties, or rather what it ought to be. There is a diffusion of skills and indigenous entrepreneurship spread throughout the economy, raising production and productivity in both traditional and new activities. The country would have a well-rounded economy, taking full advantage of opportunities for product and market diversification in both goods and services producing sectors. It would be an economy with trade orientation, supplying simultaneously local, regional and extra-regional markets.[9] This comment by McIntyre anticipates the discussion of the First World aspirations, which every developing country is presumed to have. In my estimation very little has been done, except in Barbados, to create the infrastructure for this comprehensive development. In Jamaica, the essential unity of the nation, considered by many as a prerequisite for that type of development, is not even on the front burner. Most of these prerequisites, like a sound education, are social actions linked more to the social and political infrastructure than to the economic.

It must be nothing short of scandalous that some countries of the world, including our own, still need considerable foreign aid after nearly 40 years of independence. There is evidence to suggest that the donor countries are beginning to become concerned about the minimal impact of massive amounts of official aid on Third World economies. It seems to me that these development and aid people were focussing on the wrong things in the matter of development. It appeared that they did not make it clear to themselves exactly what they meant by development. Development must increase the capacity of the host people to take charge of their own development. I have very little sympathy for some of the donor countries who used the opportunity to create jobs for their own residents and to get rid of obsolete equipment and technologies.

Helen McBain's criticism of postcolonial regimes also underlines the theme of institutional and organizational failure. She covers the first post-independence decade of 1962 to 1972. She finds that the role of postcolonial institutions was not essentially different from colonial ones in so far as they guaranteed expanded capital accumulation through the extraction from production of relative surplus value. The Farmers' Pro-

duction programmes were unsuccessful since they were relying on traditional mechanisms to deal with structural problems. The Land Lease
programme suffered from poor organization, an absence of quality control in securing land and a high arrears rate in the repayment of loans.[10]

Towards the First World

In *Struggle in the Periphery,* Manley describes in detail what could have
been, from the perspective of 1938, a set of honourable aims and objectives for the emerging national society. The reform of the class system, the
removal of the extremes of poverty and wealth, the elimination of racial
discrimination, the introduction of a larger measure of social mobility
and redress of the injustice of the exclusion of more than 90 per cent of
the population from the political process would have been among the
objectives.

The rejection of the plantation system and its replacement by something more laudable was also another honorable aim. These had the effect
of uniting the patriots. According to him, these impulses led to the formation of the PNP in 1938, dedicated to self-government, independence,
the reform of the political system and the reorganization of the economy.
He observes that:

> the great imperialisms had left behind societies where the majority lived in
> dismal poverty with little education, inadequate health services, and squalid
> housing. Independence had not been won for bread alone: but bread in the
> sense of hope and the reality of material betterment, was always the largest
> part of the equation. Independence had to be followed by material progress
> for the majority who had never known it, indeed could never know it, while
> part of the colonial experience.

The tragedy of Michael Manley's eight years of government is that at
its end, and two other regimes later, the majority of the citizens of
Jamaica still do not know it. While deploring the complete dependency
of the South (Third World) upon the North (industrialized world), he
pursued policies in which the outcomes left his country even more dependent. Singapore, faced with the same dilemma in 1965, solved it by
making the country economically strong thereby joining the First World.[11]
The question which now arises is the extent to which Lee Kuan Yew
could have achieved these aims by an alliance with the Second (or socialist) World.

The concept of the enrichment of Jamaica, of moving from a Third
to a First World country seems never to have occurred to any Jamaican

government or leaders of intellectual thinking, with the possible exception of Marcus Garvey. Thinking on the development of Jamaica has been fixated at the level of incrementalism. Three attitudes appear to account for this behaviour: the first, that it is impossible; the second, that it is undesirable and the third, that is has already been achieved and therefore no need exists for such a movement. Current Jamaican attitudes and intellectual achievements are considered absolutes, like skin colour, impossible to change. There is no recognition that attitudes are a reflection of culture, reinforced by experiences. The belief that things are impossible to change acts as a self-fulfilling prophecy.[12]

One may elaborate somewhat on the three propositions advanced in the previous paragraph. First there is a very powerful group which is convinced and believe very strongly that this sort of development for Jamaica is impossible. With this belief they make sure that their prophecy is fulfilled. They make no provision for a high level of technological education to become available, since they are convinced that the local black Jamaican is incapable of learning anyway. In some strange way they equate the African heritage with ignorance. This is one of the relics of slavery and colonialism which the society has not only retained, but also reinforced.

Secondly, there are those who believe that even if it were possible it would not be desirable for Jamaicans. They simply cannot accept the idea that the ordinary Jamaican is entitled to all the courtesies, which arise from his status as a citizen. Civil behaviour is a privilege, which must be accorded to certain people, based on ascriptive criteria, such as race and class. Thus a minister of state can declare that a hospital unfit for humans is perfectly adequate, because he can fly his family to Miami for treatment. A prime minister also can summon up a helicopter to fly him to the airport when desperate citizens, without the ability to have access to their 'representative', have to resort to law breaking to get their message across. Finally, there are those who believe that Jamaica already enjoys First World status and therefore there is very little that needs be done in any fundamental way. Thus a national debt of billions is explained away and the fact that nearly two-thirds of the budget has to be used for debt service is treated as insignificant. After all, they argue quite truthfully that the United States is the greatest debtor nation in the world!

In Jamaica, this group of critics will point with pride at our recent successes (1998, but not 2001) in the World Cup and the Spelling Bee, at the sophistication of our dwellings and the 'crispness' of our cars as evidence of our having arrived. They forget about the illiterates who pour out of our educational system (including the tertiary levels), the grinding poverty and high level of savage crime which the authorities try to ensure is kept out of the world's news gathering networks.

Two comments by citizens should nullify any perception that Jamaica is already in the ranks of the First World. The first report concerns the degree of pressure on young and old, which may have negative effects on the quality of life for individuals. It is a forecast of the highest rate of suicide for this year. The causes are mostly living alone and depression. "Sometimes the pressures of life get too intense and individuals decide to take their own lives". Many of those attempting suicide are not mentally ill.[13] The second report is again on the quality of life and the impact of culture. There are frequent complaints about loud music on buses and the response of the passengers and driver to requests to turn it down. The reporter calls on the police and the authorities to deal with the situation.[14]

For several issues in 1999, the back page of *Flair* magazine carried an advertisement for Dehring, Bunting and Golding, in which a very beautiful Jamaican girl, about six years old, was made to say, "I want Jamaica to be a First World country by the time I grow up", implying that if one used the services offered by the advertiser, such a condition would arise sooner than later. Advertising puffery aside, the sentiment about being a First World country in 20 years is one that should be taken seriously by all well thinking Jamaicans. Between the wish and the deed, however, there is a lifetime of vision, entrepreneurship, hard work and the facing of reality, much of which is not common currency in the Jamaican society. In the Caribbean, Barbados and Trinidad are well on their way towards achieving this status: a Barbadian prime minister has privately admitted that his early work in a Jamaican government department has enabled him to help Barbados to avoid the mistakes that Jamaica continues to make.

III: The Ordinary People of Jamaica

Our society does not create wealth
A component quite vital for health
What you cannot afford
To expect is absurd
And you only can get it by stealth

National movements in Jamaica, from the time of the 1920s and 1930s, had to contend with a very subtle and insidious enemy, the blind hostility towards the ordinary people and the black majority of the Jamaican colonial system and its controlling forces, who generally buttressed their position with a plethora of racist arguments. Even today (July 2001) the prime vehicle for crime fighting is reliance on further force. One may wonder to what extent the modern governments (note the plural) of Jamaica regard themselves as embattled and besieged by the black majority, to the extent that when the road to the airport is blocked, one takes a helicopter there.

The level of contempt for the ordinary people of Jamaica by its government (colonial or independent) can also be gauged from the treatment of the parochial boards (now parish councils). During the nineteenth century the boards, despite the limited popular representation they enjoyed, were regularly dissolved and replaced by commissioners. In 1964, just two years after independence, the Kingston and St Andrew Corporation was dissolved and replaced by commissioners. Today the neglect of parish councils and the belittling of the concerns of the people they represent, take the form of failure to have the local government elections on time, especially where the ruling political party sees no immediate electoral advantage from the exercise.

John Rapley, in discussing the history of development tends to put a great deal of emphasis on political and economic processes at the highest level and does not bother too much about the people who are undergoing the development process. Occasionally, as now, he relaxes that professional stance and concedes that the people do seem to have some part to play. For him the really troubling questions are those not posed by the left or the right, but those raised by the experiences of the people in much, perhaps most, of the Third World who have benefited little from the development debate and are unlikely to do so soon.[15] It is a basic tenet of my approach that any development, which is not rooted in the culture of the people nor accepted by them is doomed to failure. A major prerequisite to the institution of any such programme should be knowledge of how the people would respond to such initiatives. This is a measure of its feasibility and social soundness. Michael Manley did the right thing in finding out about the Jamaican people.

Unfortunately for Jamaicans, this knowledge seems to have been acquired after he demitted office. Manley noted that there was a natural tendency of Jamaicans to be disputatious and individualistic, but to accept a majority vote as conclusive. On the other hand, they have a strong distrust of authority, after emerging from a background of total tyranny. He also believes that the Westminster model builds upon the Jamaican tendency towards containment of authority.[16]

During a genuine process of nation building, institutions could have been designed to restore social patterns destroyed by slavery and to remove the distrust of authority engendered by colonialism. Instead, the new institutions continued to practise the behaviour of the old tyrants. The expediency of a quick decision in Parliament was made to override the distribution of political power favoured by the American system. On the other hand, legislative gridlock has positive results for the organization. It forces all the combatants to seek compromise and consensus, generally resulting in a programme that everyone can live with. Despite popular (and scholarly) belief, the Westminster model has not been permitted to work in Jamaica. "Authority continued to be the instrument of oppression." If this is so today, it can only be attributed to the postcolonial authorities in Jamaica.[17]

Welfare versus achievement

The immediate aftermath of the 1938 disturbances could either have laid the foundations of a totally new political culture or reinforced the existing institutions for maintenance of the old political culture. The latter prevails today and this author will argue that this wrong choice accounts for all the social, political and economic weaknesses of the country.

Doubtless, this choice was considered the most feasible at the time from those available to the leaders of Jamaica, Alexander Bustamante and Norman Manley, when they emerged upon the national scene. Norman Manley's work with Jamaica Welfare Ltd and his collaboration with the United Fruit Company were no doubt born of a deep concern about the physical and social conditions of the ordinary Jamaican workers. Alexander Bustamante's pioneering work in the organization of a trade union also reflected his deep concern. Unfortunately for Jamaica, both of them accepted that the current structure of society, based on race and class, would continue to be the natural order of things. Bustamante was more overt in his early opposition to the idea of independence.

Neither political leader quite embraced the notion of a partnership with the ordinary people of Jamaica: both operated under a notion similar to those of the racist colonials that the ordinary people of Jamaica could never evolve into a technologically competent people, capable of generating high levels of wealth. This amounts to a betrayal of the ideals of Marcus Garvey.

This very shortsighted version of the national aims and objectives of an emerging country has been built into the national psyche and culture of the Jamaican and has so far stultified every effort at national economic regeneration. The neglect of or lip service paid to the development process by every subsequent government has left the country divided and mired in a dependency syndrome, which is in turn deplored by the very people who created it and are the prime beneficiaries of it.

Today this preference for poverty alleviation rather than poverty elimination and wealth creation probably accounts for the abundance of voluntary social services in Jamaica. The most recent handbook of the Council of Voluntary Social Services lists 163 organizations engaged in social work activities of some sort. On the one hand, this may be interpreted as a sign that Jamaicans are a caring people; on the other hand, it may be an admission of weakness in that the society has generated so few job and wealth creating opportunities that an abundance of charitable organizations has to exist to alleviate the inevitable poverty. One side effect of this is to create a syndrome of dependency and lack of initiative and creativity.

In a vibrant economy these demands for social welfare can normally be easily accommodated, but given the economic crises that have been the lot of Jamaica over the past 25 years or so, the sources of voluntary contributions have been fast drying up. Even advanced economies can suffer greatly when forced to bear too large a burden in social welfare. Britain almost went bankrupt in the 1960s from the burden of the welfare state. At first Singapore and the Tigers of the Far East did not have, or need, any government sponsored social security system. Families were expected to take care of the needy, the handicapped and the elderly. Since this was first written, most of the countries of the Far East, including Singapore, have now modified social welfare schemes. Back in Jamaica, these voluntary organizations have to rely more and more on government funds, a hopeless move, since the government is broke anyway.

Jamaican society – then and now

The rest of this section discusses the theme of Jamaican society then and now. It was of course impossible for the founding fathers to predict the future identity of Jamaicans of quality, but they could have arranged institutions to give them scope to develop their talents. Many men and women of talent emerged in the 1940s: Philip Sherlock, Eddie Burke, Thom Girvan, Edwin Allen, O.T. Fairclough, to name a few from memory. Bustamante and Manley were not the only ones. The late 1930s through to the 1950s coincided with the emergence of a budding nationalism. The possibilities inherent in the latent talent only emerged much later, when the circumstances were favourable, mostly abroad and not in Jamaica.

Gordon Lewis declares that Jamaica has always been accorded the leadership role in the Caribbean, primarily because of its size, population, antiquity and its past economic importance, which it is now rapidly losing. This positive perception of Jamaica in the past continues today. This role has been somewhat tarnished by the choice made in 1959 by Norman Manley, with respect to his service in the late West Indies Federation. In spite of our membership of CARICOM, isolationist tendencies tend to arise in Jamaican leaders from time to time.[18]

Lewis also comments on the "realization that the *Moyne Report* was nothing more than a futile proposal to make charitable social services do duty for economic, political and social reform, and finally demonstrated the truth that Jamaican hopes would depend on Jamaican efforts". How early this realization came to our founding fathers and how they responded to it are not clear. One can only infer from the subsequent history. To this writer, it seems that the second part has been rejected and has not become the basis of our political culture, while the first part has become overwhelmingly so. Whatever the motives may have been, the outcomes are evident. The result, as Lewis puts it, is "a two-party system in which both parties, although necessarily based on a mass basis, are fundamentally bourgeois in spirit, led by a foreign educated middle class leadership". If that is so, then the leadership may be faced with the dilemma of promoting something alien to their own class interests. Furthermore, as Richardson points out, the underlying racial stratification is not completely masked by our motto.[19]

Circumstances like these give more fuel to the idea of a non-meritorious society, based on patronage rather than performance. Carl Stone's studies on the Jamaican class structure makes this point clear.[20] The society is still shaped by a colonialist heritage. At worst it is matter of choice, but there is an absence of any real sense of belonging as Morrissey discovered, in studying the country preferences of a group of school children.[21]

Examples abound of latent talent blossoming forth once the circumstances are propitious. The major failure of successive Jamaican governments has been in creating fostering institutions. For every extraordinary story there are dozens of ordinary successes. The United States government regularly publishes figures to show the contribution of recent minority migrants to the country, reckoned in billions of dollars to the economy. The lack of suitable institutions to tap this abundance of talent has been our administration's most dismal failure. We believe that too much attention has been paid to our past history and not enough to our future potential. Excellence in achievement is no stranger to Jamaicans. However, there is a special pride in the achievements of a fellow Jamaican who has worked up the economic, social and political ladder to become mayor of an English town. His is the standard rags to riches story.[22]

The next citation further examines the potential for creativity and growth. Jamaica ranks number one in functional literacy in a survey involving 89 developing countries as Errol Miller quotes from a UNESCO report. He cannot find any evidence to support the contention that children in today's primary schools are not as advanced as their counterparts before them. He maintains that children today are brighter and more advanced than those in the 1960s and 1970s. The minister of state is wrong in linking literacy only with rich and productive states.[23] There is some doubt in my mind as to the meaning of 'functional literacy'. I have seen it described as the ability to write and read one's own name. Such a standard would be woefully inadequate if citizens are to contribute meaningfully to their own development. The term is actually reserved for a level of literacy which will allow the individual to 'function' properly in a modern society. It is the minimum standard.

Sometimes hopeful signs occur sporadically that the Jamaican situation is not completely beyond redemption. The maiden speech of a newly appointed senator is perhaps one such occasion. The member has not yet been sullied by the existing political culture. He is not yet aware that the political culture does not encourage the admission of mistakes, much less the correction of them. The descent of Jamaica from a Caribbean leader to a position of penury is not accidental: it was designed and intended, perhaps not deliberately, but by default. Everything, including the fortunes of a nation, has been made to serve the short-term interests of politics. He does not attribute the flaws to the political culture. After all, he is seeking to join the club.

Since this is the main area of interest of the new senator, he gives a thorough review of the problems of agriculture, including sugar, citrus, bananas, coffee and commodity boards, even giving some unsolicited advice to Roger Clarke, the minister. "We have seen in one short generation our shameful descent from being top of the Caribbean heap to vying for last place with Haiti". In passing, he also condemns the role of political favouritism in the appointment of board members.[24]

Institution building is the theme of the three articles that will be cited in the remainder of this section. Having observed the tremendous amount of energy released over the preparations for Jamaica's successful participation in the 1998 World Cup, Lloyd Smith attempts to move the argument from football to national development. There must first be "inspiring leadership, that cares, is committed: leadership that takes the high road to discipline, honesty and hard work". The media would like to play the role of the watchdogs, but they have been rendered toothless. If they bark or bite, that is the road to ostracism. Journalists are being intimidated in subtle ways.[25]

There is much in this comment to lend support to the unwanted workings of the current political culture. I agree with him as to the need for inspiring leadership, but one needs to look at it not only as a property of an individual but also as a process. How the leader organizes his systems and gets the best performance out of his followers is the crucial test. In this context the prime minister ought not only to be a leader but a manager as well. Watchdogs and corrective measures have to be built into the system. The current system of selecting candidates makes it impossible for parliament to play the watchdog role.

Vision is a key factor in the process of institution building, but to the writer of this article, the vision appears to be missing. The writer notes the critical economic conditions and asks for a stable exchange rate, deplores the multi-tax regime and calls for the elimination of double standards. In answering, my comment is that these are not possible unless the political culture is reformed. The present proposals look good, but serve only to alleviate symptoms. The causes of the present behaviour of the government and people lie much deeper and must be sought out.[26]

We may cite one more letter to close this section. The writer notes that the minister has invited well thinking Jamaicans to support his stance on roadblocks. Heads would roll in many countries if officials allowed the mob to take over city streets. By contrast in Jamaica incompetent officials are rewarded and promoted.[27] The response of the public to block the streets is a political rather than a legal matter. The political imperative of permitting the voice of the people to be heard by their government has pitted the rule of law against the rights and expectations of citizens. Historically, many persons of the lower classes have seen the law as a device for the oppression of the poor and weak. That the political culture has the effect of rewarding incompetent officials is a major issue in this book, a practice aided and abetted by the absence of any corrective mechanism.

The creation of wealth

The welfare oriented approach to solving the economic problems of an emerging country is based merely upon the alleviation of present and persistent poverty which George Beckford describes in a book of similar title.[28] As Beckford eloquently argues, the persistence of the poverty is based upon a number of structural features, the elimination of which played very little part in the programme put in train by our emerging leaders. Latifundia agriculture had provided the basis on which the Jamaican class structure firmly rested. Reforming this sector was and still is faced with great difficulties. The alternative was industry and technology. According to Farrell, parts of the *Moyne Report* made provisions for some technological opportunities, which were only partially implemented, thereby retaining the class structure.[29]

Gordon Lewis suggests that the welfare orientation might have had further impact. In the presence of slave revolts, maroons, and other unsettling factors one might well ask how these rebellious forces were pacified. The settlers might have bought them off, thus reinforcing the insidious influence of welfare politics.[30] He believes that Bustamante lost the ideological elements of positive nationalism and racial pride, both of which he credits to Marcus Garvey. For the PNP, there was a gradual surrender of its early anti-imperialist stance in favour of a policy of collaboration with the British ruling class. One outcome of this new stance was that constitutional and other advancements were seen as gifts rather than as victories on the part of the national task force at the independence negotiations. Poll reports from 1998 and 1999 have found that a majority of persons regard the pre-independence quality of life better than the post-independence, despite the lowering of their expectations and aspirations.

The founding of the PNP and BITU in the late thirties was a necessary step in the process of institution building to organize the march towards self-government and independence. Bustamante's original opposition to self-government is rather ironical in the context. Henry believes that fortuitous circumstances rather than the efficacy of internal economic policy was the major causative factor for growth in the Commonwealth Caribbean, for example, oil prices in Trinidad in 1973 and following and Bauxite expansion in Jamaica in 1960s.[31]

He gives a summary of the Arthur Lewis intervention (1950) under the heading of an industrial strategy for the Commonwealth Caribbean. As we shall see this strategy was only half implemented but Lewis has been blamed for the consequences. On the other hand, Hong Kong and Singapore (1960s and 1970s) brilliantly carried it through to the second and perhaps third and final stages. Jamaica is still bungling the first stage of import substitution and in the process has dismantled all the work of Robert Lightbourne. This comment by Henry gives strong support to my internal response theory that the major causative factor is not external circumstance (pushed ad nauseam in Manley's *Periphery* and Barry, Wood and Preusch's *The Other side of Paradise*), but how the country responds to the opportunities and threats which beset it.[32] Barbados intends to make strides in taking advantage of the technological opportunities in computers with their Edu-Tech 2000 and is mobilizing the entire country by way of the Smart Partnership idea.[33]

IV: Aspects of Social Structure

If we don't recognize equal worth
Our folks they will opt to go North
If our leader not heeds
And fails to meet needs
In a programme they ought to set forth

Social structure may be considered an intervening variable between the people and their development. It is so important that it might lead one to the frightening conclusion that economic development is impossible for some peoples, given the persistence of certain social structures. Social structure serves as a means by which the development process can be furthered. If the social structure inhibits the development process, it may have to be the first target of the process. The dilemma is to preserve its best features even while changing it.

Organizational change is difficult enough, even if it does deal with a relatively homogenous class which is already somewhat disposed to carry out a programme for their common survival. Yet it was done at the national level in Barbados as well as in Singapore. In Jamaica, development, especially if based on merit and high levels of technology, will change the social structure drastically. The evidence amassed suggests that these changes will not be to the liking of powerful interest groups in our society.

In all matters of political sociology the contributions of Carl Stone can always be depended on.[34] His notion of deepening the Jamaican democracy is useful and fertile. He notes the impact of an elitist philosophy on our national life in the workplace and at the school. One of its most undesirable effects is the snobbery and social discrimination against the black majority, practised also, even by some of the established churches. This is a fallout of white domination in which authority was associated with class and racial oppression.

Populism has led to the weakening of all sorts of authority, including that of government. Society becomes more difficult to govern as populism has escalated to levels of anarchist absurdity. Focus is now on the effects of hierarchical party leadership and the rituals designed to strengthen it. Since Stone's passing, the weakening of authority has escalated even further to higher levels of absurdity. Its impact is now seen and felt everywhere on the judicial system – the phenomenon of Zekes and other dons, absurd jury verdicts and attacks on policemen. The politicians adamantly refuse to accept that their policies have had these impacts.

Brown and LeFranc also take up the theme of the peculiarities of Jamaica in their acknowledgment of major historical and cultural differences between Jamaica and Barbados, arising from their differences in topography, their post slavery experience, their access to education, and their respective structural adjustment programmes.[35] They recognize that their case study approach admits little scope for generalization. Their study accepts the general formulation of relationships that principles, values and beliefs underlie a person's approach to work, affect his work attitude and eventually work output and economic behaviour. They believe that the Protestant Ethic of work for its own sake is not current in the Caribbean and that work is valued for the return it brings. They conclude, however, that the spirit of entrepreneurship and positive work ethic does exist in the Caribbean.

The authors distinguish between work ethic and work attitude. Whether the entrepreneurship is sustainable or the work ethic will translate into positive work attitudes depends on several factors, including the necessary knowledge base and confidence to carry on in the face of obstacles. Relatively higher levels of education result in greater sustainability of business enterprise.

Black entrepreneurs in Jamaica continue to demonstrate a preoccupation with status but their performance is not affected if accompanied by high levels of education. Low levels of education in entrepreneurs have led to disastrous results in Jamaica. Entrepreneurship is also affected by more than 20 years of structural adjustment in Jamaica, which has been accompanied by the absence of social partnership in which employers and policy makers seek to share the general hardship with price freezes and/or wages which correspond to the cost of living. Adjustments and plans at the macro level seem to have little impact at the micro level, because of the differences between the scholarly theorizing and the way life is lived at that level. Gray, LeFranc and Brown should be a corrective for Jones and Mills in the first article from the same publication.

There is, within the country, a fairly broad understanding of the relationship between work and reward, which forms the basis of all motivation theory. Our attempts at forging a social partnership have not been successful. In this connection one may compare the Protocols for the Social Partnership, successfully carried out in Barbados, and the part played by non-economic factors.

Errol Miller has an alternative explanation for the low levels of entrepreneurship displayed in our society especially on the part of our men.[36] His *theory of place* accepts that an egalitarian society is a utopian ideal that can never be achieved in reality. Human societies are marked by relative inequality. In fact, inequality is the dynamic that fosters change. Society needs structure, that is, a basis on which to allocate and justify inequality. Complex criteria have been invented to justify the place any individual holds in the society, a temporary base on which inequality is justified at any given time. The operational absolutes in Jamaica since 1655 have been race, status groups, gender and age. Major changes have occurred since emancipation.

Miller claims to have tested the theory of place by using historical and other data analysis done in Jamaica upon gender changes in roles, particularly in the teaching profession. He notes the long term impact of the gender shift. These are the consequences of several social aims designed to neutralize the potential development of a militant group of black men, lessen the influence of the church in a state controlled education system, keep black men as cheap source of labour in the productive sector (agriculture), afford the black women the status of social equal but not the black men and reduce the cost of the teaching service by the lower salaries that could be commanded by women. All of these materialized in the early period of the twentieth century. These results have been perpetuated by educational development plans from 1943 to 1995, which assumed dominant female participation.

Public behaviour

In the 1970s, short-term electoral prospects made it politically important to support the people's culture. Vestiges of middle class morality and behaviour were considered undesirable, although the middle class citizens are no paragons of virtue these days. The workings of the political culture of welfare and entitlement stressed rights, but no corresponding duties. Undesirable public behaviour was more rife with official sanction then, where any demand for courtesy and good manners instead of aggression leading to violence was regarded as stifling the cultural expression of the majority classes. No thought was given to the functionality of courteous behaviour for the good order of society, nor the fact that culture is something taught by society. This suggests that the behaviour patterns of the various classes have been examined and that of the unlettered majority held up as the model.

The task of any society is to preserve the good while modifying the not so good. P.J. Patterson's promise for a more civil society is the theme of this letter. That promise, so far unfulfilled, is contrasted with the increased coarseness and glorification of 'bugu yagga' behaviour. Advertisers and the electronic media are seen as the main offenders. Shouting in conversation is abundant and no common courtesies are shown. This is a not so attractive reflection of Jamaican reality.[37]

Home and family

Miller's notion of the marginalization of the black male has echoes in this report from Patricia Watson. Jamaican fathers who are unable to care for their children financially are losing their parental rights. In this culture the man is expected to provide financially for his children and their mother: if this does not happen, then there is technical abandonment. This, in spite of the changing perspectives on parenting with a number of progressive ideas, increasingly being shared by Jamaican men.[38] This report is a blow to those politicians who believe that family problems do not have economic roots. The general impression one forms is that men want to perform their fair share of the duties, but lack the economic ability. This inability is a source of tension and abuse in the family. More marginalization occurs and a further subtraction of a crucial feature of the male role.[39]

The devastating effect that the political culture has had upon the lives and prospects of the children is illustrated in this article by MM. She starts off with a dispute between a bus conductor using abusive language and the children standing on the bus step.[40] To her, this experience leads to the questions: Who am I? What is my worth? How dispensable have I become? Children are abused by all and sundry as poor, unlearned and unwanted. Generally, they face deplorable treatment all round. Further, questions arise about the responsibility for the children's education, whether of governments, opposition, business, or the ordinary worker. The children's language becomes abusive and their perception destroyed. One must add these sources to those causing the abusive and aggressive language discussed above. My contention is that the possible effects on these children were forgotten in the ladling out of privilege and patronage and welfare in the 1930s and early 1940s. This represents a betrayal of Marcus Garvey's hopes.

Worth continues to be judged by class and race, not individual merit. The political culture must provide the means of answering MM's questions, posed two paragraphs ago. That they remain unanswered after two generations shows that even when they entered the thoughts of the founding fathers, the resulting institutions had no place for the ordinary people except as targets of patronage in exchange for their votes. Our value system suggests that it was (and still is) more important for the politicians to keep their seats than for the country to progress. The norm has been the exclusion of the ordinary people from the political, social and economic development processes. This realization leads to doubt about their social identity.

Notes

1. Nettleford in Wedderburn, 159, p 1 ff.
2. Carl Stone, 146, p 1 ff.
3. Rupert Lewis, 79, pp 209–219.
4. Gordon Lewis, 77, p 167 ff.
5. Rex Nettleford, 102, p xvii.
6. Dawn Ritch "'Big Tief' Gets Away – Again" (article), *Sunday Gleaner* (28 June 1998), p 11A.
7. Diana McCaulay, "What Applies in Jamaica" (article), *Sunday Gleaner* (28 June 1998), p 9A.
8. Michael Manley, 85.
9. Alister McIntyre (Keynote Address), "The International Economic Situation: Elements for a Policy Agenda", in Norman Girvan and George Beckford, 40, p 9.
10. Helen McBain, 82, pp 141, 142, 147.
11. Lee Kuan Yew, 69, 70. His later work is pointedly titled *From Third World to First*.
12. Gordon Lewis, 77, p 167 ff.
13. "Suicide Trends Point to Record High" (report), *Daily Observer* (22 June 1998), p 5.
14. Carl Wint, "The Old Can't Stand the Pressure" (letter), *Daily Gleaner* (27 June 1998) p A5.
15. John Rapley, 126, p 3.
16. Michael Manley, 85, p 28.
17. Gladstone E Mills, 93, p 9. See also Patrick A. M. Emmanuel, 31, p 4.
18. Gordon Lewis, 77, p 184.
19. Mary Richardson, 129, p 143 ff.

20. Carl Stone, 148, p 11 ff.
21. Michael Morissey, 97, p 1 ff.
22. Keril Wright, "From Carpenter to Mayor: Another Jamaican Excels Abroad" (article), *Daily Gleaner* (Thursday 23 July 1998), p B11.
23. "Ja's Education System World Rated" (report), *Daily Gleaner* (Tuesday 21 July 1998), p A3.
24. "Give Jamaicans Good Governance" (address to Senate), *Daily Observer* (Saturday 3 October 1998), p 7.
25. Lloyd B. Smith, "The Road to Jamaica" (article), *Daily Observer* (Tuesday 7 July 1998), p 6.
26. "JMA Head Calls for National Vision" (report), *Financial Gleaner* (Friday 19 June 1998), p 8.
27. Peter Robinson, "National Insecurity" (letter), *Daily Gleaner* (Friday 23 October 1998), p A5.
28. George L Beckford, 6, p 53 ff.
29. Trevor M.A. Farrell, in Omar Davies, 27, p 6.
30. Gordon Lewis, 77, p 175.
31. Ralph M Henry, 53, p 7.
32. Michael Manley, 85. See also Tom Barry, Beth Wood and Deb Preusch, 5.
33. The Edu-Tech 2000 programmes in both Jamaica and Barbados are based on the provision of high value-added computer information technology for the developed world. The Smart Partnerships for the Creation of Wealth are based on the idea of strategic partnerships between a Barbadian firm and one in a developed country. The programme is sponsored by the Commonwealth Partnership for Technology Management.
34. Carl Stone, in Omar Davies, 27, p 90 ff. The description of the Jamaican social structure is taken from Stone, 148, p 11 ff. For a general view of the temper of Jamaican society, see Ashton Wright, 162.
35. Lynette Brown and Elsie LeFranc, 16, p 42 ff.
36. Errol Miller, 92, p 12.
37. Sonia Harrison, "For a More Civilized Society" (letter), *Daily Gleaner* (Thursday 2 April 1998), p A5.
38. Patricia Watson, "'Poor' Dads Complain" (report), *Sunday Gleaner* (21 June 1998), p 3A.
39. The classic study on parental roles was done in Jamaica by Edith Clarke, 23.
40. M.M., "That Child on the Street" (article), *Daily Gleaner* (Tuesday 7 July 1998), p A8.

3

Tools for Achievement

To seek to develop sans *People*
Is as futile as chasing a steeple
If they can't innovate
Or have talents innate
Your development's not worth a wimple!

I: Available Institutions

Having set out your aims, you need tools to achieve them. If the aims are developmental, one must involve the people, voluntarily, since development is impossible without the voluntary involvement of the people. Development, as defined by the best authorities, requires this voluntary participation of individuals who are both the targets and the instruments of development. Individuals must acquire the mental and intellectual tools: engineers must acquire greater expertise in engineering, doctors in medicine, managers in management skills. The acquisition of these skills and the willingness to use them cannot be coerced, only encouraged. The interpretations of those economists and political scientists who see coercion and dictatorial methods in the successes of Singapore are seriously flawed in this respect. Nobody achieves the status of PhD under compulsion.

Economists particularly, in their hurry to begin their calculations, frequently overlook a vital component of the development process – a highly motivated, creative and well educated populace. Their leaders must also understand the interrelationships of the various tools for development; people, machines, equipment, and the processes of finance, production management and marketing. Socialist leaning leaders are by training and temperament less likely to understand the process of wealth creation and appreciate its importance. They must face up to the dilemma of wealth creation and distribution.

It is rather ironic that Michael Manley, he of the eight years of negative growth and crawling pegs, should be the one offering sage advice about the economies of Third World countries. His book, *Struggle in the Periphery*, was published in 1982, after he had demitted office. It is unfortunate that this understanding did not arrive ten years previously.[1] He declares that those wishing to study seriously the 'economic history of the Third World must begin with an understanding of three facts:

- No attempt is made to produce what was needed by the producers, but only to produce what someone else needed.
- Trade was not a calculated exchange of surpluses but importation of everything that was needed and export of virtually everything that was produced.
- Surplus was exported abroad in the form of profits.

With his understanding of the processes by which wealth is created and maintained in a society, one would have expected that the thrust of his entire regime would have been in building institutions to deal successfully with the three features of the economy of Jamaica. In building these institutions he would be ensuring that they had the capacity for effectiveness and sustainability, and give them every encouragement of which he and his government were capable. On the contrary, a comparison of one of his arguments about the necessity of creating such institutions with the actual outcomes makes rather peculiar reading.

On pages 52 to 53, Manley adduces some convincing arguments on the usefulness of the system of local government and deplores the fact that existing parish councils are "representative, responsible but powerless". His solution, however, is to further reduce their power by creating community councils to take over. In the nature of organizations in Jamaica, especially political ones, the probabilities are high that these new creations will not survive the regime that instituted them because they are seen as political arms serving a political party and being part of the system by which the spoils of office are distributed. To paraphrase Kaufman, they have no roots in the culture of the wider society and are not socially sound.[2]

The Value of Commitment

In the same work, Manley outlines four basic commitments that a government must give to its people: to

- create an economy more independent of foreign control and more responsive to the needs of the majority of the people at home,
- work for an egalitarian society, equality of opportunity and a feeling of equal worth and value,
- develop a truly democratic society, meaning more than just manipulating votes every five years, and to
- rediscover our heritage and retrace our history. He claims the right to be judged on intentions as much as on achievements. He recognizes the existence of contrary factors both internal and external to the country. It is proper to begin with intentions.

But not to end with them, one might retort. The country has the right to expect results and outcomes, not merely intentions. As prime minister he had the choice of either creating new institutions or modifying existing ones to new purposes. His full understanding of the nuances of the Jamaican economy is shown in the discussion above.

The great gulf between intention and implementation has never been bridged. Little thought has been given about the means to these ends. Very little attempt was made to win the support and encouragement of the moneyed persons in the country. These good intentions were mainly nullified by his close embrace with Castro. He made insufficient study of the processes by which individuals and groups become committed to causes. Ideology was added as another divisive factor on top of race, class, colour etc.[3]

Beckford and Girvan in their study are aware of the possibility that the global economy is undergoing a major, long term, structural crisis of its own.[4] Long term technological and demographic changes are affecting the potential demand for Caribbean exports. McIntyre in his contribution to the same volume notes the important implication that Caribbean countries will "have to transform their patterns of development from one centred around the utilization of natural resources, to one relying on the utilization and upgrading of human resources". To this end they call for massive investment in people, with an emphasis on trust and confidence building.

In his contribution to the same publication, C.Y. Thomas notes the relationship between the continuing crisis in Guyana and its underlying social characteristics, including, *inter alia*, that the existing production structure replicates the past colonial pattern of exploitation and that no significant level of diversification has occurred since independence.[5] The main class institutions are in a condition of infancy, where the state, political parties, trade unions, ideological institutions are under the domination of the petty bourgeoisie and other intermediate social strata. He thinks that these taken together constitute a *permanent* or *ongoing crisis*, to be distinguished from *periodic crisis*, and *general crisis*. Examination of the mechanisms of economic dislocation show that these arise from two aspects of the social system: one, the rapid expansion of the state sector and two, the illegitimacy of the present (1986) Guyana government from the manipulation by US/UK/CIA in the 1960s. No blame should be attached to the world economic crisis of the mid 1970s, since there has been no collapse of export prices for rice and bauxite.

This commentary reads almost word for word with my main findings on the situation in Jamaica. Not only does it support my main thesis of the causes of the crises in Jamaica but it also suggests the way out of the dilemma. Basically it is the necessity for institution building to remove the ongoing crisis.

The remainder of the article traces the consequences of the authoritarian state. Recourse to such a system always seems to offer an easy way out of our troubles. Perhaps the experiences of Guyana have some lessons for us. Not surprisingly, Thomas does not place any emphasis on the role of the various institutions and their internal dynamics. Jamaica does not have a formal authoritarian regime, apparently maintaining the Westminster model. Very few individuals have enquired searchingly into the true nature of this model. Even Mills does not tackle the correct question, which is, to what extent has the Westminster model served the needs of the Jamaican people? [6] Our practice consistently stresses the primacy of the political party over the interests of the people.

II: Political Parties

In Jamaica the Honorable Prime Minister
Sets his face against anything sinister
The Politics of the Right
He eschews with his might
And would like it exiled to Cape Finisterre

The standard tool, which is universally considered the major means of achieving the social and economic ends laid down in the statement of aims and objectives of the society, is the political party. Political parties are convenient institutions to bring together a wide range of skills, talent, commitment and motivation vital to the economic growth and development of the emerging nation. Thus the formation of the PNP in 1938 and the JLP in 1943 was hailed as major steps forward in the growth and development of Jamaica into a modern society.

Many persons are still proud of this achievement: the major participants, Alexander Bustamante and Norman Manley, have acquired the status of national heroes. The question which must be asked 63 and 58 years later, respectively, and answered urgently is whether or not the major parties still serve the national interest as they were intended to, and might have done, in the past. The danger facing any organization like a political party is that a system designed as a means to an end may evolve into an end in itself. Thus the major preoccupation of the members and supporters of the party becomes its preservation for its own sake, conveniently forgetting why the institution was formed in the first place. To account for the phenomenon of goal displacement as illustrated here, it is useful to ask some pointed questions. To begin with:

- What is the nature of a political party?
- Are they private bodies, semi-public or public ones?
- Can anyone be a member, regardless of his political views or must he always conform to the thought processes of the leading members?
- How does the system provide for change, in outlook, ideology, policies and practice? What is the process of renewal?
- Political parties have become widespread in all societies in the world, but have their effects ever been evaluated in any serious way?
- What are their obligations towards all the people of a given society?
- Are they justified in engaging in ethnic cleansing as in Kosovo of the 1990s or political cleansing as in Rema of the 1970s?
- Is a political party a private assemblage, which has gained a monopoly over a public function? To what extent is it a private cabal, or does it represent the interest of all the people?
- Why should the citizens of a country hand over their fate to a private institution that is outside of their control?
- What gives political parties the right to have a virtual monopoly over the power of the state?
- Apparently in Jamaica they have such a monopoly, which on the face of it they gain from periodic elections. But is the electoral process sufficiently free of fraud, fear, coercion and corruption to give legitimacy to the claim of representation of the majority of the people and their interests?

- And how about the diminishing number of electors who go to the polls through lack of faith in the efficacy of the system and the consequence of minority support for the so called landslide result?
- What happens when the major features of the party become dysfunctional and outdated?

Unsatisfactory answers to these questions seriously undermine the legitimacy of the political regimes we have endured in this country.

Michael Manley discovered the hard way that organizations do evolve. His misunderstanding of the nature of people and organizations led him to set up institutions and systems which were mutually incompatible. His endeavours to enlarge the public sector, particularly in strategic areas of the economy, were based on the idea that the state should control the commanding heights of the economy. Public funds were freely made available for agriculture, for public ownership in the banking sector and in areas deemed sensitive to national priorities. The distribution and marketing of sugar was done through the Sugar Industry Authority and the State Trading Corporation was created to import and distribute staples, drugs, timber, etc. A vigorous programme of land reform was also instituted. Responsibility for the remainder of the economy was left in the hands of the private sector.

A comprehensive analysis of the failures and weaknesses of many of the institutions is presented in the later pages of his work, *Struggle in the Periphery*. Shortcomings in the law, industrial relations, distribution of wealth and technology are highlighted against a social background of elitist assumptions, inadequate education and political tribalism. The superficiality of the democratic process, the alienation of the majority of the population from the decision making process, the nature of a democratic society and their effects are carefully documented. A summary of the methods used to tackle many of them include worker participation on boards, community councils, etc.[7]

The opportunity to answer some of these profound questions on the nature of political organizations was clearly not taken up by Manley. Many of the activities described above had the effect of advancing the interests of the party (and Power) over those of the People. In most cases the solutions bypassed existing institutions and depended on new, untried personnel and systems, manned by unskilled individuals whose major qualification was their commitment to party ideology. The major institutions set up to ensure their ideological suitability was the Pickersgill Accreditation Committee, which is not mentioned in *Struggle* and the Ministry of Mobilisation, which is.

One may compare the experience of Guyana in the 1980s where the list of undesirable effects reads almost like those in Jamaica in the 1970s. These include unplanned, uncoordinated expansion of and political 'diktats' in the state sector, leading to nepotism, corruption, alienation, outward migration of skilled personnel, mostly managerial and skilled operatives, poor industrial relations, growth of conflicts between government-worker, employee-worker and acute shortages of foreign exchange which affected maintenance and delayed production.[8] The differences between Guyana and Jamaica are in degree, not in kind. Both countries share the dubious distinction of being at the bottom of every Caribbean performance list.

Jamaica's political regimes are rapidly losing their legitimacy, and this has been undermined by their long history of corruption in elections. This has led to a very fundamental alienation of persons from the political regime, by persons seeking only handouts for literal survival. These official patterns of behaviour cast doubt upon the nature of Parliament, which is increasingly seen as not representative of the people. This idea is apparent in many letters, reports and articles in the daily newspapers.

With reference to the study by Mills on the Westminster model, we would have preferred to see an analysis not of the differences between the British and the Jamaican models, but of whether the Westminster-Whitehall system has been responsive to the needs of the Jamaican society and how well it has served this society. Many of the British institutions and political practices, which sustain the Westminster model were and are not transferable to the colonies. In other words we are rather amazed at the inability of the investigators to conclude that these supportive phenomena all derive from the power structure and institutions of British society. The transplanted Westminster system does not have the social and cultural support of institutions like those of its parent society: without these the colonial copies are a mere shell.

It would appear that the more the institutions come under the domination of the party, the less responsive they are to the people. Difficulties in maintaining the interest of the entire electorate in the political system all over the world reflects the people's perception that the system is becoming even more irrelevant to their needs and interests. In Jamaica the proposed constitutional reforms from the two major parties will merely increase the sense of alienation and isolation.

According to Gordon Lewis, "After the 1949 basic PNP-JLP agreement on what form the developing self-government should take, both adopted similar methods to attain roughly similar ends."[9] He holds Bustamante responsible for the "destruction of working class unity" and maintains that his essentially negative and sterile politics have had tragic consequences. Jamaica is still paying a terrible price, according to Lewis.

This is an appropriate time to pose some of the pointed questions given above about the nature of a political party and how it will adapt to serve the interests of the people. One must ask about the extent to which the institution was party rather than people oriented. We have seen results such as garrison constituencies, welfare and handout politics. A more vicious effect is the creation of a stultifying political culture, which discourages enterprise and entrepreneurship.

Political parties: faith, ideology and pragmatism

It might help us to formulate answers to some of the questions posed above about the nature of political parties and their functions within a society, if we were to examine the philosophical underpinnings of some of the ideas that underlie the political system. Ian McDonald hurls charges at both capitalism and socialism for not meeting the needs of people everywhere.[10] Capitalism must answer the question of how greed in man can be harnessed so that the poor, weak and disadvantaged are not trampled. Socialism must answer the question of how to leave untouched the essential core of freedom in man, while still harnessing the energy and individual spirit that flow from that same core of freedom. McDonald is right in pointing out that the difficulty is that both extremes lead to the untrammelled power of either corporation or state. Unchallenged power in either institution is unsuitable and unacceptable in practice. Perhaps the Chinese dichotomy leads the way out of the dilemma, by using capitalism to generate the wealth and socialism to distribute it and control the capitalists.

Mark Wignall summarizes some of the effects attendant upon the evolution of the political party system. He notes the pressures on the third term PNP government for water supplies, road repairs, youth employment, transportation and crime control. The mood of the people is now one of impatience, annoyance, bewilderment and confusion. Abdication of the role of opposition leader by Seaga and the JLP has given the PNP the leeway to tamper with the electoral machinery, despite talk of attitudes and values.[11]

Wignall notes that policies are not driven by mass based initiatives, but by pandering to those whose interest lies in maintaining the status quo. Even during the 1960s, which all admit to be the fastest period of growth in Jamaica, there was a less desirable other side. The personal earned income of the poorest 40 per cent of the population dropped from 7.2 per cent to 5.4 per cent in ten years (1958 to 1968). For the poor and uneducated, jobs, if found, provided wage levels that were guarantees of persistent poverty. This report supports our thesis that a major feature of the growth decade was that of growth without development. The ordinary people were not made capable and there was a reinforcement of class and racial superiority.

III: The Political Culture

Political parties once formed
Must make sure that they're suitably normed
For with time they change course
Go from better to worse
In such cases they must be dewormed!

The history and development of the political party system would determine the nature of the political culture prevalent in the country. We may tentatively define it as the system of values and beliefs, concerning the places that different classes of people hold in their society, as well as beliefs as to their place in the world and the way they ought to function in it. Carl Stone defines political culture as the values, beliefs, myths, ideas, behaviour patterns and underlying attitudes shared by those making up the political community. This is reflected by an analysis of the party structure, voting patterns, voter turnout, hard core and peripheral party following and the behaviour patterns of the activist core.[12]

The political culture has a major impact on the society by laying the ground rules by which actions are evaluated, programmes planned and formal and informal systems delineated. It includes the perceived and the actual distribution of power and the hidden agendas that different sectors of the society bring into interaction one with another. A non-fostering political culture is the greatest single obstacle to social and economic development of any country. The question may as well be faced right away that the political culture of certain countries, if unchanged, can never provide the basis for any kind of modern economic development.[13]

The political culture determines the role of the state. The modern belief that the state is a benevolent, fostering entity, serving the interests of the majority can never be taken for granted. The political culture gives meaning to the mix of ideology and pragmatism. Speeches, beliefs, actions and their interpretation all affect and are affected by the political culture. It sets the standards of behaviour in the society, demands conformity or relaxes the desirable behaviour patterns and may reduce or intensify the undesirable effects of the social culture. It can prepare the country (or not do so) for economic growth and development. It lays the foundation for education, academic or technical, for cooperation, and spells out the roles of various participants of the society.

Without a suitable political culture, economic growth and development are non-starters. Successful adaptation of their traditional culture to the demands of modern organization and production has been the key to success of the Far Eastern economies. So far the contribution of the political culture is largely unacknowledged. It draws upon the vision of the national founders, their beliefs about themselves and their fellow citizens, their style of leadership and their enunciation and commitment to national aims and objectives. It reflects their and their fellow citizens' hopes and aspirations and the distinctive competencies possessed by the citizens. It is shaped partly by their history, their systems of values, their attitudes, their experience and their interpretation of these experiences.[14] These forces have a mutual impact on the political culture as well since all the elements are in constant mutual interaction.

Anyone trying to assess the future prospects of Jamaica and the rest of the Caribbean would do well to identify the political culture of the society and the effect it is having upon that country. Like any human artifact, it is changeable, as Barbados has been demonstrating over the past few years and Singapore has successfully demonstrated.

Some Caribbean scholars use the term 'culture' mainly to refer to the expressive forms of the way of life of a people, especially as it is embodied in the arts. Yet political culture is far more pervasive than that. It helps us to answer questions such as: What are the values of the political and social systems, the things that they hold dear? What is the meaning and purpose of politics? What is the appropriate balance between long-term goals and short-term objectives? What role should be played by administrative expediency? Which is the stronger principle, the ease of governance or the purpose of governance? Political culture will be shown to be a tool, more vital to economic growth and development than the traditional intermixture of capital, enterprise and labour.

Characteristics of the Jamaican political culture

Historian Gordon Lewis notes the slow, tortuous growth of a Jamaican sense of national identity. This national identity did not have any place for the newly emancipated slave. Lewis quotes from a travel book by Forrest

Henderson that it was generally "believed that Negroes were incapable of self rule and that no white people would ever live in a country ruled by black men".[15] One expects that whites in post-apartheid South Africa would agree strongly with these sentiments. It is a matter of great concern to this writer that many of the behaviour patterns of our own founding fathers seemed to support this libel upon the abilities of black men. Even today it is widely perceived that the practice of the Jamaican government is to give preference to the foreigner over the black Jamaican, a practice which reinforces Miller's observations on the marginalization of the native people.

One useful source of some of the wellsprings of Jamaica's political culture can be found in the speeches of our founding fathers. Those of Norman Manley, carefully collected and edited by Rex Nettleford, delivered over some 30 years, on a variety of subjects and occasions, would not necessarily say the same things consistently.[16] On the other hand one is not about to accuse Norman Manley of insincerity. Our world-view changes considerably as we mature and gain experience, but it should be possible to gain a comprehensive view of the man and his vision from the speeches he delivered over this period, 1938 to 1968. A vast number of his ideas must have formed the basis of the political culture of the pre and immediate post independence period of Jamaica.

He was sometimes overshadowed by his more charismatic cousin Alexander Bustamante and perhaps was somewhat late in attempting to impose his own measure of intellectual power upon the political scene. By the time his influence had begun to be felt towards the beginning of the 1950s, the major factors and features of the political culture which has bedevilled all attempts at subsequent reform, had already been firmly entrenched: for good or for evil. Bustamante had already captured the imagination of the masses of the people, an advantage that the JLP did not surrender until the advent of Michael Manley, another charismatic personality. In the early 1950s Norman had, albeit reluctantly, to make drastic revisions in his party's ideological stance, in order to capture the electorate. His lieutenants had made it clear to him that he might continually stay out of office if he did not court the short-term interests of the masses of the people. Currently, Mr. Patterson is enjoying that dubious inheritance.

As mentioned earlier, the speeches of Norman Manley covered a wide variety of topics, mainly on the constitutional advances in which he played a leading role right up to independence, even dealing with the digression of the short-lived West Indies Federation. Nettleford's general introduction credits him with highly praiseworthy thoughts on the value of the ordinary man and one cannot fault sentiments like this: "Manley had an unshakeable belief in the capacity of the Jamaican people to create for themselves, to carve out their own destiny. He often declared his unending faith in the people of Jamaica." He believed too much in the intrinsic worth of the human being to write his generation off as "irredeemable zombies of colonialism". It will be always a matter of regret that Norman Manley was unable to erect structures and systems which would preserve the integrity of the party which he co-founded so as to better enable it to survive the ravages of time.

Even orthodox economists admit the impact of the political culture upon what may seem to be purely economic factors. Unexpected support is given to our thesis of institutional failure by these comments of Worrell and Bernal, the former "focussing particularly on external shocks notes that performance is worse where government spending and state ownership were expanded substantially". On the other hand, Bernal argues that structural factors rather than policy responses have been mainly responsible for poor economic performance since 1972.[17] Unfortunately, our economists, having identified these factors, rarely examine how they work to nullify the most thoughtful economic plans. They simply refuse to admit non-economic factors into their calculations. The economists are obliged to clarify what kind of structural factors are responsible for the economic performance, and whether they are internal or external to Jamaica. One would think that the purpose of appropriate policy responses is to mitigate the effects of negative structural factors. Given the blame laying mentality of previous and current administrations, the tendency has been to shift responsibility onto external factors, Michael Manley being the most vocal propounder of this view.

This response is in direct contradiction to my thesis of institutional flexibility and learning and suitability. Both government and government apologists are ready to spring to the defence of Jamaican policy responses, with no reference to the existence and quality of institutions for economic growth and development. For 25 years or more, we have witnessed a kind of crisis management response, without reform of the underlying structures of production. Far-seeing commentators agree that policy responses must depend on internal structural factors. Such a transformation, recently recommended by McIntyre (1998) is taking place on a nationwide scale in Barbados and sporadically in Jamaica. This writer has insufficient evidence to enable him to grasp the scale and scope of the effort being made in Jamaica.

At this point it is convenient to review the role of the state in national development. According to Venner, the role of the state can either be cast as (i) a neutral entity or (ii) having a partisan role in support of one class against the other. It might be the arbiter between existing conflicts or supporter of the capitalist class, supporting the property rights of this class and ensuring the exploitation of the proletariat, or sometimes after a revolution becoming the handmaiden of the proletariat.[18] The role of the state has been undergoing steady change, assuming an increased role as a provider of public goods in great demand. Evolutions of the state's role have taken different paths in Western democracies than in socialist countries, but the more significant changes have occurred in China. The effects of these developments have been to provide many choices for the Third World. An observer may comment that there are very few monoliths left, since the pressures for public and private goods and services are forcing some sort of convergence in objectives, if not in ideologies.

Carl Stone's contribution to this discussion is to trace the history of developments through the old order, the new order and the challenge of democracy, comparing the features of the old aristocratic and the new democratic orders. In his view the central theme in the development of the state in the Caribbean is the struggle for democracy, i.e. the efforts to convert the state into an administrative apparatus serving the majority classes to which government becomes accountable and under conditions which permit high levels of political participation and freedom.

> The long-term impact has been an enlargement of the role of the state in economic and social management and a shift in power from property owners to the political directorate and technocrats who control the rapidly growing domain of public power administered by state institutions.

This movement further results in the "dismantling of a state apparatus geared to express the dominance or hegemony of a European plantocracy over a black slave society and its restructuring to accommodate and reflect the majority interests of the ex-slaves".[19] Despite Stone's optimism, one has to report that these desiderata are still a far way from being achieved.

System functions and outcomes

It is salutary to learn whether the sentiments of the knowledgeable observers are the same as those of members of the public, who suffer from any deficiency that has been left in the system. By using the remarks of the public we can judge how these fine sentiments of the scholars work out in practice. This first letter raises the issue of whether or not Jamaica is a democratic country.[20] The letter writer notes that the first 100 days (since the 18 December 1997 elections) have already brought gloom and despair to an already dying nation. The hopes generated by Operation Pride have been dashed and he suggests that new elections should be held. Unfortunately for him, without significant change in the political culture further elections are not the solution. His question raises a further issue: can what passes for democracy in Jamaica be characterized by that name? What happens when there is a conflict between law and equity?

Other letters and articles from the public elaborate the theme of the functions and outcomes from our system of government, focussing on how they affect the ordinary citizen. Besides the legal questions such as whether or not a democratic regime respects the rights of citizens, there is also the issue of the sense of well-being felt by them. This has analogies with the concept of the social health of the citizens. The following article by Beverly Carey of the Maroons renders somewhat passionate support for the major theme of my book and it is an outcome of the original contempt for the ordinary people of Jamaica. She "views with alarm" the proposal to erect monuments to Bustamante, Michael Manley and Edna Manley on the grounds of the New Kings House. Credit should be given to the ordinary people who suffered. She calls on the prime minister to break down the system of privilege. She also calls for a Museum of Jamaican History, heritage and culture on the New Kings House lands, by moving the exhibits from the stables of the Old Kings House.[21]

The mechanisms for transforming visions into reality are imperfect at best. Thus Christopher Lue thinks that Michael Manley's vision of a nation of equal opportunity and social justice is not yet a reality. He also calls for a new national psyche to bring about growth. These negative effects must be replaced by positive ones, stemming from appropriate changes in the causative factors. They cannot be sustained on mere goodwill. They must be built into the system with 'natural' safeguards to maintain them.[22]

Corruption, ideology and development

Many writers on development believe that the greatest single barrier to development has been corruption. Surprisingly for some writers, corruption may also have positive values. John Rapley's work tries to capture the relationship between corruption and slowed development. He cited the cases of Zaire and South Korea in which corruption had negative and positive effects, respectively, and showed differences in practices that brought about different outcomes. Unfortunately for the developers, the negative effects are more widespread.[23]

One interesting effect of the political culture as it has developed in Jamaica is the healthy interest in ideology, especially of the leftist variety. Faced with the practical problems of running a country, leftist vituperative rhetoric against oppressors, according to Martin Henry, has been replaced by moderation and reason, recognizing many positive contributions of the British legacy.[24] According to Henry, Munroe had explained that the Jamaican left had tackled the problem not merely of how to beat down Babylon, but of how to preserve its good parts. Democracy in Jamaica was in fact facing serious challenges from lawlessness. [25]

The electoral system and its outcomes

The impact of the political culture of Jamaica is most easily seen in the conduct of general elections. These represent the mechanisms by which power is acquired and the political parties recognize no limits to their activities when such power is at stake. Every device, every corrupt practice, every piece of irrelevant trivia is used to score campaign points and to undermine the opposing party. They might sound trivial to the outside observer but are contested with deadly earnest. This is no figure of speech: the death toll from election related activities since 1980 is over 2,000.

In the face of the effective election machinery created and deployed over the years by the PNP, the opposition JLP has been reduced to sniping, in the hope of unsettling the ruling party. Thus a citizens' initiative, CAFFE, is dismissed as a compound of errors of fact, inconsistencies in the data reported, serious omissions and other procedural matters.[26] There is some justification in this allegation as other independent observers have expressed profound disquiet over the main conclusions of the CAFFE election report.

The second report is pure mischief making, designed to undermine.[27] Knowing the emotional block raised in the government merely by the initials IMF, the Opposition leader claimed that a US$48 million loan from the World Bank and other similar loans had been put on hold pending an IMF report on the soundness of the economy. The government itself might have to be bailed out and that the IMF might again be directing Jamaica's economy, even though there might be no loan from it.

Hidden agendas and political gamesmanship are part of the equipment in the campaigner's bag, according to Michael Witter. The blame for the failure to clean the drains is shifted from the Minister of Local Government to MPM, etc. He recalls how these community projects were used by the PNP against the JLP and the NDM and thinks that a repetition of the tactic is likely to be dismissed as an attempt to buy votes for local government elections. He contends that Mr. Bertram was appointed to the post of Minister of Local Government and Community Development to take on the project of winning local government elections for the PNP. The political culture and institutions are designed in such a way as to make it impossible for the citizen to have any input into the government process. The citizens cannot be blamed for failure to influence the government. Crash programmes have been used since the forties and fifties for vote gathering. These measures act as reinforcement of the welfare and handout principle.[28]

This last letter illustrates the tendency to introduce and implement a solution to problem B when the real problem is A.[29] The naive belief that because a system works in one country it will automatically work in another is perhaps responsible for more waste of development aid than corruption. Another cynical interpretation is, suppose one does not want a system that works? Suppose one wants a system that is easy to manipulate effectively? Given the local culture and the stakes in an election, the suggestions are not farfetched.

Imputing motives to individuals without bothering to find out the truth is also a characteristic of the political culture. Like many of those who object spontaneously to the idea of a university in the West Indies, Cargill takes the opportunity to attack an institution whose very existence threatens the class position.[30] His comment on the non renewal of the Grassl contract does not reflect the truth but that does not prevent him from speculating about the "Cardinal sin by quite a number of the Ivory Tower inmates at the University to question the performance of Michael Manley and the PNP in the seventies, or the performance of the PNP at any time".

On the other hand there is a definite need for informed criticism. If, as Cargill alleges, "little or nothing has been done to increase the earnings of the country and it should also be clear that we cannot go on everlastingly borrowing our way out of a fiscal hole which grows deeper and deeper", he might take heart from the fact that many of my colleagues at the university are themselves disheartened by the consistent ignoring of their best advice to the government. The truth is that no government has created any mechanism to pay attention to good analysis, whether of the right or of the left. There is no point shouting: the government cannot hear.

Ian Boxill neatly knocks the wind out of the sails of those who have formed the impression supported by some international magazines and joined in by mostly leftist academics, that the end of global capitalism is in sight.[31] Scholars are rightly focussing on the global crisis and how the world economy should be reformed. The IMF and other international lending agencies are appropriate targets for criticism, for being unwavering in their insistence that all problems need the identical remedy.

Many writers believe that they aggravated the crisis in Asia, early criticisms by local leftist economists having fallen on deaf ears. More appropriate adjustments are now being made in the system. Boxill does not believe that capitalism is dying now or anytime soon. Currently there are mostly centrist leaders in all the major industrial countries. The system will adjust when circumstances and needs change. In support of this very balanced view this writer believes that capitalism will disappear when power and wealth are no longer highly valued by society. Our recorded history is the story of wealth and power, how it was achieved, preserved, increased and lost. The leftists' error was to believe (faith, only?) that an equally flawed system, which was even then breaking up at the seams, represented the absolute desideratum.

IV. Power Distribution

An NDM leader named Bennett,
Thought that Bruce was too eager to end it
In Jamaica we find
We keep women behind
But by golly, she upped and she gained it!

Central to the theme of the efficiency and effectiveness of any organization is the part played by power.[32] No organization can function without it: it may be defined as the ability to get others to do one's wishes, whether they like to or not! Normally, power is moderated and made acceptable by the concept of legitimacy, which speaks to the acceptability of the exercise of the power, even by those over whom it is exercised. What separates democracy from all other forms of government is the general belief among the citizens that the exercise of the power is right and proper. Merely having an acceptable form of government does not ensure, however, that the exercise of the power is legitimate. Elected governments may discover that as circumstances change they may forfeit the aspect of legitimacy. In such cases they may have to rule by naked force. But that has its problems.

In Jamaica we think that the constitution legitimizes the exercise of the power of the government. It can do no such thing. All it can prescribe is the form: it is dumb with respect to the substance. Parliament, which is supposed to represent the people and therefore legitimize the power of the executive, has not done so for decades. It cannot, having been progressively sheared of all the power it might have possessed.

These abuses and mis-uses of power occur also at a much lower level, but the persons who commit them take their cue from the most prominent social and political source, the executive. These abuses are also sparked by the political culture, which treats the ordinary people as being essentially without any rights.[33] Delroy Chuck, MP, criticizes the Office of Professional Responsibility for its failure to be evenhanded in its investigation of reports of police abuse of power. He notes the tendency to clear the police in incidents by giving neither criticism nor censure and cites some instances as evidence of his contention. The tendency to protect fellow members of one's organization is in most cases a positive and powerful factor in maintaining the integrity and solidarity of the organization, particularly in a military or paramilitary force in which carrying out one's orders may lead to one's death.

The anti-popular and pro monopoly nature of the political culture is demonstrated in the next report of equipment being seized and the owner being arrested for breaches of the Public Utilities Protection Act.[34] This outcome is the result of an action by Cable and Wireless. This action seems to be in contradiction to the general policy of the government to open all economic endeavours to competition under free market rules.

V: Sectors of the Economy

In Jamaica the Chief of Tourism
Condemned roundly the natives' more-ism
Said the Chief, "It's a fact
We must clean up our act
We don't want to end up in whore-ism".

The debate has raged for decades as to the proper amount of state involvement in the economy of any country, especially a developing one. In this century we have seen all kinds of state arrangements, some successful, some not, and we believe that we have sufficient evidence to answer the question. Even then caution is recommended since the success or failure may depend heavily upon the match (or mismatch) of the state and the people. Our local political scientists have their contribution to make.

Trevor M A Farrell summarizes in two pungent paragraphs the pros and cons of state intervention.[35] First, he gives a list of reasons why the state should not be involved in the economy at all. These include entanglement in bureaucratic red tape, featherbedding, jobs for loyal constituents, fear of dismissing incompetent officials who have votes in general elections, bad management, subsidies to hide inefficiency, bungling, absence of creativity, innovation and energy and for maintaining employment of the crash programme variety. Equally revealing is the list of reasons why the state should or does play a role. These include the weakness or non-existence of the private sector, that the state is a better guarantor of business decisions, and that the success of other countries such as Japan, Korea and Singapore depended upon the state playing a critical role.

Fortunately for developers, every single one of the disadvantages is not an inherent feature of any state and each of them can be changed for the better. The inhibiting factor is the political culture. The liberating factor will be the extent to which the decision makers understand how systems work and if they want them to work. If inefficient systems exist in Jamaica, it is because someone in power wants to keep it that way. This has been the case for the past 29, possibly 39 years, but the weaknesses in these systems are now being made evident to the observer.

Role of the private sector in development

Conspicuous within Farrell's list of reasons for the intervention of the state is the absence or ineffectiveness of the private sector. Most commentators on the economic scene assume that more of the responsibility for the development of the country can be handed over to the private sector since it has proven to be the 'engine of growth' in some countries. When one examines the Jamaican version of the private sector one finds an engine in which the plugs are fouled beyond any cleaning, the pistons are shot, the gas lines are blocked and the sump is full of water. As Orwell would say, all private sectors are created equal, but some are more (or less) equal than others.[36]

John Rapley observes that the terms left and right have been used by both sides of the debate in terms of their attitude to the state's role in the process of development.[37] The left favoured using the state as an agent of social transformation. Out of an awareness of the imperfections of the market and global capitalism, development theorists proposed models that assigned states a leading role in the economy. They found, however, that industrial development consumed more resources than it generated, a waste exacerbated by inefficient states. When the postwar boom ended with the 1970s, the shortcomings of state led development became plain.

One may compare these findings with the experience of the Manley years as described by Carl Stone above. Here in Jamaica one may note the weaknesses of state-led development. Perhaps there were too many incompatible aims, inappropriate institutions, a hostile political environment, partial mobilisation, the politics of exclusion, political divisions and tribalism. The structural adjustment of the 1980s as practised by Seaga, tended to move responsibility from an inefficient state to an equally ineffective private sector. The proper course is to discover why both state and private sector are ineffective and apply such remedies to permit them to overcome their weaknesses. In either case the faults will be found within their internal arrangements and how they both respond to their external environment.

These typical flaws occurred in the private sector from imperfections in their internal arrangements and their response to their environment. In the first illustration, the political culture encourages private contractors to flout good housekeeping rules. The lax operating atmosphere permitted under the political culture delays the development of the developers and leaves them little incentive in learning to control costs.[38] Desperate attempts are then made to remedy the system by introducing new rules for prepayments and non delivery of units within the specified time.

The general low level of professionalism and motivation in the society affects both public and private sectors alike, since both sectors draw on the same flawed sources for their recruits. The general absence of care may derive from the conviction, enhanced by a divisive political culture, that certain people are not within the pale as citizens. The treatment of the public in government hospitals is even worse according to some reports.[39] This letter complains about the inadequacies of private hospitals. The expectation of more professional and personal care from such hospitals is dashed.

Occasionally the gloom under which Jamaicans live and work is enlivened by some tongue in cheek suggestion of an outlandish proposal that would presumably solve all our economic problems at one stroke. Casino gambling is one such perennial diversion, taken seriously by some or designed to raise the hackles of some group or other. In a similar vein Hamilton's proposal for legalized brothels is even more outlandish and this report is a predictable response to his kite flying from a member of the clergy. The more fundamental economic question concerning dependence upon a single source of income (monocrop culture) is shelved. Thompson records his strong opposition to any suggestion of legalizing houses of prostitution to attract tourists. He believes that the natural beauty of the country is enough attraction. "Everything and everyone cannot be for sale." [40]

The public sector in theory

The main issue arising here, in considering the civil service as the tool most expected to carry the burden of the development of the nation, is the question of whether the system has evolved sufficiently to play its role efficiently and effectively. Edwin Jones gives an analysis of the evolution of the civil service from pre-independence to independence, emphasizing the elements of administrative legacy, the translation of certain doctrines into practice and their ramifications for social formations within the public management systems. [41]

Several of his themes correspond to issues explored in this volume. One might question the very outcome of the evolutionary exercise, which was expected to shift the culture and practices from the colonial pattern to what is required in a post colonial administration. In effect what transpired was a transfer of colonial administrative culture with no consideration of whether or not it was designed for our purposes. As Jones puts it, the exercise was concluded out of "pure administrative convenience in spatial terms". The system we inherited was designed for narrow choices. The prevailing supposition was that economic development should continue on a dependent capitalist path. [42] A more far reaching result, according to Jones, was the creation of a special class or stratum of local politico-administrative functionaries, using status as the basis of rewards and promotions, thus determining the nature of the civil service. The outcome was to constrict the discussion of basically divisive issues, rather than confront and resolve them.

Jones notes that the contemporary civil service copied from the expatriates the techniques for strengthening and reproducing the system: creating and maintaining links with the private sector, acquisition of power through property and the manipulation of salary scales. They have not managed to assume the leadership of the productive process, and remained dependent on local and foreign capital, technology and ideas, being overly conscious and sensitive about their relationship with the old elite. They were thus in every way unfit to undertake a developmental process, even if such a task had been entrusted to them in the first place.

The local political directorate has cut the civil service out of the development process by its reliance on expatriate training and expertise, mostly that provided by international bodies, reinforcing the ideology that the local people are incompetent, by the denial of access to locals for leaning by participation in development processes. These, according to Stone, were some of the prime failings of both the Michael Manley and the Edward Seaga regimes. Jones mentions other tendencies, which have also contributed to unfitting the Civil Service from playing a developmental role. The focus on training in narrow technical functions does not help them to master the techniques of dealing with power relationships, primarily with ministers, local and foreign.

The tendency to focus on structures and processes rather than outcomes, perpetuated through links with international civil services (ILO, PAHO, UNESCO, UNO, World Bank), has the effect of imposing their uncreative and un-innovative approaches on other poor countries. Jones appends a list of overlapping approaches to administrative reform. The first three are process oriented, with minor acknowledgments of the presence of the client, while the fourth (and valid one) is client oriented and outcome based. Finally it is extremely difficult to infuse service and outcome ideals if the civil service members are not rewarded on their accomplishments, but by seniority as now. By contrast, in the Far East, department heads are on average two years younger than their staff, as their promotion is on merit only. Many lessons remain to be learned about institution building, adaptability, learning processes and becoming a learning organization. Singapore has recently dubbed itself the 'Learning Island'.

It is in any case doubtful whether the continuing crisis in the government is deep enough to warrant serious examination of many of these old ideas. Most of the reforms instituted in the civil service have to do with classification and reclassification of the same posts as an excuse for giving them pay in comparison with the private sector, in the firm belief that congruency in pay scales will remedy the major flaws outlined in the previous sections.

The public sector in practice

A number of these weaknesses and their outcomes are illustrated in the day-to-day experience of the citizens who witness or who are sometimes victimized by them. Sometimes other bodies try to remedy the shortcomings by taking action. Thus a warning arises from the president of the Manchester Chamber of Commerce to local government authorities and the business world to see that "issues affecting the parish are appropriately addressed by the relevant entities".[43]

Generally the absence of any system for listening to or responding positively to the justified complaints of the citizens or the power to take any corrective measures makes the complaint or the threat an exercise in hot air, since they have no power to enforce any change due to the extreme centralization of authority. An excess of caution and prudence (or timidity and a refusal to think) probably accounts for the administrative tendency to include everything in a regulation, whether relevant or not. The major and real issue, the requirement that MP's and ministers declare their assets periodically, is unenforceable, since the executive is not the servant but the master of Parliament.

Jones, above, had warned against the emphasis on procedure at the expense of the substance or outcome. An excellent example of this tendency is provided in the following report.[44] Lawyers tried to justify the role played by Mrs. Munroe, whose husband was disciplined on a charge of gross misconduct for failure to disclose his wife's real identity to the minister of agriculture. Appeals to the local Privy Council and Supreme Court had both failed. According to her lawyers, the wife had used her maiden name to ensure that she did not get preferential treatment. It is an argument that cuts both ways, since the minister may not have offered land if he had known her real identity.

This case is a rare example of the meaning and the intent prevailing over the procedures. It is a blow in favour of those who support the principles of equity in preference to the injustices of the law. It should shatter the hopes that many persons have of the assumption of privileged treatment for some connected persons. The principle of arms length transaction has been violated and the courts have rightly concluded that the whole affair smells of corruption.

The financial sector in practice

Normally the financial sector would be included in the discussion of the private sector. In a fully mature capitalist economy, that sector is primarily charged with mobilising the capital and operating funds needed for business expansion. Minimally, it provides a pool of funds so that any prudent user will not run short of capital or operating funds. In Jamaica, in the face of an immature private sector, one must note at least that the function of the financial sector will be modified to reflect the changed situation. Between 1993 and 1999 the modification proceeded in the opposite direction in such a pace that the sector seemed to have lost sight of its primary goal. What was a means became an end in itself, the acquisition of paper wealth without a corresponding increase in real wealth.

The high interest rate regime, intended according to the minister of finance to protect the value of the Jamaican dollar, fuelled an intense pursuit of marginal gains. Levels of returns were offered which were not justified by any real wealth creating mechanisms. Everyone, including the minister, cheered while the bubble inflated. The system has since collapsed wiping out both the illusory wealth and the real investments of a number of people.

The full story of a completely avoidable financial debacle remains to be told but at this time one or two observations can be made. The editor of the *Gleaner* argues that the need for bailouts shows weaknesses in four of nine of the island's commercial banks.[45] He is countered by a strong argument put forward by Minister of Finance Davies that: "Since a failed bank faced the same macroeconomic environment as its successful counterparts, factors unique to that bank must be the cause of its problems." This report confirms the supposition that connected party loans were one of the causes of the financial collapse.[46] These were not only in violation of good banking practice but of the law as well. This case provides strong indicators, if not actual proof, of the privilege versus merit and accountability thesis. The claims of the 'old boy' network, and the expectation of future favours from politicians were some of the motives for the prodigality with which loans were dispensed.

The report also reveals the scale of loans between interconnected institutions in the financial sector. It notes the doubling of the value of such loans from J$6.2b to J$15.7b and quotes from the Banking Act to show that the banks were in serious violation. The reporter also appends a table to show details of the exposure faced by particular banks. At the same time a banker opines that the "entire Jamaican banking sector cannot finance a US$100m development plan without breaching the legislation", admitting that size of the financial sector limits its capacity for financing development. In the face of such an absolute need for foreign capital a layman like me will wonder why we treat it so harshly.

Notes

1. Michael Manley, 85, pp 25, 39.
2. Michael Kaufman, 64, p 45.
3. Carl Stone, 145, p 2.
4. Norman Girvan and George Beckford (eds), 40 p ix.
5. Clive Y Thomas in Davies, (ed)., 27, p 67.
6. Gladstone Mills, 93 p 4.

7. Michael Manley, 85 pp. ix, 42.
8. Clive Y Thomas in Davies, (ed), 27, p 67.
9. Gordon Lewis, 77, p 184.
10. Ian McDonald, "Choosing Between Two Simplistic Faiths" (article), *Daily Gleaner* Friday (16 October 1998), p A4.
11. Mark Wignall, "Can It Happen Again?" (article, Part 1), *Daily Observer* (Monday 8 & 15 June 1998), p. 7.
12. Carl Stone, 145, p 54.
13. Henry S Rowen (ed), 133. See also John Naisbitt and Patricia Aburdene, 100.
14. See Chapter 5 for a full discussion on the part perception plays in behaviour.
15. Gordon Lewis, 77, p 169. Lewis quotes the reference for A. S. Forrest and John Henderson, "The Politics of a Jamaican Negro", Chapter XIII in *Jamaica* (London: Adam and Charles Black, 1906).
16. Rex Nettleford, 102. The quotation comes from p xvii.
17. The quotations from DeLisle Worrell and Richard Bernal are mentioned *en passant* by Girvan and Beckford, 40, p xi.
18. Dwight Venner, in Omar Davies (ed), 27, p 44. The comments by Dwight Nelson appear in the same volume, p 56.
19. Carl Stone, in Omar Davies (ed), 27, pp 90–92.
20. "Is Jamaica Really a Democracy?" (letter), *Daily Observer* (Monday 6 April 1998), p 8.
21. Beverly Carey of the Maroons and Friends, "Give Back the Jamaican People Their Dignity" (article), *Daily Observer* (Monday 23 March 1998), p 7.
22. Christopher Lue, "Elusive Equality and Social Justice" (letter), *Daily Observer* (Monday 23 March 1998), p 8.
23. John Rapley, "Corruption and Development" (article), *Daily Gleaner* (Friday 6 March 1998), p A4.
24. Martin Henry, "The Rule of Law" (article), *Daily Gleaner* (Thursday 15 October 1998), p A4.
25. Trevor Munroe's remark about beating down Babylon is quoted by Henry, 24.
26. "Seaga Urges CAFFE to Withdraw Election Report" (report), *Daily Gleaner* (Friday 27 March 1998), p A1.
27. "IMF Will be the Final Judge – Seaga" (report), *Daily Observer* (Friday 27 February 1998), p 22.
28. Winston Witter, "A Case of Ulterior Motives?" (article), *Sunday Observer* (15 March 1998), p 10.
29. John Sears, "Wrong Yet Again" (letter), *Daily Gleaner* (Monday 25 May 1998), p A5.
30. Morris Cargill, "A Serious Situation" (article), *Daily Gleaner* (Thursday 30 April 1998), p A4.
31. Ian Boxill, "The End of Global Capitalism?" (article), *Daily Gleaner* (Tuesday 13 October 1998), p A4.

32. Rosabeth Moss Kanter, in Pugh, 120, p 246 ff.

33. Delroy Chuck, MP, "On Abuse of Power" (report), *Daily Gleaner* (25 July 1998), p A15.

34. "Cops Raid Infochannel" (report), *Daily Observer* (Saturday 20 June 1998), p 1.

35. Trevor M.A. Farrell, in Omar Davies (ed), 27, pp. 16, 17.

36. George Orwell, 110, p 23: "all animals are equal"; p 104 "...but some are more equal than others".

37. John Rapley, 126, p 1.

38. Claudienne Edwards, "Contractors Must Prove Basis for Escalation Costs" (report), *Daily Gleaner* (Friday 3 July 1998), p A9.

39. "Private Hospitals" (letter), *Daily Gleaner* (Monday 20 July 1998), p A5.

40. On Herbert Thompson, President of West Indies College, "WIC Chief Rates Nature above Prostitutes" (report), *Daily Gleaner* (Thursday 9 July 1998), p C3.

41. Edwin Jones, 58, p 1 ff. The arguments are further elaborated in 62.

42. See Carl Stone, 147, pp 35 ff. for general support of the proposition. Since the argument alternates between the contributions of Jones and Stone, there is no need for a separate endnote each time the contributor changes.

43. "Vigilance Promised By Manchester Trade Group" (report), *Daily Gleaner* (27 July 1998), p C3.

44. "Munroe's Lawyers Explain Use of Wife's Maiden Name" (report), *Daily Observer* (Wednesday 15 July 1998), p 3.

45. "The Financial Decline",(editorial), *Daily Gleaner* (Monday 9 March 1998), p A4.

46. "Huge Increase in Connected Party Loans: Banks Exceed Limit by 20 Times" (report), *Daily Gleaner* (22 July 1998), p D1.

4

Outcomes and Consequences

his chapter attempts to show the outcome of the interaction between a vaguely conceived set of aims and objectives (or none at all)
and an unsuitable set of tools, purposelessly applied, within a stultifying political culture. Such an interaction will lead to unpleasant even if
unintended consequences. Today's headlines (January 2001) capture the
results of the interaction: shootings, murders, widespread poverty, hopelessness and despair. In this chapter we will examine the consequences in
three major areas, economic growth and development, image and appearance, and the system of justice.

I: Economic Results

There was an economist called Grassl
Whose columns each week caused a hassle
He once entered a fray
With the PSOJ
Who consigned him to Hull in a frazzle!

Economic growth and expansion

Volumes have been written about the economic fortunes of Jamaica since
its capture by the British in 1655, but my area of interest is primarily the
period after World War II. The country was in the hands of others up to
the late 1940s. Since then, Jamaicans have had an increasing share of the

responsibility. Owen Jefferson's *The Postwar Economic Development of Jamaica* does a comprehensive job of describing and documenting the results of the process and its more formal aspects.[1] He also shares with many of his fellow economists the tendency to equate growth with development. There is abundant reason to consider growth and development as complementary and interdependent, but not identical. It is quite possible to have growth without development, as has been demonstrated by the economic history of Jamaica.

Whereas economic growth is comparatively easy to define and measure, the same cannot be said for economic development. The latter is indeed associated with economic growth and advancement. My favourite definition is that development is the creation of the capacity within the people of a nation to master and continue the process of their own further economic growth and advancement. It entails the removal of dependency on others for guidance, technical direction, creativity and innovation, and control and implementation of one's own development projects. The era of the 1960s in Jamaica showed manifest growth, but little development. In another part of the world, Lee Kuan Yew was reminding his countrymen in a televised broadcast (June 1999) that Singapore was yet to create a Nobel Prize winner in physics or chemistry and wondered whether the system of schooling was producing the necessary numbers of independent and curious thinkers.

As discussed in chapters two and three, different governments of Jamaica have treated economic growth and development with varying degrees of indifference. Our founding fathers were either unaware of economic development opportunities or focussed elsewhere. They displayed a welfare, distribution and patronage orientation rather than an achievement, excellence, merit and productivity orientation. The list of contributors to the debate about the kind of economic development best suited for the Caribbean including Jamaica is almost endless. In the proceedings of a seminar about the role of the state in Caribbean Society, Dwight Venner notes that the economic history of the Caribbean reflects the role of the welfare state as an offshoot of British colonialism: "Diversification of the productive base meant adding more export crops and not industrialization". [2] The developments of the 1960s and 1970s are outlined. "While foreign investment and foreign penetration of the economies continued and were even accelerated, attempts at countervailing measures were merely symbolic". It is no wonder that the local entrepreneurs [sic] were unable to sustain the momentum of growth once the foreigners withdrew. The country had grown, but the people were not developed enough to sustain their own growth.

Trade Unionist Dwight Nelson replied, at the seminar with some observations on the present and future of the trade union movement.[3] Their immediate concern was the loss of jobs for members and they were apprehensive of the shrinkage of the public service as result of streamlining and replacement of obsolete procedures by new technologies. This response by a trade union leader is a promising prognosis that an open mind is possible even in the traditional trade union. It might not have been yet ready for a social contract (1986), but this was before the Manley Bauxite Accord.

Stone reviews some of the more conventional Western theories of development, as well as Marxist theories and dependency theories.[4] He suggests that the First World became wealthy in many different ways. He thinks that development researchers ought to look at the available evidence, noting the nature of the world economic system, the changes over the years, and the incorporation of the Third World into the world economic system. They must also examine the varying capacity of Third World economies to carry through the transformation necessary to achieve incorporation, and to open up greater development possibilities by redefining their role in the international division of labour. Also required is some assessment of the process of class formation and the development of entrepreneurial and technocratic classes able to guide the process of transformation. The most crucial part of Stone's contention is that "*failure to achieve transformation in small Third World economies is due to the absence of crucial social and political preconditions, which would permit the overcoming of those development obstacles*" (emphasis in original).

This whole book is an exposition of the theme that the political culture adopted in Jamaica makes it impossible for the necessary preconditions to come into being. One would consider some of the crucial social and political preconditions to be the presence of functional and functioning institutions. These would have the capacity to encourage entrepreneurs, to apply corrective measures where necessary, to do evaluations and to make responsibility stick to those parts of the system which need correction and adjustment. One may contend that the political system is not only devoid of these mechanisms, but has actively destroyed the base on which they could be regenerated. There has been little provision made for the people to learn the modernizing technologies of the productive process.

One of the requirements advanced by Stone is the creation of social and political preconditions. One such, not stated by him, is a high level of confidence that one's efforts will be successful, as well as a high level of commitment and motivation. The conviction that one's efforts count for something is not to be ignored. Yet the staple theme of the apologists is that one's efforts are doomed to failure because of the weak and sluggish world economy. It was alleged in 1987 that world production was not enough to fill the needs of industrialized countries, much less the Third World.[5] A picture of stagnation and negative growth was painted for all, except for Asia. Even there, simple models of export led growth were insufficient to explain these performances. In particular, they did not explain performance in China and India, where domestic agriculture has been a prime mover.

There is no obligation on any particular economic theory to explain everything. Indeed Boxill warns against theories that are too complete.[6] One might even say that Lee Kuan Yew was not aware that what he did in Singapore was 'impossible', according to the theorists, so he did it anyway. The fate of all the development aid and previous investments made in the Caribbean might have been explained by non-economic rather than economic variables. Studies need to be made of why this has taken place – of the inputs, institutions, organizations, operations, commitment, motivation and the other 'soft' disciplines, which have to do with the behaviour of people and governments.

McIntyre also agrees that the major industrial countries can do more to accelerate their own growth and thus place the world economy as a whole on a path to faster growth. This is an illustration of the old rising tide analogy, that all boats are lifted when the tide rises. Of course, this can only apply to boats that are seaworthy. But suppose your own boat is full of holes and rocks and that your country does not have the institutions and systems to take advantage of the rising tide? The only result will be that your boat will be swamped. Jamaica's performance has not mirrored the pattern of world growth over the past 25 years.

Moving from the scholarly interpretations to the observations of ordinary citizens who have no official connections and therefore no motive for massaging the figures, we find a more pessimistic but far more realistic picture.[7] For what they are worth, the figures show that the sectors contributing to Cuban economic growth are tourism, overseas remittances and a diversification of the economy. They have had to admit to shrinkage by 35 per cent since the collapse of the Soviet Union. The continued US embargo and the cutting of immature cane cause the negative factors. In spite of all these, the prospects for growth in 1998 are between 2.5 to 3.5 per cent, and for the next three to five years, between 4 and 6 per cent.

In Jamaica we have seen similar optimistic figures emanating from the official sources. Economists at the UWI prefer the more accurate compilations of the World Bank and the IMF as the basis of their computations. Probably there is a similar institute in Cuba supplying these optimistic figures. It is much easier to report these results from Cuba than from Jamaica. This factor perhaps explains part of the fascination of Caribbean leaders for things and leaders Cuban! They are spared the trauma of having to deal with dissenting voices, and they do not even have to go to the polls periodically to renew their mandate.

Commentaries from Jamaican observers are very good at giving details of social evils usually without any attempt at tracing the sources. James Walsh agrees that a link exists between the depressed socio-economic conditions of the inner city and social disorder and turmoil.[8] He concludes, however, that the demonstrators (in the Zekes incident) believe that equality before the law is not desirable. Such a belief has dire implications for the rule of law, the administration of justice and management of society. Walsh slates the shameless dependency and mendicancy that have grown in certain large segments of society but acknowledges that the present moral decay can be traced to their long-term unemployment and their exclusion for productive activity. Sources of income for distribution include drugs, illegal gambling, robbery, protection rackets and extortion. He believes that callousness or ignorance on the part of the decision makers, not the scarcity of resources, is the real reason.

One may say that this is an excellent description of today's situation. The realization that these conditions derive from the welfare and not wealth creation culture institutionalized by the party system after being introduced in the 1930s and 1940s is slowly dawning upon him. Further enlightenment will come with the realization that his own party's culture has been one of the major contributors to this sorry state of affairs and the final revelation will occur when he personally starts to take action to reform the political culture.

The themes of competition and survival and an adjustment to the demands of the free market inform this contribution from Elaine Commissiong who raises the issue of successful competition in the global market by Jamaica.[9] Good conditions for this have been taken for granted in the past and no effort made to adjust to changes. There has been an increase of direct investment in absolute terms, but it is insignificant in percentage terms. Recent figures (1991–96) show that investments in Jamaica have been at the equivalent of 3 percent of our GDP, while those of Bermuda amounted to 200 per cent of their GDP. At the same time we face challenges in bananas, manufacturing, etc. This report points to the core of the matter. It also gives the lie to the belief that investible funds have not been forthcoming on a worldwide basis after 1968. On the other hand it supports the idea that internal conditions are a greater deterrent to the destination of funds than their availability. The potential here has not been and perhaps cannot be exploited under the current political culture. My contention that the absence of enhancing structures militates against sufficient investment finds support here. Non-economic factors also appear to be at play here.[10] Trade, not aid, is normally the beginning of negotiations between developing and developed countries. Aid dependency emerges as a political lever, used by strong countries to manipulate the weak. The question that arises is: Why do we still need aid after decades of independence? The answer is that we have failed to generate growth and development by not arranging our domestic affairs. Other developing countries have bucked world trends. Jamaicans must recognize that there is no moral right to aid.

This is a useful answer to those who would make a special pleading for Jamaica's case. The lessons of other developing countries seem to be seeping through, but rather slowly. One is happy to see that the thesis of hostile world conditions as the excuse for non-development is not being taken seriously. We have seen above that the economic theory that the growth of the 1950s and 1960s reflected an abundance of capital has been refuted by the facts.

A way of disguising the failure on the part of Jamaica to invest its available funds wisely finds expression in this call for consultation on development financing, both in 1998 and 1999.[11] This call has been sparked by the decline in concessionary funds flow in recent years and this shortage has been aggravated by the debt service burden, resulting in net reverse inflows. The wording fails to disguise the fact that Jamaica from the 1970s to the 1990s has cast itself in the role of a perpetual beggar. One may wonder how a citizen can feel pride towards the eternal mendicant.

Economist Damien King has, in Gregory's view, put forward a novel proposal in a bid to highlight the process of wealth creation for growth.[12] The government's main role is to bring productive inputs together to create value. The main strategies outlined are liberal trade policies, central bank independence, infrastructure development and maintenance and stable macroeconomic policies. Other suggestions include an alternative investment market at the stock exchange and other policies to make the stock market vibrant and provide a least cost option.

Several unspoken but obvious assumptions underlie this prescription for the creation of wealth. It assumes that the government is both willing and capable of carrying out its role. We have shown extensively in chapters two and three that these are highly unlikely. This view is also based on single course thinking, which takes only economic and financial factors into consideration. The emphasis is only on growth, not development, which involves the capacity of people to create their own continued growth. As we saw earlier, there was considerable growth, but little development in the 1960s. We experienced social distribution but no growth in 1970s. The 1980s were marked by neither growth nor development. The notion of the novelty of the proposal is difficult to swallow, based on the assumption that it has never been considered before. The lesson of the impact of the political culture has yet to be learned. Its value system does not accommodate entrepreneurship, motive and commitment and the use of the appropriate tools.

It is heartening to hear that government is giving some consideration to the need for the Jamaican economy to grow, as Calvin Bowen announces.[13] No pronouncements, however, have been forthcoming about the methods of achieving this growth. Bowen notes some of problems of manufacturing in particular and the productive sector in general. The impact of high interest rates and high utility costs is noted and all the standard economic reasons for success or failure are trotted out. Missing ingredients are of course the people, their culture, their readiness, their motivation, their training and their skills. 'Giving consideration to the need' is not even a commitment, much less a programme. Government's ideology has never been oriented toward wealth creation. Again the assumption is made that growth equals development or that development is a large part of growth.

Given the documented success of the private sector throughout most of the Western world, the notion arises from time to time that the philosophy and practice of successful private businessmen and women should inform the philosophy and practices of governments. Hence the reported statement of Audley Shaw that government must think like business.[14] It is necessary to create an attractive environment for business, jobs, wealth and sustainable development for people. Our CARICOM trading partners bring in their budgets at 20 to 25 per cent of GDP; ours is at 57 per cent. The need for careful planning exists, as does targeting of those sectors with clear potential, providing incubator support.

Shutting down large unprofitable sectors of a business and throwing hundreds out of work rarely appeal to governments as a survival strategy for their enterprises. In general, such a change in philosophy and practice calls for drastic modifications in the Jamaican political culture. Many of these changes would not be feasible, even if economically desirable, because the aims of politicians are not parallel to those of business, even in Jamaica. What has the private sector done in the past with the available investible funds? The recent financial crisis demonstrated their reaction fully. They put the money into paper, not into production, nor in training, nor in retooling. High productivity was expected to come from the unassisted brawn power of the masses, not their brainpower and the exploitation of technology. In this respect alone one can compare the policies of Barbados and Singapore, which were built on entirely different premises.

This contribution by Anne Shirley underlines some fundamental changes which must be brought out by a new culture and a new way of thinking.[15] In looking for signs that the worst of the economic crisis is over, she admits to not being sure of answers to questions like: What has changed in the economy? Are we producing more? Are new jobs being created? Are people paying their bills on time? Has anything come out of the pipeline recently? She finds very few positive answers and emphasizes the need for collective effort since there is no magical turnaround or any quick and easy solution. She hints at the underlying disconnection between the economy and the financial sector, which in recent times consisted mostly of paper chasing. To compound matters, real money has been used by FINSAC to go after paper wealth. Her article raises the serious question of the suitability of our institutions for the creation of wealth. The problem of distribution will not arise if the entire citizenry participates in the creation and production of the wealth.

Economic and social development

Economic and social development is conceptually and practically different from economic growth.[16] To get our priorities right, we should always conceive of economic development as the creation of the capacity of the people of a nation or region to advance and sustain their further development without dependence on the efforts of another region or nation. This explains the massive amounts of money spent by the developed nations on research and development (R&D), to guarantee their continuing development. Development suggests changes in the qualitative aspects of life, generally leading to greater participation of the general population in the social and physical changes and improvements that have taken place as a result of the economic growth. Development also connotes a state of mind, a high level of general and technical education, a commitment to the country and its future and a level of confidence in the capacity of ourselves and of our fellow citizens.

As suggested in chapter two, perhaps one reason for our relative underdevelopment is that we as a nation have not enunciated clearly the essential features of 'development' as it is illustrated in a First World country. Off the cuff, I would mention the presence of a high level of sustainable income, both individually and nationally, derived from the application of high levels of technology to production processes and a high level of education which can sustain the level of technology. This sustained high income can be then used to maintain a high level of social services in health, transportation, roadways and highways, adequate housing and all the amenities associated with the modern Western way of life.

It happens, or perhaps it was designed that way, that the most economically advanced countries in the world practise a form of government generally called democracy. Naturally, this has led political scientists and others to question whether there is any real correlation between democracy and development. Some persons even suggest that one of the preconditions of development is for the country to have a democratic government as understood by the West. Ian Boxill examines the correlation, if any, between democracy and development and concludes that the relationship is not as clear nor as simple as some commentators make it out to be.[17] He cites the comparative failure of the Commonwealth Caribbean, nominally democratic, to develop while citing Chile, China and much of East Asia as being on the road to development, although not practising what the West calls democracy.

Anyone who is familiar with how organizations, including governments, actually work, would conclude that perhaps the wrong variables are being compared or correlated. There is need for a closer look to see how the productive forces are aligned, and that has nothing to do with democratic or authoritarian regimes. This alignment can occur just as easily within a liberal democratic framework or an authoritarian one. It all depends upon who the decision makers and implementers are and their relative power positions. In Jamaica, nominally democratic, no minister (or minister to be) can challenge the dictates of the party leader. They cannot exercise any talents they may own in any independent way.

The theory of the kitchen cabinet

The Theory of the Kitchen Cabinet is based upon the observation that no one man, however talented, can know or be an expert in everything. Most Western and Eastern business corporations have presidents or otherwise designated chief executive officers, who are normally well known, but whose expertise is supported by a small group of equally skilled and competent senior executives, any one of whom qualifies to be CEO. The outstanding characteristic of the incumbent and successful CEO is his ability to forge a team around himself. This action is abetted by the fact that the most dominant value in the group is to achieve success and in the nature of the business that success is generally measurable by quantitative data, concerning visible and tangible achievements. In government, especially in Jamaica, the dominant value is power, not achievement as business would define it. In such a value system the mark of an outstanding prime minister (CEO) is the amount of power he can exercise on a personal basis. The political culture here is very hostile to the idea of a kitchen cabinet.

We may define a kitchen cabinet as a small coterie of co-equal players, tightly grouped around a nominal leader. Each functionary is powerful enough, in status, wealth, political connections and track record in his own right, not to be dominated by the leader. The leader is truly a *primus inter pares* (first among equals). More emphasis, however, is placed on the *pares* than on the *primus*. It is extremely difficult to identify because it rarely takes on a formal appearance.

The leader of the group gets in the habit of confiding his innermost thoughts to a small select group (not more than four or five persons, regardless of the size of the cabinet or board of directors), knowing that he will get constructive criticism and an objective evaluation from it. It does not flatter, since it has nothing to gain from it. One can only infer its existence by observation. It does not advertise itself and has no formal designation. Its only justification is that it can call on the experience and expertise of a group of highly talented men and women. This happened once or twice in Jamaican history, purely by accident (late 1950s and early 1960s), under two different regimes, PNP and JLP. It is noteworthy that both these decades were marked by tremendous economic expansion and growth. Donald Harris calls this our Golden Age.[18] Orthodox explanations do not recognize the kitchen cabinet as a crucial factor. With respect to the growth in the Jamaican economy of the 1960s, as Jefferson demonstrates, the effects were masked by other factors, such as abundance of capital.[19]

The USA gives about the best example of the workings of this inner cabinet. As mentioned before it is a completely informal grouping and considerable doubt may exist at any given time as to its membership, or even its existence. During the Clinton regime in the US it seemed to consist of the president and vice president (normally not a member), and the secretaries of state, Commerce and Defence. Since the September attack on the World Trade Centre, it appears to consist of the president, the secretary of state, the secretary of defence and the attorney general. In Barbados there is the possibility that such a grouping exists consisting of Owen Arthur, Billie Miller, Mia Mottley and David Simmonds. They are very *pares,* powerful in their own right and can act independently and offer an independent critique. According to Parkinson, if you convene more than five people, you end up with speeches for effect and a public meeting is the result.[20]

Another crucial factor in development might be the nature of the private sector, which must be entrepreneurial rather than mercantile. Right wing industrialists and entrepreneurs, who knew how to organize massive enterprises, generally supported South American dictators. Long-lived dictators generally surrounded themselves with men of talent.

Closely related to the theory of the kitchen cabinet is that of the supportive leader whose counterpart is the unchallenged or undisputed leader. The unchallenged leader removes all potential challengers from party office and replaces them with persons more to his liking, especially to the extent to which they reflect his thinking and world-view. Such an organization can neither learn nor be renewed or adapt to changing cir-cumstances. Again, in the course of Jamaican economic history, the 27 years of economic decline, 1972 to 1999, coincided with essentially one-man rule or, according to my theory, were caused by it. Both Guyana under Burnham and Grenada under Gairy showed the same symptoms.

This next contributor makes some suggestions which seem to indi-cate that he would accept a supportive leader theory. Winston Barclay recommends that P.J. Patterson follow Tony Blair in a cabinet reshuffle, but not for the usual reason.[21] "There is evidence that Blair's concern was more with coordination and collaboration between ministers than with individual performance." Teams are unlikely to be effective or even exist where a single individual collects all the power unto himself. Teams need empowerment not emasculation. The British prime minister realizes he has to share power with his team to get them to coordinate and collabo-rate, but Jamaican prime ministers have not. Barclay has made an interesting point about the collaboration of ministers, a crucial factor in both my supportive leader and kitchen cabinet concepts.

This editorial goes straight to the issue of development as against growth.[22] The decisive factor to the pulling out of Hanes factory was that of productivity. It is recognized that productivity depends on several fac-tors, not just labour alone. Management, plant and equipment all contribute. My comment is that development would not only involve an understanding of these facts, but an internalization of the interrelation-ships between the various factors of production. Learning about these effects takes place over time and has to be built into the political and industrial culture. This would replicate much of what Lee Kuan Yew had to do in Singapore and it took him several years.

This address by Norman Girvan details some of the undesirable and unanticipated results of growth without development.[23] Girvan reveals the results of the pursuit of economic goals with the exclusion of social goals and vice versa. In the 1960s economic growth was high, but unem-ployment grew, inequality widened, and social and economic exclusion widened. Social problems were addressed in the 1970s, but disinvestment and capital flight occurred, leading to negative growth and falling living standards. Economic recovery in the eighties had been erratic and uneven.

The trick is to marry productive investment with steady improvement in the living standards of the majority. This points to the need for consen-sus of core values. The five-year cycle destroys such a consensus. The lesson from the developed countries was that sustained reduction of poverty was achieved only after the ruling classes recognized that it was in their inter-est to accomplish this for their own long-term survival and prosperity. Girvan cites the instance of Barbados and takes the opportunity to spell out the roles of government, private sector, labour and civil society.

Economic development would bring the majority of the people of the country into the mainstream of acquiring the skills, knowledge and experience to enable them to take part in their own development, not as mere spectators to a growth process. This simple approach focusses on the creation of wealth rather than the reduction of poverty, and will take care of the distribution problem as well. The only cure for poverty is the creation of wealth, by those designated poor, unless society believes that wealth is not good for the nation.

There are two ideas still lingering about poverty and development. The first is that one set of people will create the wealth and another set will enjoy it. This creates an indispensable role for the government as arbiter between competing claims. Asking one class to produce wealth and the other to share it will perpetuate the injustices of the past. The welfare idea is still at the background of Girvan's remedies. The major flaw in his approach is the emphasis on growth, not development for the majority of the people. Continued exclusion would remain possible. There is need for the kind of industry in which the people share in the production by becoming high productivity, even if high cost, producers. Our current policy is to become low cost and even lower productivity producers.

The second idea is that wealth creation and social goal achievement must proceed in sequential order. Much of the non-economic transformation is taking place quietly as people are taking a greater part in their own growth and development. This development still leaves the government with very comprehensive roles, but their performance would require vast changes in way of thought and practice in the political culture. To this writer, they are some 60 years overdue.

Performance and achievement

Our discussion about the kitchen cabinet evoked the view that in business the major value is performance and achievement while that of government (in Jamaica) is power. Michael Manley showed in *Struggle in the Periphery* how good intentions alone did not enable him to choose the right tools to carry out the tasks he set for his regime in 1972.

Trevor Farrell reviews the economic performance in the Caribbean in the period 1974 to 1986.[24] He notes a contraction in many of these economies, particularly Jamaica's and Guyana's. Even Trinidad and Tobago, backsliding after the oil boom, recorded a contraction of nearly 12 per cent in two years, 1982–1984. He easily concludes that:

1. Caribbean economies have failed;
2. government decisions are largely to blame; and
3. failure is our responsibility. He concedes that imperialism and rapacious capitalists and exploiters do exist. He realizes that enemies are facts of life that have to be lived with. In spite of these mitigating factors his major findings are that:
   • the failures cut across the entire political spectrum;
   • the failures were not correlated with size, or presence or absence of resources;
   • insularity and fragmentation have not helped, but the pseudo economic integration of CARICOM has not been impressive, after its first decade;
   • foreign domination is not significantly reduced; and
   • the State has come to play the dominant role.

He supports the view that many of the standard economic reasons for failure are not applicable in the Caribbean cases and leave the road open to postulate non-economic factors as possible causes of these failures. Both his conclusions and his findings help to substantiate the view that the political culture has been the major contributor to the malaise and stagnation in which the Caribbean finds itself, as exemplified in Guyana and

Jamaica. Carl Stone adds that the major problem is the "uneven development perpetuated by the dominance of the capitalist core countries and reinforced by the *failure of the Third World technocratic and entrepreneurial classes to grasp these opportunities... [and thus] maintained a system of world economic inequality*"[25] (emphasis added).

Both these scholars provide major support for the theory of internal responsibility for one's fortunes, regardless of the external situation. Singapore, South Korea, Hong Kong and Taiwan seized their opportunities, in the teeth of the twin oil shocks of the 1970s, although there is still a major misunderstanding of the role played by non-economic and behavioural factors in these transformations. Barbados in the Caribbean is laying the groundwork for massive expansion in its output with Edu-tech 2000 and Smart Partnerships for the Creation of Wealth in the Caribbean. A number of promising export opportunities has been identified, but the prime blockages are mainly "that the undeveloped and weak local bourgeoisie are unlikely to serve as the catalyst for this expansion of Caribbean economic growth".[26]

Several other considerations about the nature and possible actions of the political culture have a major bearing on the developmental issue. What if the current political regime wastes the necessary foreign investment on show projects? What is there to stop them? In May–June 1999 in Jamaica there was a furore over priorities in a proposal to spend J$700m on a new parliament building in the face of debt service requirements of 62 per cent of the budget. By way of contrast, a series of protocols shows how Barbados handled their monetary and debt crisis in 1995.[27]

II: Image and Appearance

In Jamaica we emphasize form
But of substance neglect is the norm
While to some this is swell
Others find it sheer hell
Since it tends proper thought to deform!

Recourse to buffing the image and putting in an attractive appearance to failed accomplishments has to be taken by a government such as ours, where the combination of no aims and objectives and no system in place to achieve them has been disastrous. Governments need to point to some achievements, even if fictitious and exaggerated, to persuade the voting public to support the side in the next general elections. The government may indulge in 'show' projects and make claims without any rational basis in order to deflect criticism and any close examination of its actual performance and achievements, such as forbidding the establishment of a Truth and Reconciliation Commission. A whole new profession of image builders is at the beck and call of governments who need to 'put a positive spin' on a lack-lustre performance.

For this reason, political campaigning has rarely been about performance, but about pageantry. Colours, bright lights, gospel songs, intimidating motorcades and marches take the place of reasoned proposals and achievable plans. The other side of this is the edifice complex. Dedications of buildings provide massive publicity and photo opportunities and are more spectacular than training, educational and development programmes. This is the sort of thinking which proposes a new parliament building in the face of budget stringencies. In another way, it also explains the government's intransigence over not going back to IMF, having kicked it out so unceremoniously. Generally speaking, since one cannot be good, one must look good.

The government's case

Government ministers and officials are entering into a state of denial, and have to buff their results to compensate for the lack of real accomplishments, thus maintaining their esteem and 'face'. The following is a summary of a typical bulletin emanating from the government.[28] It gives the government's point of view on matters such as inflation, (8.5 per cent), exchange rate (J$36.5 to US$1), Net International Reserves (NIRs) (US$118m) and real economic growth of 2–3 per cent. Other subjects include official perspectives on the foreign exchange market, management, ethics and corruption, education (30 per cent of budget). The government expects immediate, concrete and positive results from the productive sector. Interest rates will fall to 12 from 20 per cent.

The Minister of Finance concluded that the 1998/99 budget was predicated on the government's vision of an efficient, competitive economy. He conceded that there had been setbacks in the past but that the government has, and will continue to face each challenge aggressively. He reiterated that it is only by this resolve that sustainable levels of economic growth and improved living standards for all can be truly realized. As one would expect, this is a typical rosy view of the state of affairs in April 1998. Areas of poor government performance are not touched, including unemployment and the persistent and adverse balance of trade. It omits how economic growth and improved living standards for all can be truly realized in the face of a massive local and international debt, widespread illiteracy and a shortage of technological and productive skills.

The entire history of the Jamaican political culture has been dedicated to making sure that those desirable results cannot materialize. The setbacks in the past 10 or more years have been mostly of the governments' doing, such as the continuous shrinking in the GDP and the flight of many of our most creative people. If rumours are any indication, the migration of our best is set to further intensify (June 1999).

The government claims to be bewildered and confused when citizens fail to take their words at face value. The minister of water turns the hose on journalists by deploring the state of mind of reporters, since his efforts to get community involvement in managing its water supply have been interpreted as having some don collecting on behalf of the NWC.[29] He places blame on the "cancer that has entered the brains of some journalists". The truth, which the minister would rather not face, is that many community leaders are dons by grace of various governments. This is one of the results of the culture created by 60 years of his colleagues and predecessors attaining political domination by using the ghetto and the garrison community and all the evils that have come out of it.

Occasionally the government's side gets some unexpected and presumably well appreciated support. Michael Manley was, after all, a very impressive figure and it should surprise no one that a group of political scientists should wish to make an assessment of the man's contribution.[30] Their symposium, dedicated to "Examine the Crises, Challenges and Responses" of that era, is apposite. The 1970s were the "most dynamic era in the politics of the modern Caribbean... a period of experimentation". The expectation of uncovering pointers to an effective agenda for sustainable development and nation building is quite unexceptionable. Finding out what went wrong is a very commendable undertaking, if taken with a view to correct mistakes.

Journalists have been recruited into the entourage of political leaders from time to time to defend their actions. In this case the responsibility is not the journalist's who merely reports on the prime minister's defence of his own actions.[31] He trotted out the standard pieces about tourism interests, promotion of CARICOM/LOME IV affairs, mass marketing and meeting with European leaders. For what it's worth, the UWI had a professor who used to find that he had urgent university business in any West Indian territory in which there was a test match.

The public response

The use of figures to disclose not quite accurate information is the subject of several books, such as *How to Lie with Statistics*, by Daryl Huff. Figures themselves give an air of precision and accuracy. For this reason statistics are a favourite device used by governments when they wish to give an apparently accurate response without actually lying. Very few people would readily question a calculation done to three decimal places. People who still do that are strongly advised to study Huff.[32]

Fortunately, there are still some citizens who are not taken in by the deceptions and who can keep the thinking of the rest of us in some kind of perspective.[33] Thus Christopher Tufton urges caution with the interpretation of the latest STATIN figures showing a decline in unemployment from 16.3 per cent to 15.7 per cent October 1996 to 1997. Other figures are not fitting this picture, having little "resemblance to the reality of the economy and potentially undermined Jamaicans ability to understand the problems we face as a country and by extension the ability to develop appropriate solutions". Many UWI economists do not use the STATIN figures, regarding them as unreliable and politically biased. They depend more on those of the World Bank, the IMF and other international bodies. This is merely another example of the lowering of the credibility of the Jamaican government, a result quite possible in a country of non-readers.

A device favoured by many governments is to announce grand initiatives for which the homework has not been done, the administrative structures are not in place, or the expertise to carry out the project has not even been identified. 'Government by Announcement' is the term used. This report falls into that category.[34] No money had been voted for the construction of buildings to house the facilities for an Informatics Park, although the project had been in the planning stages for five years. It turns out that the project was not commercially viable in the short to medium term and would need to be heavily subsidized by the government to the tune of J$200m per year.

Governments like to announce these prestige projects as a substitute for the actual achievement. Part of the reason is confusion over cause and effect. Is such a park intended to be a catalyst for an electronic and computer industry or is it a mere token of achievement? If the latter, then there is something fraudulent in taking credit for something not achieved. The fact that it is commercially not viable strongly suggests that it could not be a catalyst for an electronic or computer industry. If it were, it would more than justify the initial expense and the maintenance. It is also an example of the edifice complex warned against by Matalon in a speech to the Department of Management Studies in 1988. Building an impressive headquarters has been the final straw in the back breaking of many banks and near banks. Notable among them have been Bryden and Evelyn, Life of Jamaica, Mutual Life, the Corporate Group and Island Life.

Citizens of a poor country are naturally concerned with what they perceive as the extravagance of their leaders.[35] This letter is a critique of the prime minister's taking his entourage to the most expensive hotels in France to view the World Cup games. The letter writer complains that this is becoming the norm and demands more accountability. He thinks that the people are considered 'their private fiefdom'. This good point has been echoed by thoughtful commentators and supports the contempt of the People thesis as an outcome of the political culture. The leaders' behaviour pattern supports and is supported by the political culture of privilege.

Political cartoonists deserve a section by themselves for the humour and wit they infuse into their presentations. They seem to embody the philosophy of the Roman poet Horace: what is there to prevent a man from telling the truth while laughing? The Las May cartoon caricature of the prime minister and the minister of finance shows the government giving the Reggae boys $10m, with a promise of more to come. Caption: "This should give us high marks now, eeh?"[36] This cartoon reveals that the government's preoccupation with its image has become a source of ridicule for the population. Citizens can only block roads or write futile letters to newspapers or perhaps publish futile books.[37] This letter is a citizen's critique of the prime minister and the police commissioner for being all talk and no action on the question of drug trafficking. The letter was published on 16 July 1998, a year before, almost to the day of my writing this paragraph on 14 July 1999. Faced with yet another crisis in crime, the letter-writer might want to mention the anniversary of his plaint next time he writes.

A reference to two more contributions will close this subsection. Both of them revolve around the theme of talk and image projection without the reality of achievement. Stephen Vasciannie tries to make sense of the pronouncements of ministers of foreign affairs and others.[35] Words of weighty import are uttered, totally devoid of meaning. One might consider this to be another illustration of 'Government by Obfuscation'. Vasciannie underlines the need for a change in the political culture but points up the difficulties as well.

Pauline Haughton puts the issue in an even more blunt way.[39] Her reporter credits her with a headline calling upon the government to stop

profiling and start managing. Management is about competence, not profiling. She rightly stresses the importance of a proper relationship between
managers and workers. Managers today may lack the skills needed to man-
age wealth and opportunity. Much of this advice has been the staple of
management texts and expositions, but it will be fresh to people who
have never heard it before or those who have heard it before but have never
practised it. The best management advice is completely useless unless someone puts it into practice. It is good to know that people are taking it
seriously. Profiling has a place in the old privilege and patronage regime,
but can never work as a substitute for merit. Profiling cannot endure the
discipline of a market oriented economy.

III: The System of Justice

Our system of Justice is flawed
Not because it's improperly law'd
For whatever is meant
It is quite evident
That society rates it a fraud!

The impact of the absence of national aims and objectives combined with
the inept arrangements sanctioned by the political culture, has had a marked
effect upon the system of justice prevailing in Jamaica. This system not
only takes in the courts, civil and criminal, but the whole notion of equity
in the relations between individuals and classes of individuals. There is a
strong sense of injustice and unease about ordinary life in Jamaica. Many
citizens will remark "it is not right" even if they do not have a clear sense
of what the laws might say. Justice plays a vital maintenance role in the
society. The quality of fulfilment of that role strengthens or weakens the
society. Justice acts as the watchdog of society and its job is keeping the
balance and ensuring as far as possible that no erosion occurs in the citizen's
confidence that he can exercise his rights as a citizen.

This commentary begins with a discussion of one of the institutional
arrangements, the ombudsman, which has been made to see that the cause
of justice operates at the highest level of society. It will proceed through
an examination of ways in which its provision, or lack of it, impinges on
the rights of individuals. It starts with the office and role of the various
ombudsmen and by extension the role of the various auditors and contractors general and all those offices created to preserve the system of

equity between government and citizen. The major enquiry will be how well the system balances the demands of equity against those of privilege.

Najmul Abedin gives a brief description of the ombudsman and its introduction into the Caribbean.[40] Different titles have been given to the office in different territories, but the incumbents all have duties with three essential features: (1) They are to be independent and non-partisan officers of the legislature, usually provided for in the constitution, who supervise the administration. (2) They deal with specific complaints from the public against administrative injustices and mal-administration. (3) They have the power to investigate, criticize and publicize, but not to reverse administrative action.

Some restrictions have been imposed on their ability to investigate in some countries. In Sweden and Finland, their power rests on an expression of opinion, and their success or effectiveness depends upon the support of parliament or executive, two vital considerations not readily forthcoming in the Caribbean. The rationale for their appointment is (1) increasing executive power, (2) declining parliamentary control, (3) a complicated and expensive judicial process, (4) disadvantages of administrative courts and (5) the inadequacies of executive enquiries.

The office will evolve according to the constitution and the parliamentary and administrative practices of each territory. Significant differences appear between the Caribbean and Africa, or even within the Caribbean itself. Abedin remarks that: "In Guyana, parliament is very much under the thumb of the executive authority." This might be the real situation in Jamaica where parliament is practically under the thumb (or the heel) of the executive. One tolerates the fact that it is better to have a weak protection against the injustices of administrative and executive action than no protection at all. In Jamaica the ombudsman position has been weakened because it rests on parliament which has become an institution of virtually no use.

The appointment of ombudsmen (by whatever name called) is a public admission that the much touted democratic system has failed partially or completely and this action is a desperate attempt to patch it and give it some sort of credibility. Perhaps the factor to be accused is not so much the need to appoint such persons, but their relative failure, except in the most marginal sense.

Of the five reasons given above for the rationale for their appointments, the last three are outcomes of the inadequacies of the first two. Since these two are responsible for so many other ills, in Jamaica at least, that the ombudsman cannot cure, it appears to be a more rational procedure to remedy the causes (the first two) instead of treating the outcomes (the last three). Successful treatment of the first two will reduce the load on the last three sufficiently to remove them from the problem areas. Other than speeding up the time for the handling of complaints and perhaps reducing the cost to the individual complainant there is little of substance that the ombudsman can do. For these reasons, we are advocating a preventive rather than curative role for parliament and the executive.

Contempt for the people – justice at the individual level

These citations illustrate one of the maintenance functions that the sense of justice and equity plays in preserving a civilized society. Thus a single citizen's plight becomes a critique of bureaucracy and red tape. The underlying theme is that the ordinary citizen is not regarded as having much worth in the society. The corollary is that if the ordinary citizen wants the treatment he is entitled to, he must pay (generally under the table) for it.[41] The first citation, a letter, contains indignant queries from an aggrieved citizen on the workings of the justice system. No redress has been forthcoming for a case of abuse and no summons has been served on the alleged perpetrator, despite repeated calls to the police station, the Office of Professional Responsibilities, the deputy superintendent in charge of the area and the deputy commissioner in Kingston. The letter-writer cannot help making a bitter comparison with his expected treatment in the developed world.

The same theme of the official contempt for the ordinary people arises in the second citation, an article.[42] This citizen has attended court seven times on a matter not yet settled. The absence of key characters is causing delays. He suggests stiff warnings and fines for absent personnel. The ordinary people do not matter, so their time is not of value.

Occasionally the situation arises where two individuals, facing the same legal trouble, are accorded treatment so dissimilar as to raise issues of discrimination.[43] This is the point made by Dawn Ritch who notes the different treatment meted out to Denis Lalor and Paul Chen Young. She gives figures and a history of both cases to show that the different treatments are unjustified. Here is a clear case of privilege exercised on behalf of certain institutions and not others. A cynic might offer the suggestion that a probable source of funding for party activities is being rewarded.

There is little consolation in knowing that the perception we have in Jamaica about the workings of the justice system also exists in Grenada. At least it should not surprise anyone since they adopted the same modified Westminster model and it has evolved in much the same way as ours has, for generally the same reasons. A letter from Hudson George presents us with a view from Grenada where the debate on corporal punishment has been biased and shameless.[44] This punishment apparently is afflicted only on lower class males, the poorest in the country. It is not applied to upper class males, when they steal money from institutions.

Justice: the people and the state

One of the results of the privilege and patronage society is the deep sense of injustice pervading the society. Ian Boxill comments on the spontaneous uprisings in Kingston where the demonstrators were protesting about the need for justice.[45] The call for justice has been a constant theme in the history of the country. Boxill cites a study by Derwin Munroe on the disturbances in 1965, 1966, 1968, 1971, 1979, 1980 and 1985. The details of the events are similar to those of more recent vintage in Kingston. They have been mostly about economic and/or social justice, but also about race. Some have arisen out of partisan politics. The People are no longer calling on state Power to secure their interests, but are bypassing it altogether. An unlearning government generally dismisses these demonstrations as the work of rabble-rousers and the criminal elements. This is a short-sighted reaction which may even now be contributing to the headlines in 2001. People are showing their perception that the state had no interest in them for almost sixty years.

The absence of aims and objectives highlighting wealth creation and fair treatment for the masses is another factor influencing their perception. Their exclusion from the mainstream of development has been the burden of the work of Beckford, Best, Jefferson, Girvan and many others. Adding to the citizens' indignation about the lack of justice have been the empty promises made to them during the regime of socialist oriented governments, Seaga's included, of the last 27 years to 2000. MP Jennifer Edwards' maiden speech to parliament paints the usual picture of poor housing, squatting, absence of running water, houses of cardboard and zinc and their vulnerability to flooding.[46] The belief that persons will acquire the land that they capture leads to growth in squatting. Law abiding people wait their turn in vain.

This is a general comment on the absence of aims and objectives, the failure of governments and the results of socialization over 60 years. They are the logical consequences of a political culture of not creating employment but using a welfare policy as a substitute for development. The lesson is being continually reinforced that abiding by the law is not rewarding. Actions have consequences even if they are long delayed and take forms, which are somewhat different from the expected. Martin Henry believes that the Zekes incident brings us closer to open mob rule seeing that the government has recognized the authority of the area don as being outside and above the law.[47] The prime minister's late intervention confirms the impotence of the seat of power. Zekes is more effective in running his enclave than the government in running the country.

If these interpretations are correct, they have been brought about by previous governments' policies of neglect and absence of development to serve the interests and welfare of the very people the parties were formed to protect. Successive governments have indulged in cynical manipulation of the voting power of the people, instead of leading them in ways that would give them opportunities for their own betterment. The chickens have indeed come home to roost, but not those that the rulers had envisaged.

Notes

1. Owen Jefferson, 57.
2. Dwight Venner, in Omar Davies (ed.), 27, p 34. This publication represents the proceedings of the Seminar on the State in Caribbean Society.
3. Dwight Nelson, Comment on Venner, in 27, p 56.
4. Carl Stone, 146, pp 3–5.
5. Alister McIntyre, in Norman Girvan and George Beckford, (eds), 40, p 2.
6. Ian Boxill, "Truth and Explanations" (article), *Daily Gleaner* (28 July 1998), p. A4.
7. "Cuban Economy on Track" (report), *Daily Gleaner* (9 July 1998), p A10.
8. James Walsh, "Dependence, Protest and Survival" (article), *Daily Gleaner* (Friday 16 October 1998), p A4. Zekes was an alleged don whom the police permitted to address (and disperse) a mob while he was under arrest. For further comment see "Munroe weighs in on Zekes issue" (report), *Daily Gleaner* (Friday 2 October 1998), p A3.
9. Elaine Commissiong, "Can Ja Succeed in the Global Market?" (article), *Financial Gleaner* (Friday 9 October 1998), p 7.
10. Stephen Vasciannie, "Trade, Aid and Development" (article), *Daily Gleaner* (Monday 8 June 1998), p A4.
11. "Jamaica Calls for Development Financing Confab" (report), *Daily Observer* (Thursday 1 October 1998), p 1.
12. Errol Gregory, "Wealth Creation for Growth" (article), *Financial Gleaner* (Friday 5 June 1998), p 15.

13. Calvin Bowen, "Going for Economic Growth" (article), *Daily Gleaner* (Wednesday 22 April 1998), p A8.

14. "Government Must Think Like Business – Shaw" (report), *Daily Gleaner* (Thursday 4 June 1998), p C4.

15. Anne Shirley, "Is the Worst Over?" (article), *Financial Gleaner* (Friday 19 June 1998), p 5.

16. Carl Stone, 147, p 1 ff. For a contrary view see Michael Henry, 51.

17. Ian Boxill, "Democracy and Development" (article), *Daily Gleaner* (Tuesday 21 July 1998), p A4.

18. Donald Harris, 47, p 2.

19. The achievements of this Golden Age are fully documented by Owen Jefferson, 57.

20. C. Northcote Parkinson, 114, p 177. For a plausible account of the evolution of the kitchen cabinet see Parkinson 114, p 178.

21. Winston Barclay, "PJ, Take a Leaf From Tony Blair's Book" (letter), *Daily Observer* (Monday 3 August 1998), p 8.

22. "Improving Productivity" (editorial), *Sunday Gleaner* (12 April 1998), p 8A.

23. Norman Girvan, "Growth, Equity and Social Justice" (address), *Daily Observer* (Wednesday 14 October 1998), p 9.

24. Trevor Farrell, in Omar Davies, 27, p 6.

25. Carl Stone, 146, p 9.

26. Trevor Farrell, in Omar Davies, 27, p 6. For Edu-Tech 2000 and the Smart Partnership idea see chapter three, endnote 34.

27. See Government of Barbados Protocols, 41.

28. Government Bulletin Board, "Improving Living Standards", *Daily Gleaner* (Monday 27 April 1998), p C7.

29. Karl Blythe (Minister of Water), "No 'Dons' As Community Leaders" (letter), *Daily Gleaner* (4 April 1998), p A5.

30. "UWI Symposium to Examine the 70s" (report), *Daily Gleaner* (Friday 17 July 1998), p B7.

31. Carl Wint, "PM Defends European Tour" (report), *Sunday Gleaner* (28 June 1998), p 1A.

32. Daryl Huff, 55.

33. Christopher Tufton (NDM Spokesman), "Careful with those STATIN Figures" (report), *Daily Observer* (Monday 6 April 1998), p 3.

34. "No Funds Allocated for Informatics Park" (report), *Daily Gleaner* (Friday 26 June 1998), p B9.

35. "Extravagance by PM" (letter), *Daily Gleaner* (Tuesday 23 June 1998), p A5.

36. This cartoon appeared in the *Daily Gleaner* (14 April 1998), p A4.

37. Malcolm Rowe, "They Are All Talk" (letter), *Daily Observer* (Thursday 16 July 1998), p 8.

38. Stephen Vasciannie, "The Confused Banana" (article), *Daily Gleaner* (Monday 8 June 1998), p A4.

39. "Stop Profiling and Start Managing" (report), *Daily Observer* (Friday 15 May 1998), p 26.
40. Najmul Abedin, 1, p 29.
41. "Justice in Jamaica" (letter), *Daily Gleaner* (Wednesday 24 June 1998), p A5.
42. Dwight Whylie, "More Contempt for Court" (article), *Daily Gleaner* (Saturday 18 April 1998), p A8.
43. Dawn Ritch, "Different Strokes for Different Folks?" *Sunday Gleaner* (8 March 1998), p 9A.
44. Hudson George, "Cat-O-Nine Should Be Blind" (letter), *Daily Gleaner* (Friday 8 May 1998), p A5.
45. Ian Boxill, "The People and the State", *Daily Gleaner* (Tuesday 29 September 1998), p A4.
46. Luke Douglas, "MP Pleads for Proper Housing Aid for Poor" (report), *Daily Gleaner* (Monday 22 June 1998), p A11.
47. Martin Henry, "Chickens Coming Home to Roost" (article), *Daily Gleaner* (Thursday 1 October 1998), p A4.

5

Perceptions, Attitudes and Values

In establishing values and attitudes
Nothing works quite as well as beatitudes
Some will push for recourse
To large helpings of force
To this end they'll demand quite broad latitudes!

ttitudes and values are derived from the totality of the experience *and* the response of the individual member of the society to that experience. One must be careful of explanations that postulate certain dramatic and possible traumatic experiences as the only or main catalyst of the attitudes and values of an entire people. The people of the West Indies have been in fact traumatized by the experience of slavery. The crucial factor is not the slavery itself but how the people of the West Indies have responded to it. Some 160 years after its abolition some people of the West Indies still attribute a number of behavioural shortcomings to its effects.

In 1982, Blackman[1] noted that the people of the West Indies were suffering from a deep cultural inferiority complex. By contrast, as far as the outcomes went, the people of Singapore suffered two equally traumatic events, the Japanese occupation, 1942 to 1945 and the enforced separation from Malaysia in 1965. Under enlightened leadership they have moved not just into the First World but to a position of second in productivity only to the USA. Under similar enlightened leadership, Jamaica could have done the same.

In recognition of the major part played by the attitudes and values of a people in the exercise of nation building and development, Prime Minister P.J. Patterson led off by asking for a major change in the values and attitudes of the Jamaican people and convened a national consultation on the subject. Obviously he recognized the importance of the correct attitudes and values as a precondition for development. If the prime minister wants to see changes in the attitudes and values of the Jamaican people, he must first change their experiences and hope that they respond to the changed experiences in a positive way.

Economists will tell the tale of developments mostly in terms of figures of investments and economic forces, but they have already been preempted by Max Weber who had explained the phenomenal growth of Europe and America by revealing the part played by the Protestant Ethic in infusing the Spirit of Capitalism. It simply states that without motive there will be no investment and no growth whatsoever. It is a mistake, according to Weber and like-minded sociologists, to think that the prospect of economic return is the sole motive driving the activities of the entrepreneur.[2] Economists recognize no other motive.

The motive and the drive for economic growth must either have already been built into the target population as a result of their experience of and their response to it, or it must be shrewdly inserted by a leader, or leaders, who understand the process of attitude formation. Development calls for a mental state, an open mind, curiosity and a willingness to take risks. A critical mass of the people of the developed countries possesses many of these characteristics. One may examine the profile of attitudes of any people for those that are compatible with development, on the one hand, and those not compatible, being discouraged, inhibited or destroyed by the political culture. With respect to the requirements for development, we must also determine with as much accuracy as possible the sources of popular perceptions and stereotypes and how they are reinforced, or not, in the society.

Several original scholars have already enquired into many of these attitudes. Carl Stone and Kenneth Carter have explored our attitudes to work and the values which inform them. Other researchers have examined the current and prevailing attitudes of others towards their bosses, subordinates, co-workers, school and education, crime and public order. Some scholars have discussed the idea of a social contract. Carl Stone and Don Anderson have developed the art of political polling to establish the attitudes of the people to political parties and voting practices.[3]

Mary Richardson,[4] in examining the aspiration or reality of our national motto, presents an account of stereotypes held by each racial group of each other group and the reasons for this. She traces the history of the darkening complexion of official Jamaica in stores, banks and the government service. She notes the ambivalence towards things European, and the general resentment felt towards them as colonialist oppressors, yet things European are given preference (hair, complexion, straight noses, etc.) However, in later research among school children she uncovers that Africans (black Jamaicans) are the most accepted of all groups on both the Social Distance and the Attitude to Minorities scale, towards whom most favourable attitudes have been expressed, followed by European, Indian, Chinese (on Social Distance), Jews, Syrians and Rastafarians. The differences in scores make the point that all groups are not equally ranked.

As a nation, we have not yet achieved the aspiration of *One People*, but there is some acceptance of all groups. She admits that the sample is biased toward a section of the population, the middle class or those about to join its ranks. She feels that the motto is an ideal worth striving for, if not yet attained. If these findings are a true reflection of the development of more mature and tolerant attitudes of the citizens of the country towards each other, then this is good news indeed, suggesting that the striving middle class admits that there is room for others. The black majority should not feel that the bias could not be removed with the exposure to education, as has been shown in many countries. This bids fair for the removal of one of the perceived disabilities towards black achievement.

I: Systems Theory

Of the types of info we receive
Just some fraction of it we perceive
A mistake in our sentiment
Merely works to our detriment
And we hardly know what to believe

Earlier we remarked that attitudes were derived from the totality of the experience of the individual and his response to the experience. Since it is impossible either to predict the exact influence of any one source or even to trace an attitude to a particular origin, the analyst needs a frame of reference that will minimize the attribution errors. Such a framework is provided by Systems Theory. In a small Caribbean society, the government is by far the greatest influence upon the formation of attitudes. Here we must understand government in its widest definition.

Following C Y Thomas[5] we take it to mean not just the regime or the government in power, but all its arms of administration, in the widest sense of the word, including the judiciary, security, sub-central government and legislature. Thomas approves that in its operation it should rely on ideology as a first resort, leaving force as the last resort. He goes on to analyse the state as it has evolved in Caribbean society, highlighting the characteristics and instruments of the ruling class given the non-homogeneity of most Caribbean countries. The state often has to function as a mediating factor. He lists five desiderata, which states are not expected to violate if they are to maintain their fundamental character.

As mentioned above, one of the most important of the forces that form attitudes and values, is the state itself, being the single most powerful and pervasive influence in the Caribbean. The question that must arise is whether observation has confirmed that these characteristics and their corresponding behaviours are being practised. The citations forming the staple of this work provide much of my evidence to the contrary.

The experience of Michael Manley, according to Stone, underlines the danger of not looking at society from a systems point of view and of not recognizing the impact of apparently unconnected events and developments. His aims were nullified by his exaggeration of the perceived strength of popular support. He believed that a basic shift had taken place in political values, whereby 'democratic' changes *per se* would elicit strong support independently of perceived benefits from the economy, the state and the existing patronage networks. Stone believed, however, that the most important democratic gain from this exercise was the creation of an active public opinion, with a closer view of the management of the public domain and that this gain was unlikely to be reversed in the future.[6]

Since Stone wrote this, there have been mixed results on the question of the sustainability of an active and strong public opinion. Allegations and counter charges of political influence based on rumour or wishful thinking, rather than on careful research, pervade the political discussion. Columnists are perceived now to be actively pushing the party line. Ironically, this will probably get worse, not better, with the Freedom of Information Act. (Some think that Freedom from Information would be a more appropriate title.)

One can now turn to some of the expressions of the attitudes and values which (are alleged to) abound in the Jamaican people. This editorial is a comment on Roger Clarke's (minister of agriculture) pronouncements concerning 'Lazy Jamaica'. The editor believes that Clarke is right, and that Jamaicans suffer from both physical and mental laziness.[7] In reply, one might say that it has been demonstrated in the move from hunting to herding to cultivation to industry that most productivity gains have been achieved through the regular substitution of technology for human brawn. Both the editor and Clarke have demanded productivity at the level of field labourers, but not at other technological levels.

The dependency syndrome and the handout mentality are so flourishing in Jamaica that even foreign firms share in the largesse. Even where the evidence is not substantiated, as suggested in this report, it has very little impact upon the popular perception and attitude. This assurance to the public that the Spanish firm got its contracts based on its impressive track record in Europe has not been accepted in the light of its poor job performance in Jamaica on the Negril sewerage scheme. The European Union says the government asked for its recommendation of a contractor after the choice was made: the Government of Jamaica says the request was made before.[8]

In addition to the light thrown on perception and attitudes, the issues it raises are good questions for research. It exposes the limits of the technology transfer and shows that the weaknesses of the transferee are just as crucial as those of the transferor. How much examination of the causative operational factors has been done before now? This writer is positive that the researcher will find traces of the influence of the Jamaican political and social culture in the reasons for the results.

The process of perception

Briefly, perception covers the way we understand the reality of our environment, and thus describe or respond to events and other people. It does not matter whether this perception is flawed or idiosyncratic or whatever: it is the perception of the reality which governs behaviour, and not the reality itself. Attribution is the way in which we assign causes to events, as well as the way we understand and thus analyse or diagnose events and people. Learning is a process of using past experiences and the acquisition of knowledge to influence the description and the diagnosis. Attitude is the result of these processes and describes the way we form impressions based on perceptions, understanding, and experience.

Thousands of stimuli in the shape of conversation, reading, interaction with people and observation bombard us daily through the medium of our five senses. We have to select and organize these stimuli to make sense of our world. Many habits and traits influence the criteria for selection of any stimulus. We tend to select according to our own internal state or cultural experiences. We also tend to select according to our own education or experience in viewing key events. Accordingly, the way we select which stimuli to respond to may be a function of our social class and educational background.

In discussing the cultural influences on perception, Geert Hofstede has proposed a model to clarify the dimensions of national cultures. The first dimension of the culture is power distance, which refers to the extent to which society accepts, as legitimate, the fact that power in institutions and organizations is distributed unequally. Uncertainty avoidance describes the degree to which members of the society put a high value on career stability and formal rules, are very intolerant of deviancy, have great trust in absolutism and believe strongly in expertise as a means of personal goal attainment. Individualism is our third cultural dimension. This dimension would range from the rugged individualism of the legendary American west to the collectivism, which is seen to pervade Asian societies. Collectivists would prefer a tight social framework, within which in-groups and out-groups can be clearly distinguished. The claims of relatives and clan members may prevail over those of the organization and loyalty to the collectivity may be perceived as absolute. Masculinity, our fourth dimension, would include assertiveness and a leaning toward the acquisition of money and things, including power, while showing a lesser concern for relationships.[9]

Unfortunately, Jamaica was not one of the countries examined by Hofstede and therefore no evidence exists in that article as to how that theory would apply to us. One may attempt to create a profile for Jamaica by combining aspects of our culture from those countries which we generally agree have had some influence on us. However, to state exactly what dimensions of the culture we have adopted and what is the mix of the various influences can only be speculative and therefore useless, if not dangerously misleading.

II: Cultural Influences

If our children's behaviour's not sociable
They may find their position's not tenable
Such regard, as a rule,
Comes from home and from school
From the church and communities viable

The socialization process

The motive and drive for economic growth and development has been traced to positive characteristics either inherent in or socialized into a

target population. In this connection the presence of a negative characteristic may be dysfunctional. Mary Richardson explains that early research
by McClelland and his colleagues in 1953 identified a concept called *Fear
of Success* (FOS) or motive to avoid success and showed that the construct
was generated different for men and women.[10] Others defined it as a type
of anxiety. In women this led to the inhibition of their need to achieve
through their fears of possible negative results such as the loss of feminin-
ity or social rejection if they were to succeed in areas often regarded as the
preserve of men.

Further research recognized that men, as well as women, expressed
negative reactions toward success in the ratio of 65 per cent women and
10 per cent men. Research among a black sample, however, showed reversed scores for men and women. In black communities, the result may
be explained through sociological and historical factors, where women
have been the financial providers and the stable elements of the family
circle. It is rational that black men would regard their women more as an
economic asset than as a threat to their ego. Black women should have
less cause to expect negative consequences from their success. Work has
also been done in Jamaica on achievement motivation, but on separate
sexes.[11] Much of the discussion revolves around differences between males
and females from coed or single sex schools. The researchers are not clear
as to extent of the FOS syndrome, but attest to its existence. One indicator is that girls from the lower and emerging middle class showed more
achievement need than girls from the traditional middle class.

Home and family

It is sometimes difficult to find articles which are able to distinguish
between the home and the school as the source of many of the attitudes
and values from which the children draw their own. Perhaps that is because the particular source of the contribution cannot be isolated. Miller[12]
thus examines the socialization patterns of home and school. Parents and
teachers give more attention to those more likely to succeed, based on
their estimate of the child's life chances as determined by society. The
structure of mobility opportunities open to blacks has shifted mostly in
favour of females. Miller's Theory of Place maintains that the basic motivation in society for individuals is to gain and maintain place.

Leo-Rhynie describes Jamaican family patterns as falling into three
main types, legal, common law and visiting. The evolution of the third
type sometimes takes place into the second or first. Accompanying features of these patterns and their probable effects include the dominant

role of women, the marginality and irresponsibility of men, the high inci-
dence of children born out of wedlock and the prevalence of non-legal
child bearing family formation.[13]

She continues that the stability of these patterns suggests that the
existing forms are responses to economic factors such as poverty, unemployment and other adverse conditions. A list of reasons is given for the
women's avoidance of permanent or semi-permanent relationships. In
the absence of the father and erratic financial support, the children develop a sense of trust and security with their mother, almost exclusively.
Some observers find it difficult to understand the paradox of very religious Jamaicans ignoring the dogma of the church where cohabitation or
childbearing out of wedlock is regarded as sin. It will be fairly clear that
the attitudes and values arising from these experiences will hardly be similar to those of other more fortunate members of the society. By the same
token, plans for economic growth and development, which ignore these
realities, are doomed to failure. The overt behaviour and its underlying
justification are deeply rooted in their survival needs in the face of ever
narrowing economic opportunities. There is very little point in deploring the reality of the situation and blaming it on the disadvantaged.

The school

As mentioned above, it is somewhat difficult to separate the effects of the
socialization forces of the school from those of the home and family.
Ideally, they should reinforce each other, to present the child with a high
standard set of values and attitudes towards every subsequent event or
interaction. The deficiencies of the school system are precisely those of the
home and one cannot expect much help from the other. Nevertheless, the
school is expected to reinforce the lesson of the home and to take responsibility where the home is deficient.[14] Minister of Finance Davies reiterates
the desideratum that honesty begins at school. He directs his attack towards people who disregard ethical standards, for example, pharmacists
who sell time expired drugs. He notes that education is the "only way for
a socially or economically deprived community to lift itself systematically
over time".

No reasonably sane Jamaican can quarrel with these sentiments. Their
quarrel must be with the absence of a supporting culture and environment. The political culture has done everything in its power to nullify the
letter and spirit of these sentiments. It supports the hustler mentality, a
supposed product of slavery. Although honesty should begin at school, it
should not end at anytime in one's career, even if one becomes a minister

of government! If government and business are perceived to be corrupt, such behaviour will be regarded as sanctioned and acceptable, and therefore to be imitated by others.

Errol Miller reviews the introduction of early childhood education, particularly through the agencies of the DRB Grant and the Van Leer Foundations. Early enrolment is not the significant factor in subsequent literacy, but attendance is very important. The non-attendance at grades 1 and 2 correlates best with subsequent illiteracy. Learning programmes should be targetted at these grades. To put the remedies into operation one needs to take a systems approach. The economic and social position of parents, their attitudes to education, the availability of uniforms, books, food and transport, are all factors which may determine attendance. Stress factors from police action and gunmen shooting have been added to the equation.[15] Unless *all* the factors are taken care of simultaneously, the rate of attendance will not increase. The major responsibility for many of these limiting factors lies in the hands of different ministries and departments that are notorious for their inability to cooperate with one another.

The church

We have not found much literature in our usual sources (the works of social scientists) about the role of the church in the process of the socialization of citizens. Occasionally, its teaching conflicts with desirable social movements and it can then be accused of contributing to the backwardness of the society. Ian Boxill mounts a strong critique of the ancient gender relations imposed by the Church and wonders whether they should serve as a desirable guide to modern gender relations. An influential part of it still promotes a narrow role for women.[16]

In certain parts of our society the church, traditional or evangelical, remains one of the dominant shapers and formers of our cultural and social values. My own strictures on churches are for preaching the acceptance and tolerance of appalling physical and economic conditions. The theology preached by some fundamentalists amounts to exploitation and betrayal of an unsophisticated, ignorant and illiterate people.

The more orthodox interpretation of the role of the church in its possible contribution to the cohesion and therefore the good order of society is led off in this article by Anya Elliot. She notes the role of religion in fostering a prosperous society.[17] Again this writer has no quarrel with the general sentiments, although it is doubtful that a divided church can play that role in the face of the much stronger divisive elements of tribalism, political culture and economic strictures.

The workplace

Kenneth Carter's book, *Why Workers Won't Work*, is a study of work motivation and attitudes of the Jamaican worker.[18] His theoretical framework,
gleaned from a variety of sources rests upon three generally accepted propositions. First, the higher the level of motivation, the higher the level of
work orientation. Second, the higher the level of demotivation, the lower
the level of work orientation. Third, the higher the level of environmental
disincentives, the greater the difficulty associated with motivating the
worker towards viable levels of work orientation.

He also notes that 82 per cent of the interviewed managers identified
the attitudes of workers as their main problem. Trade unions were held to
be largely responsible for this state of affairs. He then analyses an attitude
into its three components, noting that it had a cognitive element (a fact
or belief), an affective element (feeling towards an object) and a behavioural
element (a predisposition to act a certain way towards the attitude object). More important is the finding that attitudes are rarely isolated, but
come in clusters and that any attitude is extremely difficult to change, if it
is repugnant to another attitude of the cluster. This knowledge should
make it clear that the type and extent of attitude change the prime minister would like to see is not going to be easy, even if the experience of the
people improves.

Some of the insights of Panton's article may be useful here in evaluat-
ing whether attitudes were changed and the process that was used to
change them.[19] Panton links an attitude of mutual respect for workers and
managers to the high values promoted by the company as well as to the
bottom line of productivity. This mutual respect is promoted in many
ways through the system of corporate values, their programme of industrial and employee relations, communications, meetings, shop talks,
in-house publications, employee involvement programmes, their concern
for safety and their productivity incentive programme. Practitioners in the
art of management also support these theoretical points about the workplace as a disseminator of attitudes and values. Thus Richard Coe, CEO
of Courts (Jamaica) Ltd. notes that this is the time for "a complete change
in the local corporate culture". He believes, as Panton does, that Jamaican
workers respond positively to training by creditable performance. It is a
myth that Jamaicans do not like to serve people.[20]

Community and institutions

Since the community embraces home, school, church and workplace, it is
to be expected that their combined influence will have a major impact

upon the attitudes and values of the citizens. Leo-Rhynie again guides us through the thickets and leaves us with a coherent picture.[21] She demonstrates that family structure influences the opinions of children, their attitudes and values and their types of behaviour. Societal, subcultural, group and individual behaviours have been traced to the development of attitudes resulting from childhood experiences. Jamaican women assume motherhood readily since they gain status and identity within their communities on the basis of motherhood rather than marriage. Teenage births are conclusive proof in establishing fertility and avoiding the accusation of barrenness.

The absentee father (physically or psychologically) provides the negative role model of a father as an itinerant or detached male figure who provides erratic rather than consistent support for any sort of family. Children who have been shifted (from parents to grandparents or other mother substitutes) develop no stable, continuous human relationships as they are reared in several homes during infancy, childhood and adolescence. Such children spend most of their formative years in a state of anxiety, as they recognize that they are not part of a cohesive family unit and that ties can be severed at any time.

The quality of the interaction between adults and children and the frequency of negative feedback also contribute to the subsequent fate of the child or young adult. As Carter also shows, the child's experience and perception have an impact on its motivation and creativity. The perception of the environment as unfriendly and hostile may lead to crime and violence and the development of a distorted world-view.[22] The lack of verbal interaction with adults, where children are excluded from adult social conversation and told to 'shut up' (children should be seen and not heard) may have undesireable effects on their subsequent behaviour. All these are probably major factors in creating the type of passive, uncreative and violent society we endure.

National institutions

A Stone column of 24 March 1992 examines the issue of values in connection with the explosive growth of violent crime in the early 1960s. It rejects the simplistic explanation that there is an exclusive link between poverty and crime and shows that whether a poor country will have violent crime will depend upon the value system of the people and the choices which that value system will induce them to make.

He shows that a combination of some six factors were responsible for the growth of violent crime in the 1960s. One of them is of course purely economic, three of the six have their basis in changes of economic status and the response of individuals to the changed status, the fifth being the introduction of guns into political rivalry and the last being their increasing availability. The wave of crime was mostly triggered not when the poverty was at its most harsh, but when many people detected that there was some easing up of the harshness of the poverty, as in the early 1960s, a time of hope and rising aspirations. As Stone put it:

> Increased youth unemployment among males with secondary education created new formations of young people with intelligence, leadership potential and enormous confidence in themselves and aspirations for middle and upper class lifestyles but without legitimate opportunities to achieve them, hence the resort to guns and violence. The gap between their aspirations and blocked social opportunities created the motivation for violence.[23]

This is the background against which all our subsequent institutions have to operate. This is why there is a great sense of betrayal and extreme difficulty in getting the lower classes, in particular, to cooperate with the authorities in any sustained way. Calvin Bowen records his commendation of Commissioner Forbes' approach to police work, for opening up duties to include traffic and personnel management, community policing, as well as restructuring service and ethics.[24] The commissioner wants to shift emphasis from crime detection to crime prevention and make the force more people friendly. From a behavioural point of view, one fails to understand what the question of availability of funds has to do with making changes in the behaviour of the force. If it is to learn the lessons of financial and resource management, it must learn from its present predicament and make the limited funds it already has work more efficiently and effectively.

The way in which the citizen experiences his encounters with officialdom, especially the police, will contribute considerably to his attitude towards them and towards all authority. It is widely believed that policemen tend always to defend their arrest methods, claiming to follow the letter of the law. The constitutional position on police powers needs amendment. They may arrest on suspicion, but it is unclear how soon the charge must be brought. According to one lawyer's advice, if you have not been told the reason, you have the right to walk away. Police take people into custody daily without giving them a reason.

Cultural influences at the national level

The value system and attitudes of a people are determined at the national level and are reflected in the local variations, which are manifested in the home and family, the school, the workplace and the other institutions, which we have examined. In Singapore, they started the process of establishing their national values by examining those of the three great civilizations that are represented in today's Singapore – the Chinese, the Malay and the Indian – and choosing only those which all the groups consider as core values.[25]

In the Jamaican case, the establishment of national values has not been subject to any official intervention. Our values have also been affected by the fads and fashions in living and the changes that have and are taking place in the USA. One may also argue that if these values are subject to change by the fads and fashions of the Americans, then they are not core values at all. The national penchant for blaming outsiders gleefully puts most of the blame on the Americans. It would be no surprise to me to hear the Americans being blamed for the growth of crime. After all, most of the guns originate there.

Economic stringency or economic opportunities sometimes motivate behaviour, the nature of which is determined by the value system and attitudes of the individual in question. Avia Ustanny's feature article about single mothers returning to school, demonstrates that similar values and attitudes of peer groups tend to reinforce the behaviour patterns, for better or for worse.[26] Women are fighting to compete in careers. Continuing education is becoming the lifestyle of single mothers who seem to have ruled out marriage as a major goal. Further academic studies tend to discourage childbearing. Pregnant young girls, however, often descend into the vicious cycle of poverty. They are punished for their mistakes by being neglected by relatives and friends. The Women's Centre Foundation of Jamaica helps in placing girls in schools after the birth of the child. Further education, though costly, is one way to help secure the future of both mother and child.

The political culture

The prime minister is finding out the hard way that it is of no effect to make changes in the attitudes and values of the population if they are not reinforced and enhanced by those of the political culture. It is a fact of life that in a small, developing country the greatest source of influence is the government of the day. It can literally determine the survival or destruction of the members of the society. It must confirm and support the impact of the attitudes and values of other institutions such as the family, the school and the workplace. The current political culture acts to negate or confound every value taught by the family and the school today.

The two articles in this section comment on the corruption emanating from the political culture, which is surely and rapidly destroying what is left of Jamaican society. The first illustrates how the political culture systematically undermines the efforts of all the other institutions. Carl Wint refers to new legislation – the Corruption (Prevention) Act – instigated by the OAS. This Act is the successor to the Parliament (Integrity of Members) Act described as a toothless tiger.[27] Only enforcement of the law, if it ever comes, will inculcate the values and attitudes theme so dear to the heart of the prime minister. This case illustrates how the values and attitudes theme works in practice and emphasizes the role of experience in its inculcation.

The second article illustrates more consequences of our political culture of privilege and patronage. Being totally unaware of the effects of the political culture to which she subscribes, Senator Henry-Wilson calls for a "partnership that will enable government to create a quality society in which the majority of citizens will feel a sense of ownership in the national development process". According to her, the party's manifesto commits the administration to "creating a quality society, built on the foundation of education and training with the pillars of information technology, modern and appropriate physical infrastructure, timely and effective social service delivery and positive values and attitudes".[28]

The history and evolution of the political culture since 1944 objectively deny every single one of these aims and objectives. The senator does not realize that the achievement of these objectives would mean the abandonment of the entire political culture, which the governments have exploited over the past 60 years. She does not know that neither the PNP nor the JLP as currently constituted can deliver on these promises and that the current political culture makes it impossible to reform them so that they can deliver.

III: Norms, Standards and Expected Behaviour

> An American sportsman called Bennis
> Once enquired if I knew Mr Dennis
> For horse racing they say
> Makes a great holiday
> While Jamaicans don't even play tennis!

Norms and standards are what the value system aims at achieving for the good order of the society. They include the behaviour patterns sanctioned and approved by civilized societies everywhere. One of the more appropriate markers of the level of development and civilization is not crispness of the cars or the fittings and furnishings of the elaborate and expensive houses of the residents, but their good manners. In Jamaica good manners are thought to be a relic of a bourgeois society best relegated to oblivion. On the other hand, good manners may simply be the signs of a thoughtful and caring society that puts a high value on the rights and comforts of others. The thinking behind the prime minister's consultation for the renewal and inculcation of new attitudes and values was that the movement would initiate new norms and standards, and their corresponding patterns of behaviour, in accordance with the theory that attitudes have a behavioural component. As part of a development process, economically and socially, the new behaviours, norms, and standards were expected to play a vital role.

This section of the chapter examines the behaviours, norms and standards that have actually emerged and how they work in practice. We shall be particularly interested, where the evidence allows, in those behaviours having a direct bearing on the process of economic growth and development.

Carl Stone's (1986) explanation of the evolution of norms, standards and behaviour in a democratic society will provide a useful general framework into which to fit the details unearthed in my own observations:[29]

> Initiatives toward democratization are weakened by tendencies towards indiscipline and the association of all authority with oppressive manipulation and by corruption and weak leadership cadres. The general weakening of authority in schools, production, public institutions and political life has led to increasing resort to violence and intimidation as ultimate means of resolving personal and group conflicts. Democratization efforts encourage anarchic tendencies where weak authority systems prevailed.

Errol Miller's Theory of Place may explain some of the forces that operate to constrain the expected behaviours of individuals, in spite of nominal changes in their set of norms, standards and values:[30]

> Still race, class, gender and age have remained as absolutes for the placement of inequality. But today, class and race have shifted position, class being now the principal absolute, while race/colour operate within class. This leads to very complex relationships and results.

Poverty maintaining behaviour now appears justified by the limited opportunities offered by the implications of the Theory of Place. Other

forms of motivation are now conditioned by acquiring what it now takes
to gain and maintain place. Respect and ranking now fit into the theory
very neatly. One may add that the ruthless drive to acquire and maintain
place is rightly condemned as boorish behaviour and has no place among
the norms and standards of civilized society.

Public occasions: the decline of standards

The combined effects of norms, standards and expected behaviour show
up most clearly in the public behaviour of citizens. Those approved by
society are expected to have a demonstration effect and to influence the
behaviour of observers and interactors for the better. In too many cases,
undesirable behaviour has a more lasting demonstration effect. This article by J.J. Green takes an aggressive stand against sub-standard patterns
of behaviour.[31] He expresses his point blank refusal to accommodate sub-
standard behaviour, language, service and his refusal to further "develop
my morality, my intellect, my very existence to accommodate the 'common people' since what I have accomplished is no more than assisting in
the descent of human life into savagery". That article showed at least one
citizen's defiance and refusal to compromise his personal standards.

These two contributions can only comment on the decline. J Fisher
notes that morality is on the decline in today's world and expresses her
concern for double standards.[32] She rightly objects as these affect the quality
of her life. I also object to the music currently supplied on the airwaves,
not on moral grounds, but that it is not music. A summary of the various
areas of life in which norms and standards are declining is given in this
article by Lloyd Smith.[33] The Patterson administration has failed to maintain law and order. Jamaica is fast becoming ungovernable. Uplifting values
and attitudes has been thrown out the window. The country is seeing the
results of the distribution of spoils and scarce resources.

Selective rule enforcement

The following issue is a major irritant to those seeking a just society and
one which every civilized community tries to avoid, though not always
successfully. Incidentally, it supports John Maxwell's thesis that the 1962
constitution preserved the society of privilege and patronage.[34] There is
afoot a process of amendment to prison regulations, defining flogging
and whipping. Maxwell thinks that the crown is embedding barbarism
into the criminal justice system. He objects to the notorious clause in the
1962 constitution "saving" this pre 1962 punishment from being cruel
and inhuman.

Selective rule enforcement cannot be tolerated in a civilized society. Some persons seem destined to benefit from lax rule enforcement, while others have to suffer their feelings of injustice in silence. McCaulay[35] recalls an instance where other passengers were ignoring the seat number boarding rules, so she resolves to do the same. She was reprimanded for so doing. Another example, cited in the same article, is a KSAC "prohibition of such use" notice served on a gym at Haining Road. There are, however, no residential properties there and the area is overwhelmingly commercial.

The proposal to stop the minute allowance to jurors arouses the ire of another citizen.[36] This is in reference to Chief Justice Wolfe's proposal that jurors should not be paid at all. The citizen thinks the suggestion is poor and that the judiciary has suffered a loss of respect since the announcement. On the contrary, he thinks the amenities should be improved by the provision of hygienic bathrooms, lunch and medical and first aid facilities. This proposal is cast in the same perception that ordinary People can endure anything. The proposer believes that the poorer classes do not have rights as citizens, only duties. The corollary is that some citizens have rights, but no duties. This is a mark of a privilege versus merit society. It betrays the same reaction as that pilloried by the cartoonist in the *Observer* who drew three booths side by side labelled 'Salt Water Fish, Fresh Water Fish, Sewage Water Fish, approved by the Westmoreland Health Department'. As Orwell would maintain, "All animals are equal, but some are more equal than others."[37]

Outcomes of socialization: home and family

As we discussed earlier the purpose of inculcating appropriate attitudes and values is to ensure that they are displayed in equally appropriate behaviour. It is a sad fact that domestic violence is one of our major classifications of violent crime, and much of it can be traced to violation of many of what other people take to be the simple rules of courtesy and good manners.[38] If manners are important on public occasions, they are even more so in the interaction with family and friends.

The comparative neglect of the problems men face is one of the reasons behind the founding of Fathers Incorporated. This group has found that it is their most difficult task to get men to admit there is a problem. The members intend to spread the word by organizing conferences on parenting, crime and violence and micro-enterprise development. This effort is very good as most philanthropic enterprises go, as it is filling a severe need. But one must question the need for the intervention in the first place. Our experience has shown that somewhere in the background, economic instability lurks as an unadmitted cause. Global comparisons show that most of these needs arise among the poor and economically disadvantaged.[39]

Unfortunately for the following correspondent, *man bites dog* has always been more newsworthy than *dog bites man*. I remember years ago reading about a newspaper that was founded in the USA to publish only good news. I have not heard of it since. Marlane Brice[40] records a strong critique of the media for its crude coverage of burning tyres, blocked roads and demonstrations. There is little follow up for the human side of a story, for example, that of the man shot at Manor Park after stealing corned beef and rice, the fate of individual members of the Jamaica Broilers' redundant staff and Private Ferguson.

Tokenism and corruption

Somewhere in the process of socialization and the formation of attitudes and values that are based on the experiences and the interpretation of those experiences, some massive interference must have occurred. As a result, the single most remarkable development in the Jamaican society is its acceptance of corruption and sharp practice in the business and government worlds. We would widen its meaning to include not only fraud and dishonesty in the matter of monetary transactions, but any situation in which the People have had to settle for less than their entitlement because somebody, somewhere, has taken away some part by less than fair means.

A teacher who fails to teach his students well, after taking payment to do so, is as guilty of corruption as the man who transfers money to his own account after being entrusted with it by other individuals. Condoning these actions also renders an individual guilty on such a charge. Putting individuals into jobs that they are clearly incapable of doing smacks of corruption, since it is cheating the public by delivering far less than was bargained and paid for. Corruption covers not only the misuse of money, but also, even more insidiously, the misuse of power. This is an area of temptation not only for government officials but for private businessmen as well.

Tokenism is another form of corruption in which a self-serving interpretation is made of a set of facts that cannot bear the significance accorded to it. At best, tokenism is a sort of half-truth that conceals more than it reveals. Raw numbers do not tell the whole story, as some government apologists seem to believe. One has to factor in the new experiences of those made redundant and the quality and value of their new jobs. These traumatic experiences may contribute to the formation of negative attitudes and their corresponding behaviour. This report does not bear the name of its writer, but it tries to put the best face upon a situation which it tries to explain away. It tries to give the impression that a defeat is a victory. It notes that there is a net loss of 65,000 jobs or 20 per cent of the labour market in three years.[41] It gives examples of structured outplacement exercises by some firms. The recipients of outplacement end up with reduced income and prospects.

Raising the hopes of our young people and making promises about their future which one has neither the will nor the means to accomplish, is a species of corruption which destroys the credibility of governments and saps the confidence of the young persons. These sentiments are well expressed by the minister of labour, in a speech to school leavers, that poverty can be escaped through a driving desire for success and hard work.[42] The minister properly lays the stress on Aptitude, Ability and Ambition. The historical anti-wealth creation bias of governments, especially socialist, welfare and handout oriented ones, now comes back to haunt them.

The myth of the lazy Jamaican

One corollary of a society based on privilege is that there is little place for the majority. By definition, only a small percentage (less than 10 per cent, say) can occupy the top places. A society based on merit makes some room for newcomers by a process of upward (and downward) social mobility. Enough people have to be dislodged from their perch at the top to make room for those coming up from below, since the top can only accommodate that limited number.

Unwilling to make space at the top for newcomers, the privileged few justify the exclusion of the many by the allegations that they lack the incentive or the means to make the ascent. Hence the myth of the *Lazy Jamaican*. Stereotyping is a useful substitute for thought and analysis.[43] According to this report from Sylvia Lee, Roger Clarke reacts indignantly to public comments on his "Jamaicans are lazy" pronouncement. He deplores the low production and productivity. One may comment that he is apparently unaware of the structural and motivational impediments to production, for example, government's cheap food policy, an open door to agricultural imports and the comparative lack of technology and research, which he concedes as 'needed'. No mention is made of the inadequate provision of these services and the education of farmers.

Fortunately a loyal Jamaican springs to the defence of his countrymen. Hugh Dunbar, firmly convinced that Jamaicans are anything but lazy,[44] notes a completely different behaviour pattern from Jamaicans abroad than at home. Jamaicans will work simultaneously at many jobs to acquire car, house, education for children, and pretty clothes. They are motivated by the promise that the money earned will not devalue overnight. He believes that most Jamaicans want the opportunity to excel. Equal opportunities are needed in Jamaica for them to do so. We are in full agreement, based on the experience of many others, that this position is more representative of the truth. The Jamaican domestic political culture does not encourage personal excellence, but rather gives preferment on the basis of race, class and party connections

Education

The observation that some persons in the society seem to prefer name brand shoes to education brings into consideration the dichotomy between the cost and the value of an education. Those of us who have personally benefited from higher education will easily look at the cost of education as an investment. For the majority of the population, given the prospects of no satisfying returns on their investment, and the choice of migrating or stagnating, it would follow that the current generation would not have the same attitude to education as an earlier one. One result is that the Students' Loan Bureau is finding great difficulty in collecting repayments on its loans.[45] It is faced with a mass of delinquent borrowers under the old scheme. All sorts of difficulties face collectors, including changes of addresses. The techniques for collection may be the best available, but the reluctance to repay probably stems from days when education was regarded as free in the 1970s and the money is still looked upon as a grant and not a loan.

Considerations of the cost against the value of education are not the only factors at work in the next case.[46] UTECH students are reported to have blocked the main gate in protest over a 1700 per cent increase in their re-sit fees. Here, the issue of the cost and value of an education is buried under additional irritants. The roadblock appears as a communication device to present and enforce a demand for consultation before decisions having great impact on the students' finances were made. All authorities in Jamaica that are capable of learning, must know that these last minute impositions, whether gas prices, hospital fees and so on will be met with protest.

Community

It is one of the marks of a civilized society that the citizens are expected to cooperate with the authorities in the solution of social problems, especially when they pose threats to the entire community. How the community responds is a function of the confidence it has in the authorities that their proposed action will actually have the results desired. In a health crisis the behaviour of the Jamaican authorities and the response of the citizens have generally been exemplary.

It is rather ironic that in July 1999 the minister was calling upon Jamaicans to step forward for duty in a war against crime, just as he had done in June 1998.[47] According to this report, Minister of Security Knight was calling for a total national effort. He announced the targeting of gangs, a new bail policy and a white-collar crackdown. Action was promised on side issues such as dangerously overcrowded jails and lock-ups. Things then quieted down for a few months during which the country went about its "lawful business". A year later, almost to the day, a new war on crime is called for. Even at this late stage we may get some help from Carl Stone who laid down six causes for the spectacular increase in crime in the early sixties, four of them having economic bases.[48] One of the rarely tackled causes is the lack of legal economic activities in a recession largely induced by the political culture. In addition, very little attempt is made to change the experience of the young people to try to influence the attitudes and standards of behaviour.

The overall status of citizens' rights is generally shown in stark relief when different classes separate into different geographical and residential areas of the major cities. Carl Stone pointed out that one of the causes of the spectacular increase in crime was the social and geographic separation that took place in the 1960s. Heroic efforts are made today to deny that the growth and persistence of crime have any economic roots at all. The separation into geographical areas might have been slowed down if the wealth creation effects had percolated throughout the entire society. It may have given both the motive and the means for the lower income families to upgrade the quality of their houses as well as the quality of their lives.

Traditional

Traditional authority, based on the observance of the norms and standards and the behavioural patterns of one's ancestors, has long been recognized by Max Weber as one of three authority sources in any society.[49] Persons outside of the Far East completely underestimate the effect of traditional behaviour upon the contemporary generation. The much feared 'discipline and regimentation' of Singapore rests upon the traditional values of China, India and Malaya. Every developed country has laws against criminal and undesirable civic behaviour. In Singapore the people observe them, including a taxi driver this writer inadvertently tried to induce to cut a corner in his behaviour.

Traditional authority is always vulnerable to challenge by charismatic individuals. Michael Manley in the 1970s destroyed many aspects of the traditional norms and standards and behaviour. This is the theme of an article by a well known citizen.[50] Mr Reid believes that instances of ethical confusion are now coming to light. In the 1970s there was a calculated contempt for traditional moralities and values. Among other things, they were ridiculed as imported bourgeois morality not necessarily appropriate for our 'revolutionary society'. Citizens with some visible possessions were targetted as members of the oppressing class and therefore legitimate objects for plunder. The property of the state was categorized as belonging to the people and this led to the vandalizing of public property.

An invasion of squatters occurred on public and private property leading to the illegal occupation of public housing. This was aggravated by the coarsening of the behaviour of top ministers, with Minister DK Duncan suggesting that the newly opened German Automotive School was too clean and that it ought to be "desanitized". Tremendous adverse pressure was placed on traditional values and attitudes. One wonders where the present prime minister was when the destruction of positive values and attitudes was taking place. He might have saved himself the trouble of having to reinstate them, by preserving them in the first place.

Mao Zedong's Cultural Revolution tried to destroy many of China's traditional values and attitudes, especially to the artifacts of the past. Five thousand years of culture proved too much for him. Today's Chinese have shrugged off the Maoist aberration and proudly share their history and heritage with the world. As much of this chapter showed, experience is the origin and reinforcer of attitudes and values. The call for changes in attitudes and values, hence behaviour, needs institutional support and the people will not respond to the prime minister's call without visible positive experiences.

The economically and geographically enforced separation of the classes in the 1960s described by Stone has led to a vacuum in acceptable norms and standards.[51] MP Delroy Chuck views inner-city developments with grave concern and deplores the rule of the dons even while recognizing their role as protector/provider and a reliable recourse in times of distress. The values and laws of the wider society are largely discarded and rejected by a people who have experienced only neglect and injustice. Enter the dons whose obvious motive is gaining support for themselves. They fund their operations with protection money, not traceable to politics.

Chuck is correct in noting that the dons easily entered the political vacuum left by the welfare oriented politicians. Formerly, they were in business for the politicians in the garrison constituencies, to bring out the vote: now they are in business for themselves. This is a logical, if unintended, consequence of the welfare and distribution system. This writer often wonders how much Chuck is aware that the seed of many of these effects have been sown and nourished by his charismatic leader, Bustamante. By the 1950s the handout expectation was enough to affect Norman Manley's choices if he wanted to win at the polls.

Professional

The expected behaviour pattern of professionals arising from their internalization of the norms and standards of the profession may be one of the last bastions in the cause of preserving the integrity of the society. In exchange for this they are given considerable freedom of action and autonomy. The professions of law and medicine were pioneers in the movement toward self-regulation. Other professions moved to enforce their claims. The results have been a mixed bag, since many of them merely demand the perks of the profession, while refusing to accept the discipline and responsibility. Norms and standards of behaviour generally consist of both negatively and positively stated elements. The individual is enjoined to do some positive acts and to refrain from doing negative ones. Since much of what emerges in public is the result of violation of a negative element (Thou Shalt Not), the public might get the impression that the prohibition against aberrant action is more typical of the form of the norms and standards.

This contribution by Betty Jane Punnett airs the more positive aspect of professionalism, what the professional is expected to do, actively, than what he is prohibited from doing. Her area of interest is not the traditional fields of law or medicine, but management.[52] Her focus on improved management is expected to lead to improved organizational performance. General or culture specific approaches to the study are available and she thinks that a combination of both is most appropriate for the Caribbean. Her findings are that goal setting has been shown to be related to performance while the need for achievement has not. Goal setting could have significant impact on performance and thus have the potential for practical implementation. Monotonous, tiring jobs with little intrinsic motivation might benefit from goal setting. According to Ken Carter, an increase in earnings of almost any magnitude can contribute to individual welfare, when the workers are poor.[53]

This article by Errol Miller has both negative and positive elements, with the positive elements prevailing.[53] He does chide the violations, but is more constructive in helping others to observe the more positive aspects of their professional code. He finds it objectionable when other writers and talkers approach a subject they know little about with an air of authority. Listeners ignorant of the subject are impressed with the confident and authoritative manner. Miller does us a service in reminding us that form often overrides substance not only in politics but in learning and journalism as well. In politics one recalls the ability of Bustamante, Norman Manley and Michael Manley to hold people spellbound with their oratory, even while talking the most arrant nonsense. This destructive tendency has been built into our subsequent political culture. Jamaica provides an extremely fertile ground, for this is a society based upon the authority of class and social structures rather than knowledge and reason.

The next two examples are more typical of the negative behaviour among professionals. One is the concern raised by the chief justice and the other is a *Gleaner* editorial in support. The chief justice complains, in a speech to law school graduates, that some lawyers are bringing the profession into disrepute.[54] In this society, success in law is measured by the money amassed. The response of the valedictorian at the graduation is that this corruption is experienced daily by the people. The *Gleaner* editorial elaborates on the theme.[55] The lawyers are more preoccupied with making money than pursuing the lofty ideals of their profession. Since lawyers have to function in every level of modern society, their lack of integrity is a major concern.

The same media report incorporating the chief justice's complaint indeed shows that among the charges brought against lawyers there were 14 cases of fraud. The Bar Association received 232 complaints involving 144 attorneys in 1997. (This is surely a case of *gross* moral turpitude!) The frequency of corruption cases is partly a function of the lack of despatch in handling, since delays may mean avoidance of the charges, with consequent loss of confidence in the profession. Commitment must be supported by an environment that enhances these high ideals. With corruption so widespread it is easier to join it than to fight it.

Another report also takes up the issue of the failure to observe the norms and standards of a profession, this time that of management in the banking industry. The arrest of and charges against Fullerton leave one dismayed over selective applications of justice, given that so many were involved in the recent financial debacle and so few were charged with any malfeasance.[56] Fullerton was one of the few to be charged with breaches of the Financial Institutions Act. To some, this charge may be a welcome sign of the breakdown of the privileged society thesis and the violation of the code of the old boy network which has acted as the sustaining culture of the country. This case demonstrates the social failure of interlocking directorships, where favours are given by connections instead of being earned by merit.

Notes

1. Courtney Blackman, 11, p 2. He mentions a deep cultural inferiority complex as one of three factors inhibiting Caribbean development, the other two being bad scholarship and ideological aberration.
2. Weber, 157, p 47 ff.
3. Carl Stone, 151. See also Kenneth Carter, 20.
4. Mary Richardson, 129, p 144 ff.
5. C. Y. Thomas, in Davies 27, p 63.
6. Carl Stone, in Davies 27, p 133.
7. "Fruits of Laziness" (editorial), *Daily Gleaner* (Saturday 11 July 1998), p A4.
8. Garwin Davis, "Spanish Firm Got Local Contracts Based on Record" (report), *Daily Gleaner* (Thursday 4 June 1998), p B8.
9. Geert Hofstede, in Pugh, 54, p 473 ff.
10. Mary Richardson, 130, p 64.
11. See the works of Errol Miller, Mary Richardson, Marlene Hamilton, and Elsa Leo-Rhynie.
12. Errol Miller, 92, p 113.
13. Elsa Leo-Rhynie, 72, p 4.
14. "Honesty Begins at School – Davies" (report), *Daily Observer* (10 March 1998), p 21.
15. Errol Miller, "Importance of the Early Years" (article), *Daily Gleaner* (Thursday 25 June 1998), p A4.
16. Ian Boxill, "The Dinosaur Church" (article), *Daily Gleaner* (23 June 1998), p A4.
17. Anya Elliott, "Religion as Social Cement" (letter), *Daily Gleaner* (9 July 1998), p C11.
18. Kenneth Carter, 20, pp 3–4, 6.
19. Keith Panton, 112, p 15 ff.

20. Richard Coe, "Time to Revolutionise Thinking" (report), *Daily Gleaner* (29 July 1998).

21. Elsa Leo-Rhynie, 72, pp 11–14.

22. Thomas Harris, 48, supports Leo-Rhynie on the strong influence of this perception.

23. Carl Stone, 153, p 32.

24. Calvin Bowen, "A New Charter for the Police" (article), *Daily Gleaner* (Wednesday 24 June 1998), p A8.

25. John S.T. Quah (ed), 125, p 91 ff. The components of the National Values are summarized in Appendix B, p 117.

26. Avia Ustanny, "Single Moms Head Back to School" (article), *Sunday Gleaner* (29 March 1998), p 1D.

27. Carl Wint, "Cynicism about Corruption" (article), *Daily Gleaner* (Tuesday 10 March 1998), p A4.

28. "Henry-Wilson Tackles Challenges of Production" (report), *Daily Gleaner* (Wednesday 11 March 1998), p A3.

29. Carl Stone, in Davies 27, p 133.

30. Miller, 92, p 120.

31. J.J. Green, "I Shall Lower My Standards No Longer" (article), *Outlook (Gleaner)* (Sunday 11 January 1998), p 11.

32. J. Fisher, "Morality and Double Standards" (letter), *Daily Gleaner* (Tuesday April 14 1998), p A5.

33. Lloyd B. Smith, "Minister Knight and a New Day" (article), *Daily Observer* (Tuesday 29 September 1998), p 6.

34. John Maxwell, "Flogging Live Men and Dead Horses" (article), *Sunday Observer* (3 May 1998), p 11.

35. Diana McCaulay, "Selectively Applied Rules" (article), *Sunday Gleaner* (17 May 1998), p 9A.

36. Letter from Former Juror, "It's an Injustice to Jurors", *Daily Observer* (Tuesday 7 April 1998), p 8.

37. Orwell, 110, p 23 "all animals are equal"; p 104 "...but some are more equal than others". The cartoon appears in the *Daily Observer* (Saturday 6 June 1998), p 6.

38. Camille Taylor, "Restoring the Marred Image of the Jamaican Father" (report), *Daily Gleaner* (Monday 15 June 1998), p A2.

39. See Barry Chevannes, books and interview and papers; also the works of Patrick Bryan and Elsie Sayle. For discussions on the dynamics of poverty; see also Galbraith, 36 and Gray, 44.

40. Marlane Brice, "Real Stories Go A-Begging" (letter), *Daily Gleaner* (Monday 12 October 1998), p A5.

41. "Redundancies Increase Self-Employment" (report), *Daily Gleaner* (Friday 11 September 1998), p A11.

42. "Graduates Urged to Work Hard to Escape Poverty" (report), *Daily Gleaner* (Friday 10 July 1998), p C12.

43. Sylvia Lee, "Clarke Raps Critics as 'Hypocrites'" (report) *Daily Gleaner* (Thursday 23 July 1998), p A1.

44. Letter from Hugh Dunbar, "Jamaicans Are Anything but Lazy", *Daily Gleaner* (Tuesday 11 August 1998), p A5.

45. "Students' Loan Bureau Still Battling With Collections" (report), *Daily Gleaner* (Wednesday 19 August 1998), p B4.

46. Ainsley Walters, "Massive Re-sit Fees" (report), *Daily Gleaner* (Wednesday 21 October 1998), p A1.

47. "Jamaica Called to Crime War" (report), *Daily Gleaner* (Thursday 25 June 1998), p A1.

48. Carl Stone, 149, p 40.

49. Weber, 158, p 328.

50. C S Reid, "A Right Thing Done a Wrong Way" (article), *Daily Gleaner* (Saturday 21 March 1998), p A8.

51. Delroy Chuck, "Turmoil in the Inner City" (article), *Daily Gleaner* (Wednesday 21 October 1998), p A4.

52. Betty Jane Punnett, 124, p 24.

53. Errol Miller, "Nonsense Spoken with Much Confidence" (article), *Daily Gleaner* (Thursday 11 June 1998), p A4.

54. "Legal Dishonesty Rapped" (report), *Daily Gleaner* (Monday 28 September 1998), p A1.

55. "Focus on Lawyers" (editorial), *Daily Gleaner* (Thursday 1 October 1998), p A4.

56. "Fullerton Arrested" (report), *Daily Observer* (Thursday 18 June 1998), p 1.

6

The Institutionalization of Poverty *or* the Income-less Society: Overview, History and Definitions

his chapter examines several aspects of the theme of poverty. The overview will introduce the topic and give a working definition of how the subject is generally regarded worldwide. The first two sections will look at the symptoms and effects of poverty in Jamaica with respect to the basic amenities that contribute to the quality of life. These include health and medical services, transport, and housing. The effects of mass poverty on the motivation and aspirations of the people will also be documented here. The leading theme will be the aspirations and expectations of the people of Jamaica as they moved towards independence in 1962 and beyond. Section three will examine a few theories and explanations of the sources and causes of poverty in Jamaica with a view to remedying and solving them at the root.

So far most of our efforts have been at the level of alleviating the symptoms and making the life of the poor a little more endurable. Among the causes poverty will be shown as the inevitable result of the absence of economic aims and objectives during the founding days of the new nation. The equilibrium of poverty, the difficulty of escape and how the maintenance of a state of poverty almost qualifies as a policy of government will feature also in section three. The last two sections will examine the available approaches to dealing with poverty. They will look at the way in which welfare has been used as a substitute for wealth creation. The chapter will end with a critique of what has been done so far and make recommendations for a more permanent and long term solution, culminating in the creation of wealth.

M G Smith gives us a working definition of poverty:[1]

Any condition that is culturally recognized as a deprivation that merits social redress was treated as an instance of need for social assistance, provided that such need attached to individuals or domestic families who could not take effective action to reduce or remove it, with the resources available to them ... The needs for social assistance include employment, cash, vocational training, land, housing, health services for adults and children, needs of the aged, destitute, indigent, handicapped, insurance coverage, help with children, literacy, etc.

In his discussion of economic conditions he tries to put poverty in Jamaica in some kind of perspective in terms of its scale and scope. He uses the official figures including income distribution, employment, labour force statistics, but comments that "the estimates of the totals of employed and unemployed... are spurious and severely misleading" (for reasons given). The official picture is complicated by our local definitions of unemployment and its relationship to the search for work. Our official definitions of employment exclude own account workers, many of whom lack the means, resources, skill and organizational supports required to take care of their own social needs as defined above.

Patrick Bryan approaches the task of describing the scale and scope of the problem by retracing the history of social welfare and community development from 1938 to 1962.[2] Ironically, capitalist society has survived because of its reluctance to seek definitive and final solutions to complex social and economic problems. This phase of state organized welfare from Britain to Jamaica was to avoid political disaffection in the colonies and to silence United States' criticisms of Britain's imperial role. The Moyne Commission had stressed the need for social reform. Social reform came, in part, on the wings of fear of social upheaval. The Colonial Office wished to defuse what seemed to be an increasingly dangerous situation arising out of discontent, increasing racial animosity and the spread of modern ideas.[3]

Bryan continues to narrate that in the post-independence period there was a tradition of partnership between voluntary action and state sponsored welfare. There is growing evidence of concern on both sides of the partnership with structures that reinforce poverty, crime and urban culture in urban subcultures. The multiplicity of agencies engaged in welfare activities is a testimony to the generous response of the Jamaican people to the problems of the poor. M.G. Smith counted over 50 welfare agencies in the 1973 edition while this writer counted 163 in the 1987 version of the Handbook of the Council for Voluntary Social Services.

I: Symptoms and effects

Some folks are resigned to their fate
When they muse on the role of the State
It defers to the classes
'Stead of serving the masses
Who remember the last time they ate

Aspirations and expectations

The question which should arise from anyone doing a more than cursory survey of the poverty scene in Jamaica is, how could the Jamaican people, more or less, patiently tolerate a state of poverty/no income/low income for 60 years, especially for the years since independence? Why has there been no major social unrest? There have been protests and demonstrations since the big one in 1938, but somehow they have been contained by the political culture and no major change occurred in the economic environment.[4] Perhaps one answer, as we saw in chapter five, is that through the experience of the years since 1938, the authorities have created and popularised a system of values in which income earning and relative economic independence were not given positive worth. It appears that the government has acted on the belief that if you cannot supply a commodity, make sure that there is no demand for it.

Another factor responsible for little being done to create wealth and eliminate poverty is reflected in the vein of fatalism, which seems to be endemic to many poor populations. Even such a prominent figure as Rex Nettleford in a book on development in the Caribbean, commenting on the achievements of the Asian Tigers, cavalierly dismisses the hopes of Jamaicans: "Forget them, they are not for you!"[5] This streak of fatalism is also summed up neatly by some verses alleged to have been part of the old Anglican hymn:

The rich man in his castle, the poor man at his gate,
God made them high and lowly, and ordered their estate!

Trying to escape from your divinely ordained fate would surely cause the wrath of God to descend on you in the full fury of fire and brimstone! The attitude of returning residents is not so apocalyptic. Overseas Jamaicans, however, express their anger at the failure of those left behind to change their fate themselves. Our achievements have fallen short of first world expectations. On the other hand, the perception of resident Jamaican masses is that the returning residents are 3M: Mad, Mean and Moneyed.

The consequences of the one-off handout show that it is effective for political manipulation and for the perpetuation of dependency. As mentioned above, the over proliferation of social services denotes failure, not success, of economic development. Perhaps some scholar may find a negative correlation between the level of economic development and the number and extent of the activities of the voluntary social services. Handouts have more long-lasting negative effects if the contribution of the potential clients is belittled as illustrated in this finding by Obika Gray:[6]

> The politics of the poor disclose the nature of their 'imagined community', its norms, social structure and internal relations. The task of those who would be allies of the poor is to understand the character and internal logic of that community and facilitate the efforts of the poor to realize the positive aspects of such a community.

The ascent from poverty

Galbraith has confirmed the notion that the ascent from poverty starts with a strong desire of the people to work themselves out of such a state.[7] It does not matter how this desire comes about. In some countries it arises as a result of some national trauma which infuses people with a sense of purpose. The 3000-year history of the Jews and their near elimination from Europe under Hitler galvanized them into seeking a homeland. Even though the acquisition of this land was fraught with peril, that in itself acted as a very strong motivator. The majority of Jamaicans have a similar history of trauma, but it seems to have had an inhibiting rather than a liberating effect. One sometimes wonders whether the behaviour of persons of African descent is the result or the cause of their slavery.

The ascent from poverty naturally has an economic side to it. The creation of wealth by those who were formerly poor is the only solution to the problem of poverty. Any economist who admits to an appalling performance record is, of course, *persona non grata* to his profession. Thus Grassl raises the ire of his colleagues.[8] His 50 columns have annoyed some persons in government circles and at the UWI, but the interest and agreement from many of the Jamaican people far outweigh the criticism attracted and even the racial and foreign overtones. Nothing has been learnt from the past and they are about to repeat the mistake of re-nationalizing the transport system. As Grassl says, the bill is always presented to the small man. Even with his departure, he still did not understand the

Jamaican economy and the Jamaican way of political rather than economic thinking and decision making. Our leaders seem to operate on the
belief that power is the only quality needed for successful leadership.

Veteran commentator Morris Cargill is as usual scathing in his criticism of the 1998 budget and the way it was handled.[9] No full explanation
has been forthcoming from government to journalists, though promised.
The choices for further taxation are unexceptional, except for the rather
puzzling practice of taxing unleaded gas more than leaded. Nothing in
the budget speaks about reducing the cost of the public sector. The minister appears quite casual. Cargill believes that the underground drug
economy is keeping us alive, but that it is best not to enquire too closely.

Having failed to deal with the aspirations and expectations of the
people ourselves, we now are calling upon those who left our shores many
years ago to try to pull us out of poverty. One notes John Small's call to
returning residents, to design equal opportunities for youth. He also stresses
the need for partnership and power sharing between the government and
the people. The treatment of citizens by public sector officials is unacceptable.[10] Some disturbing questions arise from this report. One is puzzled
as to the meaning of social capital, as used in the headline to the report.
Furthermore, the popular interpretation of equal opportunities is equal
handouts. Government as currently constituted has no intention of ever
sharing power with the people, especially after capturing and keeping it
for 60 years.

Housing and squatting

It is easier to see the impact of the policy of poverty creation on housing
and its attendant problem, squatting. M G Smith recognizes housing as a
severe national problem. His study focusses on home ownership and rental,
the mode of occupancy and overcrowding. Even using the generous criterion of over two persons per bedroom, he finds that half of the sample of
houses is overcrowded, 30 per cent clearly overcrowded and 15 per cent
grossly overcrowded.[11]

Some historical factors account for the shortage of land for building
and the solution of squatting adopted by the landless. Satchell notes that
after the Morant Bay Rebellion in 1865, planters, under pressure from
falling sugar prices, sold their lands but preferred to sell their lots intact,
rather than subdivide. There were no land settlements, which fuelled a
tendency of squatting by both small settlers and the upper classes. These
squatters were eventually dispossessed. Even when new policies led to the
development, revival and expansion of colony's trade during the late nine-

teenth century, the negative effects for small settlers continued. Small settlers were never principal purchasers of public land until late 1890s.[12]

Problems and solutions

We mentioned earlier that one man's solution (squatting) is another man's problem. This report by Gary Spaulding shows how citizens deal with the shortage of land, which Satchell shows to have been the result of deliberate government policy since 1865. Left to his own devices, the distressed citizen finds even more desperate solutions. The woes of the Gregory Park evicted continue and their narration is accompanied by stories of individual citizens in their efforts to cope.[13] The society is flagrantly lacking in structures for wealth generation. The notion that the people can generate their own if offered the opportunity, has never seemed to have occurred to governments, since 1938.

The editor of *The Observer* is most careful to state that the activities of the squatter have been forced upon him due to the inadequacies of the economy. Although sympathetic to the efforts of government, he agrees that squatters deny people the right to enjoy their land and that unplanned developments pose health and other risks. He nevertheless argues that some 15 per cent or 375,000 Jamaicans have to squat, forced by the insufficiency of shelter and the too high prices of dwellings. The economy is simply not generating enough wealth.[14]

Long Term Solutions

It is arguable that a long-term problem like housing and squatting would be best served by equally long term solutions. Even this approach is unsustainable in the absence of wealth creating mechanisms for the residents. The frequent reports of foreclosures, forced sales, auctions and other get tough actions, suggest that many residents are seriously behind in the payments. The report gives more details of proposals for housing solutions for squatters and promises that units are to be constructed all over the island. Thus this report can be interpreted by cynics to indicate that it is only another manifestation of the welfare orientation working itself out.[15]

Well-meaning MPs recognize the severe limitations imposed on a government strapped for cash, because of its previous neglect of wealth creation. Nevertheless this does not stop them from putting their bids in. After all, re-election is vital. Thus MP Jennifer Edwards' call for some reforms in the housing process, the lowering of deposits and closing costs and increasing the time for women to pay off a mortgage in spite of an earlier retirement age. Policies should be implemented in the lifetime of those governments who introduce them. The weakness of policy implementation due to failure to create responsive organizations and the lack of commitment make such efforts at alleviation hopeless.[16] We have noted that generally the speed of implementation runs in inverse ratio to the speed of legislation. One further question: How do the jobless qualify for these houses?

One measure of the activities of those who provide housing solutions is the number of family units constructed. How comfortable they are for their future occupants is not a prime concern of the builders. This report alleges that the NHT, and its construction partner, WIHCON, offer potentially hazardous one-door studios. No consideration of security in case of fire influenced the design. The builders claim that many years of occupancy are projected before any expansion is likely to be made.[17] A later story claimed that a one-door studio is a normal practice. That may be acceptable from a certain point of view, but in keeping with the remainder of my thesis it raises some troubling questions of what the aristocrats believe is tolerable for a poor individual – low income, rather, since the true poor cannot afford these houses.

Poverty may not be directly linked to crime, but Evans has evidence to show that one-room children do not learn to respect the property rights of others.[18] This open display of contempt for the low income people has been shown to lead to alienation, almost hostility toward the rest of the society, and may account for the recent change in the location of many violent crimes.

Vendors – Problems and Solutions

Illegal vending and tourist harassment join squatting as areas in which the authorities try to treat the rational solutions of citizens as problems. Until the citizens are presented with viable alternatives to their solutions, they will survive any amount of bulldozing and forcible removal from their favourite haunts.[19] The report shows the situation in Mandeville as intractable, despite warnings by Southern Parks and Markets. As implied, the vendors instinctively know that retail marketing is based solely on location. The vendors must go where the potential buyers are. Invariably the authorities move them out of the main areas of human traffic. Inevitably they filter back. Harassment is vending carried on to an annoying degree.[20] Maloney's letter reports that the main source of harassment is vendors selling unsolicited goods and services on streets. The vendors are simply trying to make a living. The clearing of the streets can only be short term. Maloney suggests education about tourism, of its benefits and pitfalls.

As he seems to hint, the reasons for the behaviour go well beyond the surface. Even the most casual observer will note that the countries which are more successful in their tourism are either those where the number of visitors overwhelms the local population (saturation theory), or where the population has something more profitable to do than harass tourists (diversion theory). If tourism is the only game in town, as government's tourism one-crop policy appears to be promoting, then every able-bodied unemployed person will seek a piece of the action.

The quality of life

Mere survival or existence on a daily basis is too little for mankind. Philosophers agree that there is more to the life of man than mere survival. Christian teaching takes its belief in the purpose of human life to a different level. Motivational theorists believe that mankind needs to fulfil its potential, whatever that means. Most of mankind lives a life best described in Hobbesian terms as 'nasty, brutish and short'.

M.G. Smith defined the poor as those whose needs for social assistance included employment, cash, vocational training, land, housing, and health services for adults and children. Other needs would encompass those of the aged, destitute, indigent, handicapped, insurance coverage, help with children, literacy and so on. These are lists of their lower order physical needs and speak mostly to their survival requirements. The second set of needs speaks to the quality of their life, after their survival and safety needs have been met. In Maslow's terms they still have to meet their higher order needs for esteem, belonging and self-fulfilment.[21] Remarkable individuals, like Gandhi, were able to bypass their lower order needs to fulfil the higher level ones. For the mass of human beings, particularly the poor in Jamaica, their needs are more mundane and run of the mill. Researchers like M G Smith concede that other identified needs include literacy, assistance in family planning and legal aid for criminal and civil issues to permit them to legalize purchases and wills and to secure their legitimate rights and claims.[22]

Smith's findings and recommendations are based, as usual, on thorough research. To bolster the claims of the poor on literacy, he found that a low ratio of urban respondents admitted partial or complete illiteracy (14.8 per cent men, 9.6 per cent women), compared with rural admission of 31 per cent men and women. With respect to family planning, the great majority does not practise it. There is a large catalogue of rural and urban poor who need legal aid, illustrating a variety of issues, conditions and outcomes, who are unable to take the necessary action. He also examined the provisions for information and mutual aid in which he discussed voluntary organizations in Jamaica and the assistance provided to them. He found that 56 per cent of the potential clients knew nothing about available assistance and never sought help; 7.2 per cent learnt from their MP, parish councillor or JP; 7 percent from kin; 4.9 per cent from neighbours; and 4.2 per cent from siblings and cousins.

Many commentators on the educational scene completely agree that education is the key to social mobility, even in a depressed economy, and cannot understand why the poor do not seem to embrace it with open arms and open minds. Glen Day believes that education may be priced out of the reach of the poorer people. September is no longer welcome, he begins. High school fees and the additions for books, lunch, uniforms and games equipment push the price out of the reach of the poor. The cost of education is a shock to children and parents as they advance through the grades.[23]

Prices are relative with respect to the happiness one gets from the purchase. Elsewhere we have commented on the phenomenon of parents sporting the latest expensive hairstyles, clothing and shoes while failing to pay school fees. The reasoning is simple: if you get little or no pleasure out of a purchase, like that of education, then any price is excessive. On the other hand, if you get maximum pleasure from a purchase, like gold bangles and chains, then they are comparatively cheap. A society which gives its rewards to class and political connections rather than merit cannot expect its people to place a high value on education. This result is a direct fallout of the absence of national aims and objectives and of the failure to create wealth.

Education and Careers

The social power of any class contributes greatly to its perceived quality of life. Many of the upper classes tend to evaluate their quality of life in terms of their connections and their material possessions. Motor cars do give considerable freedom, especially in the light of a ramshackle transport system. Obika Gray suggests that lacking possessions, the poor evaluate their social power in terms of the body. He comments:

> in opposition to 'large quantity of law' possessed by the propertied class, the people have a large quantity of power inscribed in their bodies and in their conception of an exalted self. They have the power to define their personae, protect it against attack and humiliation, and defend it against extractive

claims of the state and allied groups in civil society. The 'badness' of the ghetto poor is a form of this power, manifested also in crime, intimidation and the creation of an atmosphere of insecurity. Crime is even used as political expression.[24]

This illustrates the difficulty facing those institutions dedicated to the alleviation of poverty and the fight against crime. In other words, the poverty fighters can give the poor fish, but if Gray is right, they can never teach them to fish. This scenario gives some highly unwanted answers to the question of how the poor will respond to well meaning attempts to alleviate their lot on a permanent basis. What inducements can the rest of society offer to encourage them to abandon this protective but insecure society? How far do government projects reflect a knowledge of this kind of reality? The relatively high price for educational equipment and fees is one factor in the rejection by the poor of the use of this route as a way towards social mobility. A more deep seated reason is that the fact of their poverty greatly reduces the academic performance of their children and perpetuates the cycle of poverty over the generations, since the grandchildren and the great grandchildren are equally stultified educationally.

Mitchelmore and Clarke's findings showed that contrary to expectations, it did not matter whether there were significant differences between boys and girls. They found that both sexes showed identical results. What mattered was their nutrition status, especially in the matter of regular and full breakfast, something the poor simply cannot provide. Results showed that the upper achievement group was significantly taller for their age and had a higher breakfast rating than the lower achievement group. *All socioeconomic variables showed significantly higher means in the upper achievement group* (emphasis added). Significant gender differences were rarer.[25]

In spite of the establishment by experts of the optimum conditions under which Jamaican children learn and make the best use of their educational opportunities, there are some self-styled 'experts' who take a small part of a real experts' finding, ignore the context and arrive at illogical conclusions. Garwin Davis argues that hungry children can learn: "Limited resources can be a deterrent to a child's educational development but should not be the underlying factor that determines success or failure in the classroom."[26] Since a little poverty is no bar to literacy, then perhaps more poverty will enhance literacy. This article provides great scope for many false conclusions and spurious logic. Research cannot establish that limited resources *should not* be an underlying factor. If the research establishes that limited resources *are indeed* an underlying factor as Mitchelmore and Clarke appear to have; no one can pontificate as to whether it should not be such. The same sort of reasoning marks the debate about poverty. Since poverty is not a direct cause of crime, we can ignore it. Poverty elimination or better, wealth creation, is not considered an end in itself, but only as a means to other ends.

Wealth creation is therefore far from consideration. It is true that money is not directly connected to success, but can it not buy more willing and competent teachers and upgrade the equipment and books? Must teachers remain poor in order to be competent? The Americans' finding of a correlation between available money and success must surely depend upon whom it is available to. Mitchelmore and Clarke have demonstrated that if the money were available to poor parents to provide an adequate breakfast for the students, the impact on success in the classroom would be astonishing.

Both the emotional and the developmental arguments surrounding the dialect spoken by most Jamaicans are aired between these two contributions. Audley Foster's article advances the usual arguments about the appropriateness of dialect in national affairs and cites the popularity of Witter in support. Allan Foreman's letter counters that we will be worse off with patois. He agrees that the use of English in Parliament and official documents does shut (some) people out of participation in politics. He thinks that the use of technical terms is deliberately done to confuse the people of Jamaica, who support Parliament out of ignorance.[27,28]

To take the article first, the same romantic arguments pale before one economic fact. If Jamaica wants to get into the mainstream of development and come to equal terms with the world, it had better come to terms with English. English triumphed not because of any inherent superiority, but because it was spoken and written by some of the most creative people the world has ever seen.

The North American people reinforced its importance by making it the language of commerce. In today's world, over 90 per cent of the world's business is conducted in English, the same percentage of scientific journals is published therein; all computer software is generally first written in English, even by native speakers of Swedish, Dutch or Japanese. No one is going to write any technical or managerial treatise in Jamaican patois.

To respond to the letter, technical terms have to be a staple of government or any other technical discipline. The first language of Singapore is English, with the second being the people's native tongue.[29] The Chinese are discovering that, in the face of some 6,000 dialects and 1.2 billion people, it is better if everyone spoke English. All of Europe, except the French for historical reasons, speaks English. Even the Russians and Arabs write their protest demonstration placards in English. One final prophecy: if Jamaica persists in failing to teach literacy in English, it will face another 60 years of economic stagnation.

II: Sources and causes

The best troops in the fight against poverty
Are the ones who're bereft of all property
For they need to be taught
The behaviours they ought
And to naturally do them from puberty!

Theories of poverty

One of the explanations for poverty consists of the behaviour patterns of the entities, whether of the individual human being or of whole nations. Many economic arguments suggest that national wealth existed because of the possession of some natural resource which was marketable on the world market. These arguments have been firmly challenged by the experiences of the twentieth century, which have shown beyond a reasonable doubt that the source of wealth is not the possession of natural resources but of the ability to use skills and technologies to 'add value to things'. It is the recognition of this factor that has made value added tax a popular fiscal measure in the Caribbean and other places.[30] It would seem that the creation of national wealth is more a function of the use of skills and technologies, that is, the behavioural pattern of individuals and groups, than the possession of raw material resources.

We think that there is a good case for extending the argument to explain the poverty of individuals in a society as well. We are proposing a hypothesis that three pertinent sets of behaviours explain the phenomenon of the creation of wealth and the persistence of poverty. These are poverty causing or poverty seeking behaviours, poverty avoiding behaviours and wealth seeking or wealth creating behaviours. These behaviours operate at both the individual and the national levels as well at the intermediate levels, that is groups and organizations. At the individual level they explain that poverty is the consequence of certain poverty seeking patterns. Many of these behaviours are controllable by the individual: some are only controllable at the societal level and not by the individual. The best the individual can do is to control those behaviours, which he can, such as by acquiring an education, and then placing himself in positions where the favourable societal behaviour patterns, which he cannot control, may work in his interest.

The theory needs some modification in the light of the findings of other researchers and theorists. The efforts of the individual to lift himself by the bootstraps, so to speak, are more than hampered by the creation and reinforcement, by the ruling political culture, of the national dependency syndrome, which the same politicians now deplore. Scattered individual efforts of the Horatio Alger type, admirable as they may be, may not be enough to break the 'equilibrium of poverty'. Galbraith shows also that the reason for the apparent 'poverty seeking behaviour' may stem from the 'accommodation' of the poor to their plight. Being dashed to the ground more than once, the poor yield to their experience and cease trying. The conviction that the individual effort is doomed anyway strengthens the inhibition of creativity.[31,32]

To resume the behavioural theory, the same scheme operates at the national level. Among the factors controllable by the nation are the creation of realistic development plans, an attractive investment climate and the presence of people and organizations prepared and motivated to carry out the development process. At the national level a philosophy of development must incorporate a meaning of development, which recognizes that economic growth is not the same as economic development. As discussed previously, in the late 1950s and throughout the 1960s there was remarkable growth in the Jamaican economy, but very little development. To elaborate the definition of development, it can only mean the creation of the capacity in the people of Jamaica for seizing the opportunities available, based on a realistic perception of trends and developments in the world.

C.Y. Thomas in his *Typology of Poverty* offers us another analytical framework within which to understand the anatomy and physiology of poverty. He identifies three categories of 'poor', each with its own dynamics, requiring distinct modes of intervention. The first is the hard core systemic poor, who are born poor and remain poor over their lifetime, mainly because of their manner of insertion into the system of production and asset ownership. The second group are the newly poor or structurally adjusted poor, becoming so largely because of stabilization and structural adjustment programmes in operation. The third group is the transient poor, varying in number, form and content from year to year and from season to season.[33]

This is a good framework for the analysis and recognition of the need for different ways of handling the clients, including taking into consideration how the poor respond to their condition. It is not likely that they will be equally affected by or contribute to economic growth and development. This leads to an apparently silly question of whether poverty can be reduced if the entire economy remains poor. Most persons would answer "no", but all the governments of Jamaica since 1972 have been operating on a "yes" answer.

Galbraith's contribution provides much support for my modified theory. He rejects many of the standard explanations of poverty and by implication, their prescribed remedies. He seems to favour an explanation based on accommodation, the equilibrium of poverty and the attitude of the community to risk. *Accommodation* resembles the behaviour pattern that is the theme of Patterson's *Children of Sisyphus.*[34] Having tried and failed to escape poverty, generation after generation, they stop trying. They become what Thomas calls the hard core systemic poor. The *equilibrium* of poverty illustrates the cruelty of fate. A good example from Galbraith discusses the results of a massive irrigation system introduced by the British in India. It had the effect of increasing the income of the farmers and their families. This led to an increased birth rate and decreased infant mortality. The increased population ate up the increased income and returned the people to the previous level of deprivation. *Risk Aversion* completes the trilogy. Much of the world's poverty exists in rural areas and in developing countries. The farmers simply cannot afford the risk of technological change. If agricultural corporations such as Dole or Archer Daniels Midland in the USA experience crop failure, they are inconvenienced but not endangered. If an agricultural community in a developing country like Afghanistan or Sudan experiences the same crop failure, it faces famine or extinction or both. It is therefore highly risk averse and will not readily welcome new methods of cultivation.

The sum of all these theories is that the capacity of the poor to display the necessary behaviour under the circumstances facing them is crucially limited. As Galbraith suggests, their doubts as to the long-term sustainability of any interventions make them cling to these poverty-causing behaviours and provide fodder for the intergenerational socialization which perpetuates the poverty. Circumstances and their experience may mean that the behaviour is forced instead of voluntary or chosen, but the effects are the same. Finally, one must refer to the contributions of Obika Gray to review the defence mechanisms the poor of Jamaica have used to maintain their own status and integrity and to resist the efforts of outsiders who would attempt to change that status.

III: Breaking the Cycle of Poverty

The cycle of poverty's dysfunctional
To avoid all behaviours irrational
One must want to be wealthy
In no way it's unhealthy
Fitting well with our purposes national

In the light of Galbraith's theory of accommodation to and the equilibrium of poverty, along with risk aversion, the task of breaking the cycle of poverty becomes a formidable one. It is more difficult to break when self-imposed. The theories quoted rather support the notion that much of the manifestation of poverty is behavioural. Breaking the cycle of poverty, for individuals or for the nation, consists of changing the behaviour pattern of both. Most poverty alleviation programmes tend more to confirm and reinforce the present behaviour. Behavioural change is possible but the inducements must be strong. As a general rule, the longer the behaviour persists, the stronger must be the inducement. It is difficult for the people to make the change without the support of the political culture of a sympathetic and transformational leadership. That too was supplied to the people of Singapore. From 1938 onwards the practice and precepts of the prevailing Jamaican culture, as shown in chapters two to four, encouraged poverty seeking rather than wealth creating behaviour. The people were faced with hesitations, partial commitment, mostly in words and standard excuses, which were used abundantly to conceal a basic unwillingness.

Marjorie Newman-Williams and Fabio Sabatini in discussing the issue of child centred development and social progress in the Caribbean, observe that the intergenerational cycle of deprivation and poverty has to be broken at some point. They argue that if policies, which induce the desired behavioural change, are put in place for a single generation, they would have tremendous effect. Full satisfaction of the basic needs of children and their participation in society would be enhanced by such an intervention. The parents' time, health and education and parenting skills would then interact with the values, attitudes and practice at the household and community level. These policies might even help with the crime problem we are experiencing at the moment.[35] Poverty may not be a direct cause of crime, but so many of the side effects of poverty create conditions that have been shown to lead to crime, that it may as well be cited as a cause.[36] Even when sincere efforts are made to break the cycle it cannot be done without the active co-operation of the poor.

Persons in authority tend to ignore the requests of the poor on the grounds that the authorities know their needs better than their clients. Newman-Williams and Sabatini warn us that the poor develop short-term coping strategies which help them deal with the crisis of the moment and they develop systems for survival that often constitute barriers that isolate them from society, feeding off the inter-generational reproduction of poverty. These compare well with Obika Gray's findings on the defence mechanisms of the poor.

Theory into practice

Errol Gregory's article "Breaking the Cycle of Poverty" conveniently offers its title to this section. Gregory begins with a comment on minimum wage discussions that highlighted the absence of buoyancy in the economy and our inability to match wages with living costs. Parliamentary pensions were increased to J$25,000 per month, creating further imbalance in income distribution. He quotes two of the many reasons for Jamaica getting to this point of relative national poverty. He notes that Charles Ross blames inappropriate macro-economic policies over 25 years and that Dennis Morrison goes back further. For Morrison the problem that started in the early 1950s is linked to our failure to obey two economic laws, that the rate of rise in income should be linked to increases in productivity and that we cannot ignore the relationship between savings and increases in productivity.[37]

A number of questions are raised from this writer's behaviourist point of view. What mechanisms existed then or exist now to ensure that the government does not break the laws of economics and pursue inappropriate policies? If such corrective mechanisms do exist, why have they not worked? Why has the government failed to mobilize savings? Is the cultural resistance to savings innate, or were the people taught that they need not save because government would attend to their every need? All behaviour is caused, even if the causes are not economic.

Solution by reclassification

The British comedy series 'Yes, Minister' contains a scene in which the minister, reflecting Cabinet concerns about the overstaffing in the civil service generally, decides to make drastic cuts in the staff of the Department of Administrative Affairs. His permanent secretary is entrusted with the job. The minister reports his success to Parliament, only to discover that his PS has simply reduced the numbers by reclassification.[38] Morris Cargill in a number of his articles has always claimed that he does not make jokes over serious matters in Jamaica, because his most outlandish suggestions eventually become administrative policy. Cargill's fears have come true with a vengeance. No doubt the flap over the forced deportation of mentally ill street people was caused because some very junior police officer was told to 'do something about the presence' of the mentally ill on the streets of Montego Bay. He did.

The aim of reducing poverty is not achieved merely by cutting numbers. This is a classic case of poverty alleviation by reclassification.[39] In spite of the fact that the value of dole is $30 to $100 weekly, the inspector of the poor wants to reduce the number of recipients, grown from 2,173 persons (up to June 1997) to 2,225 (June 1998). He needs to define who is poor. He appears sincere about wanting to break the cycle of poverty and to alleviate the plight of the children of paupers. The chances are high that, following the practice of delegation as it works in the government service, he too was told to do something about the cost of poor relief, with no guidelines from his superiors, who found this an excellent way to avoid responsibility.

Techniques and effects

The change process as described by Lewin says that behavioural change goes through three phases: unfreezing, moving and refreezing.[40] Others have elaborated the model to as many as seven stages, but the basic process is untouched. Stripped of its jargon, it merely means that the behaviours as presently practised must first be uprooted, destroyed or otherwise removed from the profile of the individual's or group's behaviour. The second phase involves moving to a new desired behaviour. Refreezing means reinforcing the new behaviour by practice.

Unfreezing the old behaviour involves some very heavy and consistent work, especially where the rewards for new behaviours have, rarely if ever, materialized. The Jamaican people are likely to become very cynical and skeptical, and refuse to cooperate, in accordance with Galbraith's theory of accommodation. Moving to a new behaviour needs the commitment of the individual or group undergoing the change. Refreezing the new behaviour into place needs constant reinforcement not only from those in close interaction with the change agent, but from the entire community and society. Singapore successfully got all its citizens to go through the process. Lee Kuan Yew, on television in June 1999, was somewhat dissatisfied with the new behaviour and believed that it ought to change to yet another level. He now needs to unfreeze some of those patterns that he had carefully frozen into place over nearly 30 years.

The provision of crash programmes, a staple of political intervention since the forties, will freeze the existing undesirable behaviour of the majority of the people even more solidly into place, thus making even more work for the change agent. A newspaper editor's proviso that the programme should give value for money is perhaps justified on the grounds that editors have to fill the space available.[41] A policy of economic growth and development should never be based upon what the workers *are*, but what they *can be*. *All* workers in the Newly Industrializing Economies (NIEs) of Asia were originally low skill and low wage workers. The policy of basing development upon the existing skills of the people is doomed. In the past 37 years we have been building an infrastructure of poverty which is needed to support the current political culture.

Treating the symptoms

Symptoms and manifestations have the quality of being impressive, frightening, urgent and immediate, calling upon someone in authority *to do something now*. Most people go into a panic and the thing done rarely solves the problem, but may lead to the creation of others. In reality the symptom may simply be the outward manifestation of a condition that may have been implanted years ago. If one uses Carl Stone's ideas, the crime wave of the 1990s had been brewing since the 1960s. Yet there are loud and insistent demands for Minister of National Security and Justice K.D. Knight's head. The best we can do is to start now to avoid the crime wave of the 2030s.

This report is simply one of the many efforts to *do something now* to deal with squatters. The writer has the grace to admit that the squatter colonies are 'chronic'. It describes a proposal to remove squatters, especially those sitting on joint venture holdings and other sensitive areas.[42] The proposer needs to pay close regard to my explanation that *solution* is the other side of *problem*. Chronic squatters result from chronically poor economic conditions brought on by the welfare policy.

The next report illustrates the fairly common fallacy of finding a strong correlation between two sets of data and concluding that one is the cause of the other. The truth is that both may result from a third, common cause.[43] Because tourist harassment is at an all time high, MP Danny Melville thinks that squatting is the root cause. He calls on three ministries to seriously tackle the problem. Hotelier Wyman remarks that "our people have become desperate and are looking for a way to access money. They come far and wide to the place where they believe money is in abundance and that is the resort areas". Unless there is some gainful alternative employment for those who harass, they simply will not stop doing what he described as a very lucrative business.

Except for the logical gaffe of failing to realize that both squatting and tourist harassment spring from the same cause of economic stringency, it is refreshing to see a realistic assessment of the problem, which is the solution to the economic conditions of the people. Official Jamaica, including the prime minister, simply will not accept this explanation. Their apologists prefer to attribute both problems to the 'wickedness and bad mindedness' of the Jamaican people. Wyman's observation provides some grounds for my tourism diversion theory.

Living conditions: status and change

At least one other regular writer, Martin Henry, appears to agree with me that the outcome, if not the aim, of government policy and practice has been the impoverishment of the people. The budget option most favoured by the government is a continuation of the wealth transfer from the poor to the rich in the blind quest for macro-economic stability. He quotes government MP Ronnie Thwaites as stating that: "Every government since Emancipation – colonial legislature, Crown Colony, internal self-government, independent government, JLP, PNP – has encouraged the poverty of the many by preserving the status quo of wealth and power, wittingly or unwittingly, or by choking wealth creation by bad ideology or by bad public policy."[44]

The following citations show how the poor and apparently hopeless living conditions may also contribute to the lessening of efforts to break the cycle of poverty. Good health, avoidance of chronic and preventable diseases, affordable accommodation and positive prospects for the future, especially among young men, provide the minimum conditions necessary for the efforts to be sustained. The reality of the poor is far different. Jamaica's sick head to Cuba for treatment unavailable here and too costly elsewhere.[45] The Jamaican system works too slowly and needs much improvement. The deteriorating economy and the living conditions it engenders would have been quite avoidable if the country had embarked on a wealth creating policy. The current political system, not just the ruling party, lacks the capacity to change. The survey of living conditions suggests that negative trends are affecting all social groups. There are emerging signs of chronic and preventable diseases.[46]

IV: The Creation of Wealth

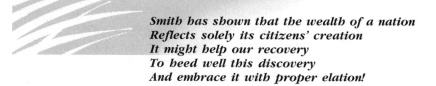

Smith has shown that the wealth of a nation
Reflects solely its citizens' creation
It might help our recovery
To heed well this discovery
And embrace it with proper elation!

The only real economic, political, social and long-term solution for the presence of poverty is the creation of wealth. It is not merely enough for the society to create the wealth and distribute it to the poor. The poor must take an active part in the creation of their share of the wealth; otherwise they still remain poor. The Marxist position is right in so far as it insists that the poor must have access to the means of production. In modern terms, however, the means of production is coming less to mean the massive machines and heavy equipment requiring large capital expenditures and more to mean the possession, by the worker, of the skills, enthusiasm and creativity of the modern productive cycle. The leading countries have gone through muscle power, to machine power, to brainpower.

The typical socialist position assumes that wealth exists independently of its creation and must simply be shared out equally. No correlation is believed to exist between the creators of wealth and those who enjoy it: the defining belief is that the workers create it and the capitalists enjoy it. In the older industrial countries that was only partly true and did not reckon with the activities of trade unions and labour legislation. Even revisionist China has apparently learned the lesson that wealth must first be created and that those who create it deserve to enjoy its first fruits.

In the discussion of the behavioural theory of poverty we introduced the idea that both wealth and poverty among individuals and nations was a function of the behaviour of either the individual or the nation. This is not to deny that a number of economic and other factors exist which are outside the control of the individual or the nation. Since these external factors affect all the nations of the world, the crucial variable must be how the nation responds to the threats and opportunities which occur in its environment, that is its behaviour. By the same token at the individual level, in a society like Jamaica, the very same economic factors operate for all the citizens. The crucial factor that determines individual wealth or poverty must be the response of the individual or those closely related persons whose behaviour may have dictated the subsequent fortune or misfortune of the individual. As Finance Minister Davies remarks, if all banks face the same environment, and one goes under while the others remain viable, then the fault must lie in that bank.[47] This is a lesson Mr Davies' own government adamantly refuses to learn for itself.

At this point it would be useful to separate the factors under the control of the nation or the individual from those which are not, in order to understand the impact of the response or behaviour of the nation or individual on the fortune of the appropriate entity. Those behavioural factors that are controllable by the individual include his level of education, his attendance at school and participation in learning activities, his attitude, ambition, and his fondness for or apathy towards learning or productive work. Some of these factors are controllable by his parents or guardians, for example, their aspiration levels, their ambitions for the child, their setting of standards, their inculcation of work attitudes and values and the examples they set for the child.

At the same time at the national level, there are also operating factors that are uncontrollable by any developing nation. By definition, a developing nation is one that cannot exert any meaningful control over world events and economic developments. Yet a comparison of the response – the behaviours – of two leaders of the developing world to the identical world economic trends and conditions is very instructive. While Michael Manley of Jamaica was busily chasing the chimera of a New International Economic Order, Lee Kuan Yew of Singapore was engaging his efforts in the development of his country by following the exact prescription as outlined above. Not only did he avoid poverty seeking or poverty causing behaviours, but also he also actively induced his people, by all kinds of methods, to indulge in wealth creating behaviours.

It is one of the minor tragedies of the developing world that many countries refuse to follow or learn anything from the Singapore experience simply because they do not understand it, what it was, why it happened and how it was done. Even the Singaporeans, those we interviewed, had some trouble explaining it because they were so busily engaged in it that they did not have the time to document it. Now Lee Kuan Yew is concerned about the next 100 years and his countrymen are busily documenting what they did right and how and why they did it, so as to keep their country in contention for that time. He pointedly reminded them on television (June 1999) that they have not yet produced a Nobel prize winner in physics, chemistry or medicine and he wanted to know whether their education system could do the job.

The creation and sustenance of real wealth by any developing nation calls for big thoughts and big plans, taking people out of their preoccupations with the daily trivialities of life and lifting them to the point where they think that they can tackle mountains (or mountain lions) single-handedly. The little incremental and marginal additions, such as screwing a few more tons of bananas out of some acreage will serve only to maintain the country in a state of poverty.

The Boston Consulting Group (BCG) has popularized a scheme to show what kind of investment any company should make.[48] It divides investment opportunities into four groups, cash cow, star, question mark and dog. A star has a growing share of a growing market; a question mark has not yet proved its potential, but there are high hopes attached to it; a cash cow has a fairly stable or growing share of a static market, while a dog has a decreasing share of a decreasing market. It will one day dawn upon the Caribbean (in about the 2050s perhaps) that the banana is a dog. Reports like that from Garwin Davis of the plight of the banana farmers in St Mary illustrate the dog at work. St Mary banana farmers now need a bailout and are struggling to recover from the massive drought in 1997. Government assistance has not been forthcoming.[49]

Economic growth and development

This is one of the most vexed questions that have faced the Caribbean over the last 50 years. Generations of economists and other social scientists have contributed numerous ideas on the ways the Caribbean can get on the path of economic growth and development. Those Caribbean countries that have jumped upon the twin bandwagons of financial services, offshore banking and other such activities, have reaped a considerably better harvest than others. Jamaica and Guyana, the two largest territories of the Anglophone Caribbean seem mired in underdevelopment and backwardness.

To give the social scientists credit, many of them have gone as far as the canons of their discipline will let them, but these norms prevent them from going far enough. One is left with unsatisfactory phrases like "we followed inappropriate macro-economic policies over 25 years" or "our failure to obey two economic laws". They never seem to ask *why*. Following an inappropriate policy for one year, or perhaps five years might be forgivable, but it strains credulity to find the same behaviour persisting for 25 years.[50]

Since none of our government regimes had, up to 1998, lasted more than ten years, it appears that both political parties and their governments followed similar inappropriate macro-economic policies or failed to obey the same two economic laws. This lends considerable support to the poverty seeking behaviour part of my theory of poverty. It also confirms my conclusion that Jamaica's economic problems, though they have economic results, do not stem from economic causes. The implication is they will never be solved by economic measures alone.

Norman Girvan's mostly economic analysis emphasises the impact of the global and regional economy on the poor. Much of this part of his exposition is an examination of the relationship between social and economic development, stagnation, inflation, the new working poor, as against the systemic poor (the result of landlessness in rural areas) and urban unemployment. Most importantly for my major theses, he examines the role of social exclusion of the majority of population. He accepts the notion that empowerment of the poor is a vital precondition and defines empowerment as an improvement in the ability of people to design and participate in the processes and events that shape their lives. Bureaucratic paternalism is a major obstacle to empowerment, for ignoring the views of clients and thinking that the providers know best.[51]

C.Y. Thomas' essay "The Inter-relationship between Economic and Social Development" examines the effects of recent structural adjustment programmes as experienced in the Caribbean.[52] The positive economic effects have not 'trickled down' to the point where a significant dent in poverty has been noticed. In this connection one may note that economic development, which includes growth, but not *vice versa,* has a set of pre-conditions without which it cannot begin at all, a set of co-conditions without which it cannot be sustained during its progress and a set of post conditions without which it can neither be sustained nor accelerated in the future. The problem with using solely economic approaches to economic development is that these tend to ignore totally these conditions, since in most cases they are not economic in nature at all. Some social conditions, not just political stability and other orthodox requirements *must* precede economic development, as the donor agencies are finding out.

To change the subject, if the Human Development Index (HDI) actually measures only the provision of services and not their impact upon the quality of life of the citizens of a society, the results would be very misleading. The contention that economic growth cannot be equated with economic development is supported by the following contribution. Henry and Mondesire note that the most recent growth policies have not delivered the promised outcomes of prosperity for the majority of the people. Having said that, they proceed to clutter up their thought pro-

cesses by providing a lengthy excursus of the history of global intervention and end up blaming Reaganomics and Thatcherism, and introduce a
very irrelevant but dogmatic thought, that the new globalization of production must be followed by full freedom of movement by peoples. They
exclude East Asia from the general debacle but do not say why this should
be so.[53]

One of their statements seems to suggest that one must wait for the
perfect model to arise, since they all have flaws when experienced by different countries. They concede that although income gaps might be
widening even in the developed countries, total income is growing at a
tremendous pace. Most astonishingly, they reveal that the miracle of East
Asia, which some people are now calling the Myth of East Asia, *was largely
a failed attempt to defend the neo-classical position.* One would have thought
that the focus would be on what the East Asian miracle was, how it worked
and to what extent it was replicable, instead of trying to see whether it
fitted into any particular model of development. It appears that an experience, which does not fit a model but works, is less preferable to one
which fits the model well, but does not work! This says volumes about
the type of evaluation that is acceptable to our Caribbean decision makers, who accept only the evidence which confirms their prejudices.

Growth without development

These articles and reports provide evidence in Jamaica of what the scholars report on a global scale. In some cases illuminating comparisons are
made with conditions in Jamaica. James Walsh reports that the equity gap
is increasing in the Caribbean, in contrast to Latin America and that the
economic growth of the 1990s has been reducing poverty in Latin America,
but not in the Caribbean. Different degrees of income inequality exist in
different countries. In the Caribbean below poverty line percentage ranges
from 12 to 42. Growth had little impact on job creation or job quality,
since the bulk of the increase in jobs was of low productivity type.[54]

Research is most likely to show a correlation between economic development (not growth) and reductions of the income inequality. Countries
with narrowing gaps are more likely to be those in which the majority of
the population is taking part in the growth through development of the
people and their capacity for better paying jobs. If the jobs are of the low
productivity, low paying type, then income inequality will increase and
more people will slip below the poverty line, in spite of the increasing
wealth to the country as a whole. The *trickle down* theory has been replaced in those countries with small equity gaps by a *flood up* theory.

The real state of development of a country like Jamaica is concealed and confused by rankings and ratings in some restricted field, which has very little to do with economic development. We suppose that after being subjected to a flood of negative statistics, it does the heart well to observe that the country has succeeded in some minor category. The table of football standings immediately after the World Cup (1998) provided such a euphoric feeling![55] Football standings are not the only popular substitutes for income earning capability. Others include national pride, relying on displays and gimmicks, for example, the massive reggae football, thereby getting overwhelming international exposure, sports achievements, national cultural curiosities like dance and music, Rastafari, the social and psychic income of being the largest Anglophone country in the Caribbean, thereby claiming leadership of CARICOM, and the 'photo-ops' along with the President of the United States (first Seaga and now Patterson).

Preconditions for development

Earlier in this section we mentioned that economic development had some preconditions before it can even begin. That is not strictly true because putting the preconditions into place is the start of the process of economic development. These conditions tend to be non-economic. This article lists some of these preconditions. Walsh quotes research findings on the profile of Jamaican workers and notes that the existing one is considerably at variance with that necessary for desired levels of economic performance. There is a shortage of communication and problem solving skills, a shortage of multi-skilled personnel and low levels of creativity. Low literacy levels and lack of interest in further education and training create poor ability to acquire and evaluate information.[56]

None of these preconditions could be fulfilled by a welfare orientation. Unfortunately ,the neglect of the school system began in the nineteenth century, shortly after emancipation, according to Miller.[57] Walsh has listed a catalogue of signs pointing to the absence of a coherent policy for wealth creation. The emphasis on the garment industry is misplaced since it depends on a permanent cheap labour policy, now unravelling at the seams. The absence of imagination and creativity is rife among ministers and parliamentarians. The absence of co-conditions is the reason for this result. One of the puzzling things to this writer is the explanation of the de-industrialization of Jamaica since the late 1960s. The co-condition theory, which speaks to the necessary maintenance environment, may provide such an answer. The Hanes pullout has left 570 workers out of jobs. The explanation cites reducing capacity and consolidating operations. It thinks that it will continue with subcontracting. The cost of production here is high compared to Mexico.[58]

The people would respond in a hostile manner to the feeble, if true, explanations by the minister. It should have occurred to him that his job was to get the market forces to work in Jamaica's favour, not against it. He holds out no prospect of action to be taken to preserve productive capacity and to find jobs to replace those lost. The minister simply does not appreciate the value of an investment. The British have a scheme of giving successful new companies, after five years, a cash bonus of £500,000 as a reward for success. The minister has rejected such a suggestion for Jamaica out of hand. The notion of rewarding success is still not understood by socialists.

Preconditions arising from macroeconomic, fiscal and monetary arrangements are more recognized in orthodox economic discussion. That these preconditions are not in place is the burden of this article from MP Delroy Chuck. He does not gain a sense of hope from the 1998 Budget and no relief from the black economic mood. In spite of this, Finance Minister Davies is happy that we are on right track.[59] The partisan bias is notably absent from MP Chuck's comments this time. Economic based conditions are a necessary, but not a sufficient condition for development. One needs to look at how the entire political culture and policy keep the country poor. The opposition policy does not examine the structural and organizational weaknesses of the country. Their policy rests on the belief that the nation will respond to displays of power and braggadocio. It is not unreasonable to expect this, since it has happened many times before.

Preconditions: aims and objectives

Whether or not one approaches the business of development in a systematic manner will determine the success or failure of the enterprise. The requirement that the government should think like a business is a plea to adopt the systematic approach used by successful businesses all over the world. The proposer, Audley Shaw, believes that will create an attractive environment for business. This approach will create jobs, wealth and sustainable development for the people.[60] In reply, one must point out that this is not likely in Jamaica since business and government have different aims and objectives. In Jamaica it is more likely to discover businesses thinking more like government. It appears that here at least the aims of government and business have converged, to enjoy and exercise power.

Results do not matter. Third (and fourth) terms and personal promotions do.

The theme that governments of Jamaica since 1962 have consistently chosen short-term political advantage over long-term benefits for the country has been exemplified many times. Here its effects upon the prospects for wealth creation and poverty eradication are discussed. Cargill reacts to a piece on limiting the importation of dairy products in order to protect the local dairy industry. He notes that everything we produce can be imported more cheaply from abroad [61] Regarding the source of the money to pay for the imports, it merely leads to an inflated balance of payments deficit. Continued importation would lead to further impoverishment.

Notes

[1.] M G Smith, 141, p 1.

[2.] Patrick E. Bryan, 17, pp 51–54, 67.

[3.] See Bryan, 17, p 34 for the reference to Howard Johnson's contribution.

[4.] See Boxill, end note #45 to chapter four for Derwin Munroe's discussions on minor uprisings and riots.

[5.] See John Kenneth Galbraith, 36, pp 61–75, on the accommodation to poverty. The quotation by Nettleford is taken from Wedderburn, 159, pp 16–17. For a further discussion on the workings of fatalism in Britain, see Seabrook, 134.

[6.] Obika Gray, 44, p 189.

[7.] Galbraith, 36, p 100.

[8.] Wolfgang Grassl, "Celebrating the Diversity of Opinions" (article), *Daily Gleaner* (Wednesday 10 June 1998), p D3.

[9.] Morris Cargill, "Fool's Budget" (article), *Daily Gleaner* (Thursday 23 April 1998), p A4.

[10.] "Invest In 'Social Capital" (report), *Daily Gleaner* (Saturday 20 June 1998), p A3.

[11.] M.G. Smith, 141, pp 67, 70.

[12.] Veront Satchell, 134, p 152.

[13.] Gary Spaulding, "From Squatting to Kotching" (report), *Daily Gleaner* (Saturday 13 June 1998), p B7.

[14.] "Squatting: A Reflection on the Economy" (editorial), *Daily Observer* (Wednesday 15 April 1998), p 6.

[15.] "GOV'T Joint Venture Houses for Squatters" (report), *Daily Gleaner* (Friday 6 March 1988), p B5.

16. "Edwards Calls for Lower Deposits on Houses" (report), *Daily Observer* (Friday 19 June 1998), p 5.
17. Reginald Allen, "Housing Blunder" (report), *Sunday Gleaner* (2 August 1998), p 1A.
18. Hyacinth Evans, 32, p 182.
19. "Vendors Face Removal Threat" (report), *Daily Gleaner* (Wednesday 24 June 1998), p C11.
20. G.A. Maloney, "Tourist Harassment" (letter), *Daily Gleaner* (Monday 11 May 1998), p A5.
21. A. H. Maslow, 87, pp 370–396.
22. M. G. Smith, 141, p 1.
23. Glen Day, "Is Education Priced Beyond Reach?" (article), *Sunday Gleaner* (18 October 1998), p 8A.
24. Obika Gray, 44, p 186. See also Horace Levy, 73.
25. Michael Mitchelmore and Naomi Clarke, 96, p 123.
26. Garwin Davis, " 'Hungry' Children Can Learn" (report), *Daily Gleaner* (Thursday 23 July 1998), p A3.
27. Audley Foster, "Aren't We Bilingual?" (article), *Daily Observer* (Friday 29 May 1998), p 7.
28. Allan Foreman, "We'd Be Worse off with Patois" (letter), *Daily Observer* (Friday 29 May 1998), p 8.
29. Lee Kuan Yew, 70, pp 145–167, describes how he successfully handled the question of diverse languages and cultures.
30. See Lalta and Freckleton, 68, p 297.
31. See end note #10 to Introduction for Horatio Alger.
32. Galbraith, 36, p 57. Galbraith's arguments are referred to over the next few pages.
33. C.Y. Thomas, 155, p 37. Also in Girvan 39, p 37.
34. This is the theme of Orlando Patterson's fictional work, 116.
35. Marjorie Newman-Williams and Fabio Sabatini, in Girvan, 39, p 57.
36. For a full discussion of crime as it affects Jamaica and the Caribbean, see Stone, 149; Chuck, 21; Headley, 50; and Harriott, 46.
37. Errol Gregory, "Breaking the Cycle of Poverty" (article), *Financial Gleaner* (Friday 10 July 1998), p 14.
38. Lynn and Jay, 81, p 174.
39. "Inspector of Poor Wants Fewer People on the Dole" (report), *Daily Gleaner* (Monday 20 July 1998), p A12.
40. Lewin, 74, p 228.
41. "We Must Get Value for Our Money" (editorial), *Daily Observer* (Tuesday 23 June 1998), p 6.
42. "100,000 Problem Squatters Targeted" (report), *Daily Observer* (Tuesday 14 April 1998), p 1.
43. Garwin Davis, "Squatting the Root Cause of Tourist Harassment" (report), *Daily Gleaner* (Thursday 2 April 1998), p A20. The quotations from Wyman and Melville appear in this report.

44. Martin Henry, "The Impoverishment of the People" (article), *Daily Gleaner* (Thursday 2 April 1998), p A5.
45. "Jamaica's Sick Head to Cuba" (report), *Sunday Gleaner* (7 June 1998), p 1A.
46. Carl Wint, "Policy Makers Should Rethink Strategies" (article), *Daily Gleaner* (Monday 27 April 1998), p A1.
47. The newspaper report of Davies' comment on a failed bank is quoted in "Financial Decline" (editorial), *Daily Gleaner* (Monday 9 March 1998), p A4.
48. Plunkett and Attner, 120, p 166–167.
49. Garwin Davis, "Banana Farmers Bewail Lost Ground" (report), *Daily Gleaner* (Friday 17 April 1998), p B5.
50. Henry Rowen, 133, p 1, in his overview of the performance of the Far Eastern countries.
51. Norman Girvan, 39, p 2 ff.
52. CY Thomas, in Girvan, 39, p 21.
53. Ralph Henry and Alicia Mondesire, in Girvan, 39, pp 101, 104.
54. James Walsh, "Poverty and Equity" (article), *Daily Gleaner* (Friday 6 March 1998), p A4.
55. "Table of Standings" *Daily Observer* (Thursday 16 April 1998), p 28.
56. James Walsh, "Weak Worker Profiles" (article), *Daily Gleaner* (Friday 22 May 1998), p A4.
57. Errol Miller, 90, p 53 ff.
58. "Hanes Pulls Out" (report), *Daily Observer* (Tuesday 7 April 1998), p 1.
59. Delroy Chuck, "Heading for Bankruptcy" (article), *Daily Gleaner* (Wednesday 22 April 1998), p A4.
60. "Government Must Think Like Business – Shaw" (report), *Daily Gleaner* (Thursday 4 June 1998), p C4.
61. Morris Cargill, "The Rocky Road to Ruin" (article), *Sunday Gleaner* (5 July 1998), p 9A.

7

Administrative Impact Today

his chapter provides a rather more detailed examination of the performance of the tools (chapter three) which have been designed to secure the benefits of national and economic growth and development for the people of Jamaica. It will examine the impact of the political culture upon the major tools – the private sector and the public service, including the political directorate – to see why all of them failed to deliver. It will also examine some of the sustaining institutions of the society including the Constitution and the House of Representatives. A prime area of evaluation is the question of their fitness for their tasks. We need a thorough examination of the informal and real, not just the formal and official, nature of the entity. Organizational theorists use the analogy of the iceberg to illustrate the real nature of an organization. Only one-tenth of icebergs and organizations appear above the surface. As the captain and owners of the *Titanic* discovered, it is what you do not see that will sink you.

This chapter will also examine the effects of organizational dysfunction. It will compare the impact of procedures on purpose and examine why goals are not met. In regard to the public sector it will demonstrate that the absence of a profit motive does not mean that the civil service has no goals or objectives: they are merely more difficult to identify and measure. The chapter will examine how the locus of power in organizations changes over time and the impact these changes have upon the nature and culture of the organization.

The theory of the necessity of pre, co, and post conditions will be used to illustrate why the efforts of the Jamaican governments, the political directorate and the public sector, along with the private sector have failed in the development process, official denials and euphoria notwithstanding. It will demonstrate the necessity of having a supportive environment. It will lay great emphasis on the substance of organizations in contrast to their form, and stress the human side of enterprise.

I. National Development

If a system's designed for production
All observers can make such deduction
Any hint of welfare
Makes a new atmosphere
And may lead to a difference in function

Development policy

John Rapley makes several contributions to explaining the theory and practice of development. Any acknowledgment of the role played by the human side is conspicuous by its absence. Nevertheless we can still benefit from his analysis. He notes in his introduction that the idea of using the State as an agent of social transformation has been favoured by communists, socialists and modern liberals alike.[1]

This was based on the belief that the State could embody the collective will more effectively than the market, which favoured privileged interests. In the postwar period, the new right has been looking at the State as a potential tyrant and has venerated the freedom and productive potential of the market. One may comment that the evidence of the past 50 years in Jamaica is not overwhelming for any side of this argument. Both private capitalists and state functionaries will favour privileged interests. Both of them suffer from the imperfections of organizations. A better way is to let no group, private or public, gain a stranglehold of power over the resources. In Jamaica, the imperfections of the market have been perfectly matched by the imperfections of the State where institutions designed for service have become equally oppressive, whether private or state run. These are mainly the results of the dynamics of organizations. People who know how organizations work and are willing and able to take the necessary corrective measures in time, can avoid them.

Rapley's profile of the developmental state is an abstraction from the experience of many states and may not fit any state exactly. The features of the developmental state are too numerous to quote here in full, but these two are typical: 1) the State makes development its top priority, encour-ages people to forego the benefits of growth so as to maximize investment, and uses repression, if need be, to achieve this goal; 2) the State invests heavily in human capital formation, particularly in targeting the develop-ment of the technical and engineering corps necessary for modern industry. The political scientist in him respects power, but little else. He seems unable to understand the limitations of power in an organization. Many of these features of the modern developmental state have been experi-enced in Jamaica. One very important omission is the way in which a majority of the country cooperated with the imperatives of the develop-ment programme. These must be a purely economic caricature of what actually took place in the country.

To give Rapley credit, many persons believed that Lee Kuan Yew achieved his impressive results in Singapore by massive doses of force, repression and by taking away the civil liberties of his people. That is obviously why they have reelected his party eight times since the 1960s in elections that the UN organizations have declared to be the cleanest in the world and why some 90 per cent of all ethnic groups claimed never to have even thought about migration.

Behind every successful development programme lie some common elements, such as the recognition, by a significant ratio of the population, of the country's national aims and objectives, commitment to a programme, preparation of individuals and gaining the co-operation of a majority. It is not possible to force an individual to complete a PhD in chemical engineering. On the other hand, we experienced a lot of these strictures during the Manley regime.

Obviously, these new statists believe that power and coercion solve every problem. Power and coercion seem to offer a short-cut favoured by those who do not really believe in the freedom of the individual. Vasciannie demonstrates that the use of force to solve the problems of crime could lead to the loss of civil liberties for the entire population.[2] The statists also believe that cooperation and commitment contribute little, or nothing, to performance.

The section on the political directorate and the Constitution will show that, contrary to the intent and practice of the Westminster model in Britain, the Jamaican version has evolved to confer almost dictatorial powers on the prime minister. One important consequence of this mo-nopoly of power enjoyed by the Prime Minister is that there has been, and can be, no national consensus or cooperation and commitment with re-spect to the development path that the country should pursue. Since the

Prime Minister has all the power, he is not obliged to listen to any ideas from other people, no matter how good they are. Except when he invites public participation, his ideas and those designed to please him are the only ones which are given any kind of consideration. After a while the other citizens become frustrated and stop offering any solutions. An atmosphere of cynicism pervades where there should be an air of commitment and shared responsibility. After a while the population falls into the same mode. They greet with skepticism any initiative the government puts forward.

Human relations: communication and motivation

Development policy must be clear and understandable to all those who are expected to participate in its implementation. It should be communicated in such a way that it not only informs the potential participants but elicits their cooperation and commitment. This is one of the prime preconditions for economic development. Without cooperation and commitment the attitude dissolves into one of disbelief and lack of trust.

The government may be tempted to use coercive methods, but one cannot coerce creativity. Communication, motivation and the presence of trust are vital elements in the effective functioning of organizations. The concentration or distribution of power in the system, if it distorts the relationships of the participants, has a deleterious effect upon its functioning. Shaun Johnson thinks that the PM, now having "total control of our political system" should summon Seaga and Golding to chart a course of moving country forward. He should also seek help from other organizations – church, PSOJ, JMA, SBAJ and other similar entities.[3] This would be an excellent idea, if the well-being of the country was the main aim of the parties. For all his power, the Prime Minister cannot summon leaders of other parties. Furthermore, an individual who believes he has total power will not seek the help of anyone. The inability to come to agreement over 50 years is caused by much deeper forces.

The theme of the distortion in relationships among members of the society rises again in Howard Hamilton's address to the PSOJ. He opines that an evaluation of past performance is a necessary step in charting the course forward. It is time for all local private sector organizations to talk with one voice. Agriculture, manufacturing and tourism have worked for other countries and there is no reason they should not work for Jamaica. He thinks that a social partnership is the answer.[4]

An evaluation of the past would be much more useful if it focussed not only on economic data but examined thoroughly the nature of different organizations and institutions, and their motives, not only those on the surface, but the hidden ones as well. The main reason why agriculture and other areas have not worked for Jamaica is that this society, from the political directorate downward, was never organized or designed for productivity, only for welfare.

We have steadfastly invited our most educated and experienced people to go abroad. They leave because we have created no place for them. Economic research recognizes this factor as the brain drain, but shrugs it off as one of those inevitable things. The brain drain has causes and can be remedied or prevented.

Systems and structural suitability

Hamilton's address (cited above) notes the desideratum that all private sector organizations should speak with one voice. This suggests quite clearly that he sees the PSOJ as a political pressure group and little else. It is true that the organization was founded in the socialist 1970s to enhance the survival capabilities of the private sector. Over 20 years, in a different economic environment, the notion of a changed mission would have long been put into operational terms. A real entrepreneurial private sector would have broken free, as some few Jamaican enterprises have done, and taken their fate into their own hands. Instead they wait around with palms outstretched for gifts from the government. Indeed, one of the author's close friends defines the national tree of Jamaica as the 'outstretched palm'!

They know that the path embarked upon by the government will lead to disaster, but they are content merely to warn an unseeing government. In the years ahead, they complain, they see further decline instead of growth, if the government continues on a similar path.[5] The truth is that this path of decline is not peculiar to the PNP and P.J. Patterson. Its seeds were sown in the late 1960s with the disintegration of the Shearer government. It was watered into full flower by Manley, repotted by Seaga and further fertilized by Patterson. The causes of the decline cannot simply be a matter of personality nor of party ideology, since it was common to all four regimes. One needs to discover what feature of the government and the productive sector has strongly persisted over 30 continuous years. Something built into the system, so to speak.

The electorate has learnt that there is little point in getting rid of the PNP government since the JLP under Seaga will continue along the same path, with a difference only in style, rather than substance. Here is a clue for students of organizational behaviour. Why does everything go to the Prime Minister for decisions and action? Why not to the ministers?

The practice in many corporations in most of the developed world is to fund their original and basic financial needs with the use of equity rather than debt. The use of debt financing also feeds the tendency of foreign investors to use local resources and pull out when it is convenient to do so, leaving a mountain of debt behind, as in the recent financial meltdown.[6] One major reason for this preference is that the tax system favours debt.

The other side to the debt financing choice, having a more direct effect upon the financial sector, is illustrated here. It is clear from the following report that the debt was not used to finance the creation of real wealth but for speculative ventures. Some 24 per cent of loans system-wide are bad. Commercial banks' bad loan portfolio represents $14.4bn and 24 per cent of their total portfolio. Of loan amounts to agriculture, mining, manufacturing, construction, tourism and transport, all but two showed declines last year.[7]

This subsection ends with a preliminary examination of the nature and the role of the private sector and whether it can serve as the engine of growth. The short answer to Gordon's question as to whether privatization has worked is, no, except in a few special cases.[8] The reason is that the private sector is suffering from the same organizational deficiencies and dysfunctions as the public sector and for the same reasons. As we shall see, the local private sector, being mostly non-entrepreneurial, is not in the mood for complicated enterprises, preferring straight buying and selling, what they know best.

The government is still trying to privatize services, including motor registration, but the alternative of government paper as an investment (no work, but guaranteed returns) has had negative effects. The experience of some privatized companies confirms the failure of the programme. Carib Steel has lost all its shareholders' equity, the last sale being at 26 cents. Carib Cement shares went below par value, but have now recovered to $2.05. NCB is showing poor results, but surviving. Radio Jamaica and JBC have associated, but their combined results are not satisfactory. The divestment of Cable and Wireless has been successful, but is has a large foreign component. One may well ask whether private sector 'managers', for all their bluster, are basically incompetent? But then the political culture has always penalized merit and rewarded incompetence.

The enrichment of the *People*

Many economists and political scientists are slowly coming to the realization that their models which concentrate on abstracts like state power and the rate of capital formation have left one major ingredient sorely missing. Some economists represent the point of view that the trick is to ensure that the poor acquire some of the wealth created by the economic growth. There is no trick. If one incorporates the poor in the development process, they will not only create the wealth but also automatically share in it, thus ending their poverty.

Of course, the poor will have to be greatly transformed before they can help in creating the wealth. We have seen where Jamaica's low skill and low wage policy condemns the people to eternal poverty. Enrichment demands the participation of the ordinary people and participation calls for their education and preparation. The references in this section will look at some of the preconditions for the participation of the people. These preparations include fiscal and monetary probity and stability, accurate data to inform us where we are and to assist us in charting our progress, a broad vision to lead and inspire, and assessment of where we could fit into the larger world. None of the following four reporters are aware of the role that educated and committed people must play in the development process.

Moses Jackson introduces the theme of the financial world in his article. He comments that the first task is putting together a budget that balances fiscal and monetary prudence, with a catalyst for the reconstruction of Jamaica's battered economy. Internal debt is out of control and this limits the options available to Finance Minister Davies. There is nothing growth oriented in the present policies.[9]

Max Lambie notes that new research indicates that the economic performance of exporting countries should be evaluated by examining trends and risks in the merchandise trades and service sectors that are aggregated from the sectoral level using a bottom up technique. He contrasts this with the traditional macro-economic indicators. Aggregates can be misleading as a table contrasts the new (increased) employment with the old, showing a much lower value.[10]

Seaga hopes that the manner of handling an incident in Tivoli Gardens will not prejudice peace among the rival factions, and recognizes the underlying crisis of massive discontent with the economic conditions now prevailing.[11]

Using figures put out by the UNDP, Walsh shows substantial growth in consumption worldwide. This increase is a reflection of increases in global production. This consumption is not evenly spread, since there are inequalities among and within nations. The bulk of the consumption is taking place in the developed countries, up to 50 times more than that of developing countries. The latter are more likely to bear the cost of environmental degradation.[12]

Political rather than economic rationality is the hallmark of Davies' solution, as Jackson explains. The absence of growth orientation has long been a staple of patronage politics. The analysts should not assume that their frame of reference is the same as the minister's. New and more comprehensive indicators may give a more meaningful picture than the traditional ones. Care still needs to be taken in this political culture. The whole truth becomes a casualty when the figures can be manipulated by politicians to give any picture that suits their purpose. When this factor is added to a non-reading population, anything goes!

Seaga continues to disappoint with a lack of any vision that takes him from his own backyard, Tivoli Gardens. With unjustified over concern with his own seat, he fears the effects of government policy towards garrison constituencies, conveniently forgetting that he created one of the first. He does not seem to be aware that the welfare patronage orientation of the first Bustamante regime set the stage for all subsequent government behaviour.

Walsh's comment is the rehash of the old hat socialist argument. It has probably never occurred to them to look at the level of production in these developed countries, or to note that the people who consume the most in the developing countries are those who produce the most. He is still wedded to the notion that the sheer labour of the people is the main contributor to the creation of wealth in spite of abundant evidence to the contrary. He should note that the main contributors to productivity are the highly educated and technically competent. There are more illiterates in the developing world, which has been proven to have an impact upon their productivity. The whole point of being developed is to permit a country to produce and consume more.

The meaning of development must involve an increase in the capacity of the nation to fend for itself and continue its development. Governing parties in Jamaica have never considered wealth creation a priority, only welfare and distribution. Developing countries, if they play their cards right, can join the ranks of the developed countries. This is what the East Asian tigers have achieved. Lee Kuan Yew's latest book is pointedly and challengingly titled, *From Third World to First*.[13]

Participation by the *People*

All development programmes, anywhere in the world, socialist or capitalist, East or West, call for participation of the people who are both the objects and the subjects of the development process. The ruling regime determines the terms and conditions of the participation and thus they vary widely. Although it might be easier to count factories and the various infrastructures, they are not the driving elements for the change. Those professionals who concentrate on figures and dollars are measuring only the *results*, not the *causes* of growth and development. The motivation and knowledge, which must accompany every development process, must exist in the people who are resident in the country.[14]

In spite of the great to-do about the structural adjustment of the Jamaican economy during the 1970s and 1980s, what took place was only a restructuring of the finances of the government.[15] Structural adjustment was conceived and executed mostly in terms of monetary and fiscal policies, to make the books look good for the IMF. The outlook for mining, private capital reflow, revamping social and economic infrastructure was all grim and suggested the need for new financing. The policy proved, by 1983, to be unsuccessful.[16] In the meantime, the basic pillars of the economy have been left untouched. Before it was bauxite, tourism and bananas, afterwards it is still tourism, bauxite and bananas. The nascent industrialization of the country and the diversification of the economy, which generated such high hopes in the 1960s, had ground to a quiet halt.

In the meantime one must ask just what is happening to really mobilize the people of the country for more productivity and production, other than the token and emotionally laden efforts of the ministry of mobilization of the Manley years. Calls for more productivity and production are made with the regularity of a metronome. The loosening of trade restrictions has proven counterproductive in a country with a massive propensity to import. After the famines of the 1970s, each government has ensured that there are lots of goods on supermarket shelves, even if this policy leads to growing balance of payments problems. The emphasis remains on the welfare orientation, which is the basis of our political culture. The structural adjustment programme put an over-emphasis on financial factors only and no attempt was made to create a producing people, *à la* Singapore. The notions of the extensive use of technology thereby increasing the scope and size of the productive sector were strangled at birth by the welfare orientation.

The unwillingness and the inability of the political leadership to deliver the goods are having an impact on the interest and participation of the voters. The opinion polls just before the 1997 elections showed that up to 42 per cent of the potential voters had decided to opt out of the political game, because they perceived that it was not worth the effort.

To this we can add those who reported 'did not know' or 'not interested', because they did not even believe it was worth the effort to arrive at an opinion. As usual, there is no attempt to remedy the cause, but to treat the symptom. When the government therefore sets up elaborate structures and systems such as the computer based electoral system, it is going to generate a large yawn on the part of the populace, since the outcome of the election changes nothing, except perhaps the name and party affiliation of the Prime Minister. Some members of the electorate might even regard their participation in the electoral exercise as legitimizing their own exclusion from the activities of the body politic. No number of pronouncements from officials will change that attitude, because the people know from some 50 years of experience that it does not work as officialdom would like it to do.

II: Entrepreneurship and Private Sector Theory

> *To return to our private sub-sector*
> *One has no intent for to hector*
> *They have not proved their worth*
> *As an 'engine of growth'*
> *And perhaps they could use a director!*

The debate has raged inconclusively between economists of the left and right as to which is the best engine for development – the State or the private sector. The leftists have favoured the State, while the rightists have defended the private sector and the market with equal vigour. In the Caribbean the argument has been equally inconclusive because of the mixed results. What neither of the sides has done is to examine the actual practices of the successful countries and their private and public sectors. They would discover that both groups use essentially the same principles of management. To my mind, there is no such thing as public sector or private sector management: there is good management and bad management, and that can occur on both sides.

John Rapley contrasts the performance of those economies that favour less State and more market involvement. The essential thrust of structural adjustment was to move from the State to the market. The really troubling questions, not those posed by the left or the right, but raised by the experiences of people in much, perhaps most of the Third World, who have benefitted little from the development debate, and who are unlikely to do so soon. The newest model, the developmental state, has won the admiration of the left.[17] That may have been the intention of the structural adjustment programme of the 1980s in Jamaica, but it merely shifted resources from an inefficient and ineffective state sector to an equally inefficient and ineffective private sector. The early 1990s saw a shift in the opposite direction and the late 1990s are seeing a shift of the previous shift.

Robinson in his study of the structural adjustment of the 1980s noted that the import substituting oriented industries set up in the 1950s and 1960s were ill prepared to face world market: "The decline of the economy during 1972–1980 could hardly be ascribed to the external environment in any direct sense... Efforts over the period to arrest the economic decline and to offset the effects of reduced export earnings were unsuccessful."[18] In this writer's view, one explanation of these unwanted results was the methods used in the structural adjustment process. The tremendous short-term borrowing, finally from the IMF, and the massive devaluations of the dollar damaged the economy, while the economic managers neglected the fundamental export earners.

Development programmes in the Caribbean – Barbados, Trinidad, and Jamaica, among the larger islands – have a varied record. Trinidad and Barbados have forged ahead while Jamaica has fallen behind. Perhaps one of the major problems in Jamaica starting from the 1970s is this ideological battle which has raged over the role of the private and public sectors. This would be bad enough, except that *private sector* has three connotations. Many people talk about the private sector as the engine of growth and also as the party responsible for the country's backwardness. They may be talking about three different aspects of the same thing.

First, we might identify the real private sector which is the people as they are, the body of citizens, *sui generis*, of their own type, owing no allegiance to anybody, responsible and accountable to nobody but themselves, making an economic way for themselves, doing their own economic thing and making a living the best way they know, whether by hustling or not. This private sector is the ordinary citizens – some wealthy, some poor, one-man operations or corporations, from street corner vending to international operations, some persons cultivating marginal acres, others with large spreads, using large acreages and employing lots of people. This private sector can do anything it wishes, within the law, of course. It can combine if it wishes, in companies, co-operatives, corporations, or operate on its own. It is no monolith, but speaks with thousands of different voices and does not have a single political outlook. It votes for any party it likes, or does not vote as it cares. That is the real private sector. It has all the weaknesses and the strengths of any body of citizens. It can be mean, grudging, shortsighted and narrow-minded, as well as visionary and transformational, but that is its privilege.

Secondly, there is the Marxist notion of the *private sector*, the Marxist bugbear, a monolith, sinister, always operating against the best interest of the people. This leaves us with a dilemma, since the real people are the ordinary citizens and it is not possible for a body to operate against its own best interests. But it makes it very easy to arrive at an erroneous conclusion if you think of the *private sector* as something sinister, something terrible, and something very frightening.[19]

It does not matter that this is just a construct, since a large part of the world has a government and an economic system based upon the belief that the *private sector* is something awful and that it should be squashed, sat on and suppressed by whatever means possible. Whereas the Russians did not learn the difference between the Marxist bugbear and the real *private sector*, the Chinese have, and they are making waves in China, with their private sector. Of course, the man who recognized this (Deng Xiao Ping) suffered quite a bit, until he got his way and transformed China. We can continue looking in this way at the *private sector*, the Marxist bugbear, which we can do well without.

Against these we have the third *private sector*, the white knight, or perhaps in this colour conscious society, better referred to as the black knight, that is the private sector in its beneficent aspects embodying everything you wished the real private sector was but is not. That is the good side of the private sector, that is considered capable of mobilizing great amounts of capital and of organizing and creating incredible wealth, which of course ends up in the hands of the ordinary citizens, and not in the hands of the hands of one or two capitalists, as emphasized by the Marxist version. That *private sector* mostly resides in the economic textbooks, represented by 'the profit maximizing entrepreneur' or 'the engine of growth'.[20]

Except for these instances, the white knight is only a concept, a mental construct, coming into being only as a counterweight to the Marxist *private sector* which does not exist either. There is, even in Jamaica, a small number of intrepid entrepreneurs who do fit this description of the *private sector*. They generate their own resources and finance their own operations, neither asking favours nor giving them, except where these actions constitute good business practice.

In making policy, governments must understand that one cannot build a policy on something that does not exist. Policy has to be built upon something that is there, the real private sector. Of course, if you are like Lee Kuan Yew, you can transform the private sector into the *private sector* (white knight version), but this is not an easy task. In a society with a liberal democratic value system, the government cannot compel it, because it is the citizens. The government can only induce it or give it incentives.

Motivation theory will point out that not everything that most managers think is an incentive is an incentive to somebody in the private sector. These investments are not just of money, which is very important, but also of one's person, of one's reputation, one's whole concept of the self, of one's life, for a whole lifetime goes into an investment and that is what you expect to get from the private sector, as investor.

The story is told that when newly elected Prime Minister Seaga met with the members of the private sector to discuss the protection of manufactures from imports, he asked all those who were wearing foreign made shoes to leave the room and all of them had to go. That behaviour is typical of the real private sector, but it is not typical of the *private sector*, white knight version, because that white knight is not supposed to be inconsistent and irrational. Mr Seaga was making a mistake in confusing the real private sector with the white knight construct.[21] Even today the Jamaican private sector is generally not the white knight riding to the rescue of the beleaguered maiden, since for the most part it does *not* consist of entrepreneurs.

The biggest task facing any government on the road to development is to transform the real private sector into the *private sector*, the one which is the engine of growth, in other words make the citizens responsible or induce them to be responsible for their own growth. In fact they are the only people in any country who can lead the charge in the growth. We have tried industrialization by invitation. It did not catch on in Jamaica. It is a good start, but it has to catch because someone has to take it over and there is only one entity which can, and that is the private sector or the body of citizens. We tried government led growth in the 1970s and 1980s, and we have seen the limitations. Now it has to move back to where it has to be – the ordinary citizens. If we want our ordinary citizens, our ordinary people, to become a part of their own development, we have to make it worth their while, we have to sell it to them. And we probably cannot sell it to them. We have to bring them into the process from the very start.

This section will demonstrate the nature of the real, not the wished for, private sector and see how it falls short of the entrepreneurial version, which is the engine of growth. A fourth private sector may be discovered, somewhat peculiar to Jamaica – the private sector as dependent.

The role of the private sector: fact and fantasy

Support for this theory of the private sector comes from the reactions of observers who expect consistency of behaviour (one concept theory) and find confusion instead (three concept theory). Thus, Miller is befuddled by the bailouts. He deems this condition to be the result of the failure of the liberalization and privatization process in making the private sector the engine of growth.[22]

The justification for such a move was the greater efficiency of the private sector over the State. Instead, the private sector has become the biggest recipient of welfare under the name of bailout. The future of the children of Jamaica has been laid on the altar of sacrifice to atone for the plunder of the pirates. My evidence suggests that the failure of the liberalization and privatization process was caused by the governments' attempts to use the private sector as the engine of growth. They misunderstood the nature of the sector and believed that they were dealing with entrepreneurs.

Even the Chamber of Commerce and the PSOJ know that the local private sector is not an entrepreneurial one.[23] The president of JAMPRO believes that the local private sector campaigned long against foreign investment. They led the attack on the high interest rate policy. They accept that Jamaica is a high cost country, which is why manufacturers are leaving. In my opinion, they arrive at these conclusions by taking the current culture as a given, which cannot be changed. Because they are still a mercantilist private sector they do not recognize that the infrastructure is faulty.

This article by Enid Brown throws further light on the true nature of the local private sector.[24] The PSOJ having predicted doom and gloom should not be in their offices, but in the field, presumably spreading the gospel of entrepreneurship. She believes that its staff does little else than monitor figures and trends. The impression she gets is that no one at executive level even considers having meetings with sector groups. She thinks that there are no meetings to assess real and developing problems, real solutions, targets and the like. Questions arise such as are they going to do anything to reverse the trend and are they interested in doing so? This writer's own thesis rests on the belief that the answer to the last question is 'no'. He has found no convincing evidence that several of our major institutions, including the government, are sincere in their aims about the development of the country. This article suggests that the writer has doubts about the sincerity of aims of the PSOJ. It began life as a survival and pressure group to resist the ravages of 1970s. It is still protective, according to this informant and not proactive as entrepreneurs.

One Jamaican based investor has attempted to buck the trend and invest locally, calling upon his fellow Jamaicans to do likewise.[25] He explains that low inflation and stable exchange rates have influenced his decision to invest in manufacturing roof tiles. This IBM CPA has become a risk taker. He thinks that the cost of his operation is still high. He thinks that Jamaica is missing out by having others process gypsum. Only the raw material is being exported to Columbia and Venezuela. One could extend this argument to include aluminum. It has been established that it is not economically feasible to smelt, but as far as I know, Jamaicans have not gone into fabrication of artifacts for exports.

The nature of the private sector

Since the Jamaican private sector is not, except for a few companies, entrepreneurial, it is a common event to read in the media stories in which Jamaican businessmen ignore opportunities for profitable processing and export enterprises. Typical of these reports is the following.[26] In the Eastern Caribbean, there is a recorded demand for spices, jerk seasoning, hotel amenities, bath oils and the like. The figures on import and export from CARICOM support the inference that these opportunities go begging. There is also a lack of promotion and information about the availability of goods. This is a nauseatingly familiar story – the private sector waiting on someone else to take lead. In the meantime they are organizing to pressure government rather than to explore markets abroad. Going on junkets is a substitute for the patient and unspectacular development of markets.

The ambiguity of the role played by the private sector and its relative non-performance raises questions as to its credibility. The absence of credibility is founded on several basic underlying and false assumptions about the nature of the private sector, such as we have been exploring in this section. Brown admits that the sector is looking very bad and cannot give speeches calling for moral integrity in society, and such topics. A productive and vibrant sector is needed to turn the economy around. It needs a course of objective and constructive self-criticism and a critical assessment of its failures. Competent and well thought out proposals are needed. The sector and the society ought to reward companies who have been transparent, raised productivity and treated workers with a sense of decency.[27]

The part played by motivation and perception is highlighted in these reports. The Stock Exchange is trying to awaken the private sector to existing opportunities.[28] It distinguishes between people who see opportunities where others see or experience failure. Money is a consequence of success, but rarely a motivator. Alvin Wint, another contributor, reports on some 16 Jamaican entrepreneurial firms that are now international operators, including Grace, Kennedy, Eagle, Hofab, Alkali, Serv-Wel, Jamaica Producers.[29] Some have since fallen out while others are to be included. All these entrepreneurs require and take advantage of supportive outlets such as provided in the USA and the UK. These reports should clear up once and for all the distinctions called for in the private sector theory, separating the sheep from the goats. Wint's list is not typical of vast majority of Jamaican companies, just 20 or so of the lot. These should be enough to illustrate the nature of the white knight private sector and the ones run by the JCC and PSOJ types.

This real private sector does not wait on the government to create an environment for them to work in; they create it themselves. Real entrepreneurs are scathingly contemptuous of that type. Butch Stewart of Sandals is too busy expanding his enterprise to bother with politics and is independent and wealthy enough to make the grand gesture of propping up the national currency for a while and offering to intervene again.

The part played by the supporting culture on the success of an enterprise is stressed in another article. This writer refers to a previous account on a Marc Andresen at 24 years of age, who made a huge fortune within a year. This is not likely in Jamaica. Andresen was one of the class of knowledge entrepreneurs. The writer thinks that in Jamaica the best students seek a career in the universities and not the private sector. They gain lots of prestige, but little money.[30] Universities worldwide, including the UWI, need to fund more of their activities. This is an excellent idea, which works best in places where the culture encourages entrepreneurship. Our political culture is based on ascription not on merit. There is tremendous social pressure to choose security, rather than adventure and risk taking. We need a culture that stresses acquired status and prestige to counteract ascribed status and prestige.

Lobbyists and pressure groups

Confusion of the role of the private sector is compounded by the demand that it becomes a political pressure group not just to lobby for privileges for itself but also to support a particular party. It cannot carry out that task and retain its intrinsic nature and outlook, inadequate though they may be. The leader of the Opposition has lashed private sector organizations for not mounting a serious challenge to government's current policy, charging that they lack the guts of their counterparts in the 1970s. It is not forceful enough to take the government to the table and say 'this cannot continue'. Whereas government could resist the Opposition, the private sector has the wherewithal to take the government to task.[31] Obviously, the leader of the Opposition thinks that those organizations have forgotten what a JLP government was like. His memory is also selective about how he treated some members of the private sector on accession to office in 1980. We have already quoted the story of the imported shoes. Why should they do anything for him when he has done nothing for them? He is now ruing the absence of corrective mechanisms to make the government listen, a thing he would not do in the past. He seems unaware of changing needs and perceptions.

The call for unity in any segment of society is either the sign of strengthening the defences or wanting to go on the attack. The monolith idea has become dominant. The rift between the PSOJ and the JCC has been highly publicized. Cliff Cameron is concerned about the criticality of private sector unity. He defines the private sector as the hundreds of thousands outside the government sector. The private sector has been dubbed the engine of growth, but is a minority shareholder in national production with the government controlling nearly 60 per cent of GDP. The sector will have a diversity of opinion but the majority position is usually adopted. At this point he recounts the good deeds they have done.[32]

They admit to facing three challenges: achieving sustained economic growth; improving the competitiveness, productivity and efficiency of Jamaican businesses; understanding fully the requirements and changing trends in international trade and preparing to survive in the global market place. They have spoken out consistently, advocating appropriate policies for which they have research capability and access to economists and other experts. The record will show that they have consistently failed in meeting all of the three challenges. One notes a minor omission from their list of activities. They have done lots of speaking and advocating but how much impact have they had on the economy? Can they face the challenges, given the limitations of their mercantile background? They are apparently uniting as a pressure group to influence government policy rather than to build the infrastructure for successful economic growth. They make no mention of economic development and do not appear to be aware of the fundamental differences between growth and development. The Government of Jamaica, whether PNP or JLP, is not structured to be influenced, as Seaga seems to be discovering. The majority of the most vocal advocates from the private sector are still hoping for favours from government in the traditional welfare culture.

Grassl might have made a more signal contribution to the development of the Jamaican economy if he had understood the true nature of the PSOJ and the private sector. Like many superficial observers, he was carried away by the names, not by the nature of the institution. He could not understand that political considerations count far more than economic ones in decision making in Jamaica. From his point of view, the rift between the JCC and PSOJ, due to the former's endorsement of the Davies model and the latter's rejection of it, was sheer economic madness – and never mind the political considerations. He was well aware of the foundation of PSOJ as a resistance to the Manley government. The political necessity for a united private sector continues to exist. He gives a list of functions carried out by private sectors abroad that have been arrogated to the government in Jamaica. Does the Jamaican private sector want to reclaim conditions under which it can do profitable business or does it want to act on shortsighted pettiness? [33]

Both the monolith and the entrepreneurial concepts of the local private sector have been confused in Grassl's mind. He excoriates the private sector, mendicant version, for not acting like the white knight. It cannot, even if it wanted to. He also has some doubts on that score as well. The primacy of political factors in decision-making has been counterproductive over the last 30 years, but it is a foundation plank of the political culture. The functions carried out abroad have never been carried out by the private sector in Jamaica. It therefore cannot reclaim what it never owned in the first place.

The lobbying function of the private sector appears here as well. The JMA continues to lobby government to create an environment in which the manufacturing sector can compete in the global economy. Some small success has been achieved with the lowering of certain interest rates. The sector needs $30–50 billion for refinancing old projects and funding new ones.[34] One would view this small progress as an excellent start in clearing the air, but the steps are still very conservative and incremental. It is not efficient to use up lots of energy in gaining small concessions. The small scale of the outcome is not in keeping with the necessary thrust for economic development and growth.

III. The Constitution and House of Representatives

A citizen's right to a Parliament
A democracy grants without argument
In Jamaica that right
Disappears out of sight
And its lack's not deplored by the government

Orthodox economic analysis generally takes the formal constitutional model of a government as a given. Not until recently have they been exploring the part that the actual government plays in the development process. The process of enquiry started as a part of the Cold War rivalry and the competing claims of each side that its economic form and the political ideology that accompanied it were a *sine qua non* of development.

Today the realization is creeping in that the formal systems and structures have very little to do with the development process and that the crucial factors are how the systems actually work. Labels do not give an accurate picture and tend to be dangerously misleading. Thus Jamaicans will not even consider the economic model of Singapore on the ground that Lee Kuan Yew was and is a dictator. It also accounts for the equally thoughtless conclusion of many Jamaicans that our crisis requires for its solution a benevolent dictator. Unfortunately, though such a creature might exist, the country will not know it until afterward.

Orthodox opinion is that Jamaica has a Westminster model of government styled after the British parliamentary system and backed up by a Whitehall coterie of highly technically skilled and impartial civil servants. We have looked at the true nature of the Jamaican civil service and must now turn our spotlight on the Parliament and the government.[35] First off, the evidence available seems to suggest that the Jamaican Constitution is modelled on the Colonial government as it existed in 1960 rather than on the British government. The Governor was visible and all-powerful in the colony: the British government unseen. The Colonial Governor controlled his Executive Council: Jamaican Prime Ministers control their Cabinet. All the restraints, legal and traditional, which existed in the British Constitution, in theory and practice, written and unwritten, were swept away to create a colonial model in the postcolonial era.

This was very shortsighted on the part of our so-called national heroes, who are given the credit as the framers of our Constitution. What we have in Jamaica is not the Westminster model, but the Jamaican colonial model. Ironically, after Norman Manley had helped to construct the Constitution, he never enjoyed power as Prime Minister under it, and must have gone to his grave a very disappointed man.

On first approaching the problem, this writer thought that virtually all our political and thus economic difficulties were the creatures of the Constitution. The correct formulation is that the roots of most of the problems that we have in the society today were present even before our Constitution was drawn up and that our political and social systems were already showing the signs or symptoms of the existence and subsequent development of these factors.

These, along with the political practices developed prior to independence, were institutionalized, not so much by the Constitution, but in the
practices which evolved. The Constitution could not possibly have given
them birth, nor caused their existence. It is not fair to say that they grew
out of the Constitution: the most that can be said is that the Constitution
gave the political practices some form of respectability. There is evidence to
suggest that the political practices of today have totally ignored the spirit of
the Constitution, while sticking, more or less, to the letter.

One important point about the framers of the Constitution in 1962
is that the actual drafting would have been done by a set of civil servants,
law officers and others. The Jamaican framers obviously would not have
done the writing themselves. They would have read the drafts and agreed
or not agreed with certain legal positions. One does not know and will
probably never know, the extent to which the British presented the document to the framers as a take-it-or-leave-it proposition, or the extent to
which they had real choices in the matter.

The question arises, though, that in a Constitution with so many
flaws, how did the British get it past the attention of the Jamaican authorities? Another explanation is that the Jamaican authorities intentionally
put them in. Although there is no conclusive proof, there are indicators.
One participant is reported to have taken the position that the Prime
Minister would be a dictator for five years and another contributed the
thought that one minister must rule.[36]

The provisions placed in the Constitution to remove a Prime Minister from office in a case where he loses the confidence of a majority of the
of the House of Representatives are supposedly modelled on the British
Constitution. The relevant provision in the Jamaican Constitution is found
in section 71 subsection 2. This is similar to the British convention where
there is a vote of no confidence in the Prime Minister (or in the Jamaican
constitutional language, the appointment of the Prime Minister ought to
be revoked). The result is that the Prime Minister has to resign office and
a new leader is chosen by the majority party. A legal advisor has told me
that it is not clear whether the Prime Minister of Britain has the right
either to appeal or overturn the decision of the House. The same advisor
maintains that the better opinion is that he does not have that right.

In Jamaica, the Constitution gives him the right (section 71 subsection 3) and the power to overturn any House vote in favour of the revocation
of his office. That is one important point on which the Jamaican Constitution differs from the British. On other points also the parliamentary
and the political party practice follows different lines from those in Ja-

maica. In Britain the annual conference of the party confirms or reconfirms or elects the leader or new leader as the case may be and that person will be the next Prime Minister if the party wins the next election. In Britain it is the MPs or parliamentary party who decides who the next leader shall be. This seems to occur both in the Conservative and the Labour parties. A challenge to the leader may arise at the party convention and is fought out, but if the challenger fails he is not expelled from the party. In some cases the Prime Minister has to include him in his Cabinet, as a result of public or party pressure.

The practice that has arisen in Jamaica is that in the selection of candidates for election the party executive, through its power to fund the campaign, exercises significant if not decisive influence. The question that arises is whether the successful candidates represent their constituents or the party executive. Representing the interests of the constituency might make them ineligible for ministerial rank. While this is understandable, it has made a farce of the whole idea of a House of Representatives and accounts in part for the public disaffection with the entire electoral system, with the House, with the Budget debates and virtually all other government initiatives.

These constitutional defects and the parliamentary practices which have developed from them have had the effect of removing any semblance of accountability from the system. In Britain, the Prime Minister is accountable to the House which can, in the extreme, remove him from office. In Jamaica, we have already seen that the Constitution gives the Prime Minister the power to control the House.

The Auditor General has to report on the activities of the Ministers, appointed by the Prime Minister to the Members of the House who have become so, courtesy of the party executive. They are not likely to render an independent critique of ministerial activities. No wonder that nothing changes from year to year. The Public Accounts Committee has degenerated into such a farce that even they themselves do not take it seriously. These developments probably account for the absenteeism of Members of the House, since they have no meaningful role to play.

Michael Kaufman notes that the PNP was unable to transcend the limitations of existing structures of the Jamaican State in order to develop new structures and institutions of grass roots political, economic and social power.[37] New structures are essential to infuse fresh meaning and new weight into the liberal democratic traditions of Jamaican politics. New institutions are critical to transform the population from being political consumers to producers of their own political destinies. Such is a key to the transformation of social, political and economic relations, and to mobilizing the dormant energies of the population. It would also be crucial in the positive polarization of political discourse, as opposed to what Jamaicans call the tribalism of the island's paternalistic party system. This comment by Kaufman is well taken, but it is ironic that the major obstacle to this transformation was the PNP's refusal to give up the benefits of the paternalistic party system, since, after all, it was the basis of their power. Much more would have been gained from using the existing institutions, party, Parliament, in particular, and the civil service, instead of pushing them into marginality.

Nunes also sharply presents the dilemma that managerial and organizational power rested mostly with the elite, since they were the educated ones, who were the first invited to leave the country in the 1970s.[38] If Obika Gray (mentioned above) is correct, the major social power possessed by the poor is defensive of their own interests and they are not concerned with projecting this power into the society.[39]

Returning to the question of the British Constitution, it will be clear to the careful observer that the most salient feature is the relationship between the various institutions or individuals which constitute the British government, Prime Minister, Cabinet, Parliament and the Civil Service. Such an observer may be inclined towards the view that the Cabinet is of much more importance or influence than Parliament. In reply, one must note that the sheer voting power of the British House can nullify the power of the Cabinet, a probability ruled out by the fact that our Cabinet and its various Ministers of State and Parliamentary Secretaries can outvote the House.

Mills promised to note behavioural differences between the UK and the Jamaican versions of the Westminster model. In the succeeding pages he notes the major differences between the social and political backgrounds in both countries and stresses the 'supremacy of Parliament' in the UK. He also appraises the differences in the USA and UK Constitutions and gives due weight to the formal separation of powers.[40] One must respond that the concept of supremacy of Parliament does not exist in Jamaica, except in theory. The supremacy in Jamaica is vested in the Constitution.

With all due respect to the Constitution, it is only a piece of paper. Only men and women with real power can control other men and women who exercise the power of government. On that score alone, the Jamaican system is less like the UK. The practice of the UK is more like that of the USA. Whereas the USA has a formal separation of powers, backed up by the power structure of their society, the British system has a practical separation of powers, probably from a real back bench, given the numbers in Commons (650) with only about 10 per cent being ministers. The Cabinet, with all its power, can easily be outvoted by Parliament. To prevent this from happening inconveniently, the British have introduced the parliamentary Whips. British history will show that the supremacy of the sovereign was not replaced by that of the Prime Minister, but by the supremacy of Parliament, and this has worked for centuries in Britain. It is true that there are moves afoot to increase the power of the Cabinet at the expense of that of Parliament, but the British are not going to surrender their rights so easily.

Mills notes that progress in the constitutional development of Jamaica reflected a gradual whittling away of the presence and power of the Colonial Governor and ex-officio and nominated of the executive and Legislative Councils. In Britain, the parallel movement ensured a gradual erosion of the power of the Crown by Parliament, eventually attaining a position of supremacy. The changes in the Jamaica reflected the exact opposite and it was not gradual. Mills fails to show that the power taken from the Colonial Governor did not go to Parliament, but to the executive and the Prime Minister. The supremacy of the executive has become such a part of the establishment that few persons can recall a time when Parliament was not subservient to the Chief/Prime Minister. Perhaps the reason for the requirement of solidarity was the presence of the Colonial Governor and his apparatus existing all the way up to actual independence.

Parliament cannot, and perhaps was not intended to, act as a control to the Prime Minister and Cabinet. Given the small size of the government party in Parliament (about 45) and some 30 Ministers, Ministers of State and Parliamentary Secretaries, the chances are that there is no functioning back bench which could outvote the Cabinet group anyway. A much more destructive outcome is that all offices and officials which depend upon the supremacy of Parliament for their efficacy are rendered null and void, whether public accounts committees, integrity committees, parliamentary and political ombudsmen, contractor general or auditor general.

By writing these provisions into our Constitution we continue to sanction and practise them. We have seen that one of the most effective corrective mechanisms which most Parliaments have in their armoury, the vote of no confidence in the government, directed at the Prime Minister and his Cabinet, has been rendered null and void and of no effect by the same Constitution. In democratic societies a successful vote means the resignation of the government, following which the Parliament would proceed to choose a new Prime Minister and government. Such a vote is an extreme measure and some states, for example Germany, include provisions to ensure that it is not used lightly and over trivial matters. In Jamaica the constitutional position is different. In case of a successful vote of no confidence by the Parliament, the Parliament is dissolved and the Prime Minister can call general elections to choose a new Parliament, more to his liking.

Ombudsmen, public accounts committees, auditors and contractors general

The inability of the ombudsman to function effectively is a pathetic reflection upon how this device, so cherished in countries which observe the rights of citizens, is cynically undermined in Jamaica. Very few citizens are aware of the hollowness of this institution. The lowering of confidence in the legitimacy of the major institutions of our political culture does not have merely theoretical effects but practical ones on law enforcement and even the very success in the fight against crime. Those who think that controlling the growth of crime is a matter of greater firepower should think again. It has been shown that the most effective factor in the fight against crime is its prevention. The more people are satisfied that the system of justice is fair and equitable, the less likely they will engage in criminal activities.

This surely is part of the thinking behind this report of the Senate's call for the restoration of the rule of law. Senators have called upon the security forces and the citizens to resolve the current crisis. They predict tragedy if the problems are not solved in short order. The citizens should understand that the rule of law should be respected.[41] These are perfectly good sentiments, but the citizens have as much right to demand that the rulers observe the rule of law and agree to be shackled by it.

We have just made the point that any institution which rests upon Parliament for its effectiveness is for all practical purposes completely useless. The new Contractor General is already facing up to the realities of his new office.[42] In an interview with a newspaper he examines some of the issues, including the nature of the office. The scheme presupposes that Parliament will take the reports and act on them. The efficacy of the office depends upon Parliament's powers and interest. A few technical problems have delayed the tabling of the new bill, increasing his powers. The commitment from Parliament to the previous contractor general has not apparently been kept. Some problems exist in the administration of rules for contracts, for example, the office has different lists, and individual contractors are qualified in some, but not in others. He suggests that well laid down processes are not being followed.

This is a fairly well documented mess. For a 'new boy', McKoy has been active and deserves our congratulations and our gratitude. He has put his finger fairly quickly on the role of Parliament. He will discover, much to his chagrin, the Parliament simply cannot play a monitoring and corrective role. This will render the contractor general's office futile and useless, as his predecessor discovered.[43] Doubtless he possibly will achieve a few improvements in the technical administration of the contracts, but overall the effects will be transitory and superficial. A person or institution with less power simply cannot control a person or institution with more power. It has never been done.

The transparency of the electoral system and the belief that it can be trusted to reflect the will of the people is a major factor in building the citizens' confidence in the legitimacy of the major institutions of our political culture. MP Chuck believes that electoral reform is critical. He proposes two views: 1) that the issue is so fundamental and critical that no other election should be held until the reforms are completed; and 2) that expensive technology is not the answer.[44]

Impact of political culture on national development

A major issue relating to the political culture and the institutions derived therefrom is their impact on national development in its many aspects – economic, political and social, and any other that might come to the mind of the reader. One is assuming, in spite of evidence to the contrary, that governments by and large seek to promote the well-being of their citizens.

George Beckford in his study of persistent poverty offers considerable insight into the entire question. His description of the plantation organization classifies it as a total economic and social institution, a complete and self-sufficient community. Plantation economies and sub economies reveal social and political characteristics almost identical to those found within the individual plantations.[45] It should be no surprise to any careful observer that the government and social organization of Jamaica reflect the pattern of the plantation, even to the denial of real participation in the process of government. It seems not possible to have a democracy on a plantation. Besides the question of where the process of reform should come from, there is a more fundamental one of how a government which is itself a plantation can lead a reform away from the plantation. According to the pessimistic theory, the plantation can never be destroyed. Did they do it in Singapore or not?

Beckford explains the reasons why the plantation system creates persistent underdevelopment: 1) the system denies the majority of people a real stake in their country; 2) it creates a legacy of dependency because the locus of decision making resides outside the system, so that dependency syndrome is characteristic of whole population; 3) the majority of the people are not sufficiently motivated towards the development effort because of the first two considerations. No meaningful social change can take place to correct these three basic deficiencies. The plantation system must be destroyed if the people of plantation society are to secure economic, social, political and psychological advancement.

One major weakness in the critique of Beckford and others is their insistence that the system be destroyed without planning to replace it by the provision of something more desirable which can achieve what the plantation system cannot achieve. If the society and the government are the plantation system, they are not about to destroy themselves. On the contrary, throughout our recent history there have been major attempts to consolidate the features of the plantation system. Some of them represent a betrayal of the hopes and aspirations of Marcus Garvey for the people of African descent.

The interaction of power and people

The essence of a democracy is that the people have effective control of the power of the State. Government policy can be affected by the people only if their representatives are respected. In real, and not paper terms, a system of parliamentary representation of the people has not existed in Jamaica since about 1944. The Representation of the People Act has been replaced in practice by the 'Representation of the Party (Leader) Act'. Yet another citizen experiences the reality of the political culture. Lloyd Smith concedes that Davies is the most powerful man in Patterson's Cabinet, that he is personally honest and above board, that he approaches his duties with sincerity and his integrity is unquestioned. The Prime Minister must have great deal of confidence in him. But questions now are arising as to his credibility, since his predictions and projections are not working out. How much longer can the people endure his wild imaginings and madcap experiments? He must either deliver the goods or make way for one who can.[46]

Many people cannot understand the pervasive influence that a system can have on an individual. The organization is indeed many times more powerful than the man. A single good man by himself cannot defeat a corrupt and sterile system. The Jamaican political culture encourages and reinforces behaviours like his. He will not be called upon to resign or leave the system. We understand that he has actually tried to resign but it was not accepted.

One report shows how the policy of no wealth creation has back-fired into making the State unable to carry out its role as welfare provider. This report cites Senator Henry-Wilson as agreeing that the State may have given up critical aspects of its role, which may have resulted in decades of erosion of some institutions and could have contributed to this week's (September 1998) violent demonstrations in Kingston. Asked if the State had abandoned the most vulnerable who have embraced area dons as representatives of hope, Henry-Wilson expressed concern about the power of 'non-mainstream' leaders. The greatest challenge to government is to bring these persons back into the mainstream of society.[47]

The Senator expresses a most refreshing point of view, but it is hardly shared by the mainstream politicians. The statement about bringing people back is somewhat optimistic. My major contention is that they were never in the mainstream, except to be exploited for their voting power, being locked up in garrison constituencies. As a potential leader of a reform movement aimed at changing the political culture, the General Secretary has possibilities, but these can be easily be overridden by the conservative wings. Nevertheless, she may point the way towards the political and cultural renewal that many of us deem so necessary, if she is given our support and encouragement.

Notes

1. John Rapley, 126, pp 1, 125.
2. Stephen Vasciannie, "Crime and Civil Liberties" (article), *Daily Gleaner* (2 August 1999), p 4A.
3. Shawn Johnson, "SOS to the Prime Minister" (letter), *Daily Observer* (Wednesday 16 September 1998), p 10.
4. Howard Hamilton, "Fostering Prosperity and Growth" (address), *Daily Observer* (Monday 27 April 1998), p 7.
5. "PSOJ Predicts Economic Gloom, Doom" (report), *Daily Gleaner* (Thursday 21 May 1998),p A1.
6. Christopher Berry, "How to Move from Debt to Equity" (article), *Sunday Observer* (26 April 1998), p 15.
7. "$19bn Bad Loans at Banks and Building Societies" (report), *Daily Observer* (Friday 24 April 1998), p 22.
8. Raphael Gordon, "Has Privatisation Worked?" (article), *Financial Gleaner* (Friday 9 October 1998), p. 9.

9. Moses Jackson, "$150bn Internal Debt Will Cripple Budget" (article), *Daily Observer* (Wednesday 25 March 1998), p 1.

10. Max Lambie, "Current Economic Indicators Inadequate" (article), *Sunday Gleaner* (20 September 1998), p 8B.

11. "Seaga Warns against Tivoli Gardens Incident Repeat" (report), *Daily Gleaner* (Friday 25 September 1998), p A1.

12. James Walsh, "World Development 1998" (article), *Daily Gleaner* (Friday 18 September 1998), p A4.

13. Lee Kuan Yew, 70.

14. For a general background and a critique of the development process in the Caribbean, see Girvan, 39, 40. Odle, 108.

15. John W Robinson, 131, pp. 87, 88.

16. Elsie LeFranc, (ed.), 71, p. 1.

17. John Rapley, 126, p. 3.

18. John W. Robinson, 131, p 91.

19. Barry et al., 5; Beckford, 6; Beckford and Witter, 7; and Best, 10, provide more background reading.

20. See Alvin Wint, 161, for an account of the real private sector in action.

21. Nunes, 106, p. 4.

22. Errol Miller, "Befuddled by Bailouts?" (letter), *Daily Gleaner* (Thursday 2 April 1998), p A4.

23. "Lack of Foreign Investments Hurting Economy" (report), *Daily Gleaner* (Monday 27 April 1998), p A3.

24. Enid Brown, "PSOJ Can and Should Do More" (article), *Sunday Gleaner* (7 June 1998), p 8B.

25. "Private Sector Urged to Invest Locally"(report), *Sunday Gleaner* (3 May 1998), p 6C.

26. "High Demand for Jamaican Goods" (report), *Sunday Gleaner* (24 May 1998), p 9B.

27. Enid Brown, "How Can the Private Sector Restore Its Credibility?" (article), *Sunday Gleaner* (19 April 1998), p 9B.

28. "Now Is the Time for Entrepreneurs" (report), *Financial Gleaner* (Friday 26 June 1998), p 17.

29. Alvin Wint, 161.

30. Perry M Ferrie, "Business Ownership" (article) *Daily Observer* (Friday 9 October 1998), p 7.

31. "Private Sector Organizations – Seaga" (report), *Daily Gleaner* (Monday 25 May 1998), p A1.

32. Cliff Cameron, "The Need for Private Sector Unity" (article), *Sunday Gleaner* (24 May 1998), p 8B.

33. Wolfgang Grassl, "Private Sector Madness" (article), *Daily Gleaner* (Wednesday 6 May 1998), p D1.

34. Sameer Younis, "JMA Batting for Manufacturers" (report), *Financial Gleaner* (Friday 8 May 1998), p 14.

35. Patrick A.M. Emmanuel, 31, gives a searching critique while Gladstone E. Mills, 93, p 4, merely gives a description of the Westminster/Whitehall Model.

36. See Trevor Munroe, 98, for the generally undemocratic and self-serving atmosphere in which the constitutional discussions and decisions took place.

37. Michael Kaufman, 64, p 45.

38. Nunes, 105, is in general agreement with Gray (next note).

39. Gray, 44, pp 186, 189.

40. Mills, 93, p 4.

41. Luke Douglas, "Restore the Rule of Law" (report), *Daily Gleaner* (Saturday 26 September 1998), p A3.

42. "Problems Face New Contractor General" (interview), *Sunday Gleaner* (9 August 1998), p 8A.

43. See Ashton Wright, 162, p 260 ff.

44. Delroy Chuck, "Why Electoral Reform?" (article), *Daily Gleaner* (Wednesday 15 July 1998), p A4.

45. George L Beckford, 6, pp 53–55.

46. Lloyd Smith, "Dr Davies, We Need Action" (article), *Daily Observer* (Tuesday 11 August 1998), p 6.

47. Dorothy Campbell, "Inner Cities Neglected - Henry-Wilson" (report), *Daily Observer* (Saturday 26 September 1998), p 3.

8

Creating The New Political Culture

I: Aims and Objectives

To reform the political culture
Is a task that no one man can nurture
Co-operation's a must
Built on honour and trust
To ensure us a promising future

The major theme of this chapter is that the current reform attempts, such as those by the Jamaicans for Justice (JFJ), the JMA, PSOJ, JCC, NDM, PNP, JLP and UPJ, by means of such devices as prayer breakfasts, football peace and public embracing by national leaders, if carried out in isolation, will make only minor incremental changes in the total fabric of the society. Merely coming together to deal with the consequences instead of the causes of the deterioration of the society will be of no effect. At best, if these initiatives work, they will make life a little more tolerable for a small minority of the population. At worst, they will simply hasten the deterioration of the society and reduce the level of confidence in the belief that the society can heal itself, since it will be perceived that we have tried everything, and nothing has worked. At this stage Jamaica needs a grand vision which can capture the imagination and mobilize all the citizens into maximum contribution to their own cause. Singapore and the Far Eastern countries had such a vision, and they organized their societies to make it work.

Need for reform of the political culture

The address by Prime Minister Panday of Trinidad and Tobago to the CARICOM consultation held at UWI on Friday 3 September 1999 raised some profound thoughts about the prospects for the future of CARICOM as an organization and of the countries that constitute it at present. This was complemented by an address by Prime Minister Arthur of Barbados on a similar theme. Between them they used the terms 'the Caribbean Century' and 'the Creative Imagination' as themes to symbolize the promise, potential and performance of the Caribbean in the twenty-first century. A major concern was the preparedness of all the members, especially those of the Anglophone Caribbean, for this venture. Against all protocol, but out of his friendly concern for a country he loves, Prime Minister Arthur of Barbados severely criticized Jamaica for its structural weaknesses and the division and tribalization of its society as major impediments in the pursuit of these uplifting goals.

Their use of the terms highlighted above provides hints of a grand design for the Caribbean. Arthur's chastisement of Jamaica reflected the fact that the other members of the Anglophone Caribbean are very disappointed with its gradual abdication of the economic leadership of CARICOM. Though they have no real reason to be afraid, they feel more comfortable with Jamaica in the lead, especially when they are enlarging the trade bloc to include an overwhelming number of Spanish speaking people.

The 'Caribbean Century' simply asks that we provide some leadership to the poor nations of the world and prove to them that our small size and our initial poverty present no barrier to producing individuals and organizations of world class in the leadership of the movement for economic growth and social development as well as in the fields of sports, entertainment, music, and administration, as many of us claim with pride. Contrary to the feelings of their many boosters, these achievements are not substitutes for economic competence. Jamaicans must begin to feel that being at or near the bottom of every Caribbean list of development indicators is not acceptable.

To make the 'Caribbean Century' a reality, our success in the art and cultural worlds must be replicated with success in the economic world. This calls for a transformation in our attitudes and values, indeed, in our entire political culture, to use Stone's definition from an earlier chapter. We must have high hopes and aspirations and not be content with what some individuals think is good enough for us. Our pride in ourselves must be reinforced by solid, genuine and real achievements, not the spurious and paper achievements we have celebrated in the past. We must have real and not pseudo heroes and achievements. We must set high goals and then design our systems to achieve them. An unanswered charge against CARICOM, especially Jamaica and Guyana, is the failure to achieve our potential.

Part one: changing the culture

The first seven chapters of this work have made a strong case for the culpability of the political culture as the prime agent responsible for the current state of the nation. The conclusion is inescapable that the current culture and ways of doing things has outlived its usefulness and must now go. The only questions that remain are, how to do it and what to replace it with. As to the first aim, the removal or changing of the old culture, two strategies suggest themselves.

The first strategy is to actively challenge the old political culture by infiltration of the leading instruments of the current political parties and helping them to formulate new policies and cultures. Opportunities for this may arise sporadically from time to time, when the parties are seeking new candidates or whenever the existing parties give the public an opportunity to comment on their new manifesto, such as the PNP is engaging in now (2001). One hopes that it will be tabled for genuine and not showplace public discussion. Current political realities make participation in reform extremely dangerous. Recent events have demonstrated the existence of open links between politicians and dons. The power of the don is partly derived from his ability to dispense scarce benefits, on which the current political culture of handouts and welfare rests. This strategy is likely to be resisted and sabotaged by those in power.

The second strategy is to work directly on the culture and demonstrate to the parties that the old culture is no longer suitable. Although many reform programmes are busily engaged in these activities, there is little awareness among the participants that their own restricted field will not show significant improvement until the entire political culture is reformed. Thus the JFJ, in their laudable exertions to secure justice for individuals, tend to confine their efforts to the narrow administration of justice and the effects without recognizing that these effects stem from the pattern of injustice built into the society. Similarly, the JMA confines its efforts to negotiating some minor accommodation for its immediate economic problems without recognizing what it has in common with the JFJ.

Unwittingly they play into the hands of the political culture, which finds it easy to give minor concessions without changing its basic nature. As a general rule, each reform-minded institution seeks some private accommodation to its immediate concerns without seeking to reform the entire system which the first part of the work demonstrated to be the major culprit in the underdevelopment of Jamaica. It is a classic case of divide and rule, even though the divisions are self-imposed. Successful pursuit of this strategy calls for a degree of cooperation between reform minded institutions never before achieved in Jamaican history. As a first step all these institutions need to recognize the commonality of their apparently diverse causes. This is an ongoing strategy that needs pointing, clarification and organization, calling for a high level of cooperation. Polls show that about 60 per cent of electors are uncommitted to political parties. How does one get all of them aboard a reform movement?

A national target for growth

One of the best ways of eliciting cooperation among the reform minded groups is to have a common task to which they can contribute with a view to changing the economic and cultural climate which we have shown to be the major cause of the current chaos in Jamaica. Acceptance of a common task will take each group out of its narrow concerns and assist it in appreciating the big picture. It will help people to believe that they can have a significant part to play. It might also help them to realize that the economy is our business, and not merely the province of politicians, businessmen and economists.

The people of Jamaica through the interaction of their various groups need to set a target for growth. The target should be stated in terms of the earnings we must generate in order to take our people out of their penury and for all of us to enjoy the good life. Singapore did it and Barbados is doing it. Our plan must be based on achieving so much earnings over so many years. The current practice of scoring by percentage increases in the GDP, though impressive in itself, does not convey any information to the people of Jamaica as to where they are, and what effort is needed to bridge the gap between poverty and wealth. The current increases in the GDP are based on what the government believes the country can achieve at the current level of effort. This becomes the target and its attainment is greeted by both major parties with great whoops of joy. They lose sight of the fact that anybody, even the physically handicapped, can clear a hurdle when it is only one foot off the ground.

The target for earnings should make allowances:

• to eliminate the national debt totally or to bring it within manageable proportions;

- to provide enough income for future investment;
- to provide enough income for comfortable living expenses for the entire body of citizens. The notion of equitable earnings must be interpreted to mean that in narrowing the gap between the haves and the have nots, the floor be lifted considerably and the ceiling be lowered not at all. Only the imagination and the exertion of the people of Jamaica should limit the amount of wealth to be created. It is not a finite amount.
- to act as a rallying point for a national effort.

This plan calls for radically new thinking and a total break from the orthodox. As Albert Einstein is reported to have remarked, one cannot solve a problem with the same level of thinking that prevailed at the time the problem was created. The year by year growth figures have no motivational impact. They do not provide feedback to the citizen on the effect of his effort, how much he has achieved and how much farther he must go. To many persons, the annual report on the national accounts is merely an accounting exercise devoid of any practical meaning. It does not provide the spark that can galvanize a national effort. The report does not reflect that each component merely plays the incremental game without reference to the contributions they ought to make and those others are making. A national target for growth will make it clear what part the individuals and the various corporate citizens can play in the developmental effort. The presence of a tangible target is one way to get a national consensus. Handshakes and embraces by national leaders will never produce the necessary consensus.

One must begin with an exercise of the following nature. We must make a list of all the export industry sectors, and fill in the current value of their output and the share they contribute to the GDP. The next column might show the shortfall between the current value of earnings and the amount we must achieve to meet the targets set out above. During the assessment, it may be discovered that certain sectors cannot be extended sufficiently to maintain or increase their share of an expanding GDP. In others, such as the bauxite/alumina sector, the expansion will depend primarily on value added, not in an increase in quantities of raw bauxite or the first stage of alumina products. Serious consideration must be given to the fabrication of aluminium products, even if the intermediate stage of smelting is performed elsewhere. Creating high value products will call for massive inputs of human ingenuity and mastery of technological processes, as well as investments in production facilities. It is not the *quantity* of the effort that will matter, but the *quality* of that effort. A totally different mind-set is needed.

It will immediately become apparent that the current minor increments marking the growth of each sector of the industry will be woefully inadequate. Some sectors, perhaps all or most of them, will have to take a quantum leap. We will be able to put figures upon statements such as this one attributed to Dr Vin Lawrence: "The music industry can produce trillions of dollars for Jamaica!" At that level, it will not matter whether they are Jamaican or US dollars. The national growth target will show what the resources are, whether they exist now or have to be created. Obviously they cannot be acquired by massive borrowing. If the projects or programmes are viable and profitable, they will find private funding. It will be up to Jamaican individuals and firms to convince the venture capitalists of the world. The drill also requires that the government will not guarantee a single penny of any loan.

The success of any project or programme will rest solely upon the astuteness and managerial ability of the Jamaican people. They will have to learn the disciplines of finance, marketing and production. They must learn to view Planet Earth as their market. They must expect no favours, and dispense none, except where it makes good long-term business sense. There is a consensus among economists that the world's wealth has been increasing by leaps and bounds over the centuries, the last century, the twentieth, being especially productive. It is good if the targets are set higher than the minimum requirement. This will ensure that the only unlimited resource, human ingenuity, can have maximum scope for performance. To quote Franklin D Roosevelt, "The only thing we have to fear is fear itself."

This approach does not call for rigid central planning, down to the last nut and bolt as in the centrally planned economies of the Soviet era. Instead, it merely lays down a practical blueprint for a national consensus. The present poor who are non-participants in the creation of wealth must be brought into the mainstream of production by a process of education, conditioning and learning. They will not co-operate unless they are convinced that an end result is envisaged that will remove their poverty. So far the welfare and distribution orientation has given them merely the illusion of prosperity.

Part two: of visions and missions – the shape of the new political culture

Whichever strategy is adopted, one of its end results would be a change in the culture of each of the major political parties. Some comments on the culture of the major opposition party, the JLP, would help the reader to asses its prospects of providing the necessary vision, drive and dynamism required. Though the following was based on observations made in 1998 and 1999, there is little reason to believe that any significant change has taken place since then.

The perception that the PNP is in the government and therefore appears to be a viable party, capable of meeting the needs of the present and the immediate future, the early years of the twenty-first century, has shifted attention from its weaknesses to the state of the opposition JLP. Specifically, the area of focus is the question of the leadership. As one of my correspondents points out, should they form the next government in 2002, the next slated general election, Seaga will be the oldest at 72 and Karl Samuda the youngest at 60. One can wonder whether such a team is prepared for a regime of regeneration and renewal.[1] Most of the citations dealing with the future of the JLP do so in terms of the immediate disposition in the matter of Seaga's imminent or desirable resignation from the leadership. It is assumed, presumably, that it will be business as usual after the annoying distraction of the leadership issue is settled.

Two of these citations are somewhat vague calls for renewal. The writers, however, do not say just what precisely needs to be changed, the purpose of the change and how the process may be carried out.[2] Erica Virtue believes that the time for tears has passed and it is time for reconstruction. The JLP needs to re-organize, re-construct and re-invent itself to be a credible and relevant alternative to the country. John Butterworth adds that the party had a golden opportunity to make changes since it would be choosing officers and other senior positions in next few weeks. He also names several individuals who should be given responsibilities.[3]

The first citation points to some good signs, but there is much more to building a valid alternative government than merely replacing the PNP. There is absolutely nothing to be gained if the incoming regime simply repeats the programme of the other party. One needs to examine the whole political culture, what NDM calls the 'system in its constitutional presentation'. The JLP needs drastic renewal, but will not get it. They need to build a team, but the current leadership believes in one-man operations. It is organizationally impossible for one man to achieve the task of governance.

Of change and renewal

The process of change and renewal needs the capacity to implement and monitor progress and take corrective action when necessary and to conceptualize and carry out large and transformational projects, sustained over as long a time frame as required to make it realistic. The problem with the people and the so-called leaders of Jamaica is that they are afraid to think big and then to organize themselves to make the vision work. Even if such a vision is revealed, it is quickly vitiated by the handout and welfare orientation of leaders and people, and generates further waves of cynicism. Tremendous euphoria is generated over the most minimal advance. The ideal standard of anything Jamaican is what we have already achieved, not what we can achieve with a little thought and boldness.

Our developmental policy is based upon the current quality of our education, not upon what it can be if we pursued the correct educational policies. Hence the focus is on low wage unskilled labour, since this is what we have in abundance. None of the Asian tigers based their development thrust on cheap, unskilled labour. If they did at the beginning, they have now phased that policy out. In Singapore the gap between the top and the bottom earners is one of the lowest in the world.

In 1986, Carl Stone presented an eleven-point plan to move the country forward.[4] One major weakness was that such a plan needed more policy and administrative capability than the PNP displayed in the 1970s. No Jamaican government has ever been able to display the policy or administrative capability needed. If the present political culture remains intact, it will never display that capability. All of Stone's points are obvious steps in the regeneration process. If they can be achieved, they will transform the country. But the current political culture is not interested in their achievement.

Stone would like to transform the country into a state capable of creating a new dynamic, nationalistic and capitalist class. The society should develop a political and administrative capacity supporting the participation of the citizens. The country needs to tap into sources of financial support independent of conservative international capitalists. It should mobilize the productive energies of a large number of creative small producers. It needs to restore the democratic tradition, including channels for ordinary citizens to take part in public life, to remove clientelism and dependence on US interests, and to rebuild national institutions to give Jamaicans the feeling of running their own affairs. The existing debt problem should be handled by renegotiating foreign debt through rescheduling and converting some of it into equity funds.

The country should also reorganize and restore more of the public sector, thereby rationalizing human resource use, so as to develop management capability in the public sector and a diversification of enterprises. In the process of reform, minimum standards would be set for public services. The task is a formidable one, requiring a consensus on national policy, embracing leaders from various political parties and other interest groups sharing a common nationalist and democratic perspective on national development. Some of these are being carried out by the current regime, but with limited success. Foreign debt forgiveness is always being renegotiated, only to be replaced by other borrowing. Stone would like us to avoid not all the international capitalists, but the conservative ones. After all, they are the only ones who have the money.

Clientelism and dependence on US interests is the choice of Jamaica, and has not been imposed by the USA. Singapore could cane American Michael Fay for spray-painting motor cars and hang an Australian for drug trafficking because firms from both countries are lining up to do business in the country. That country owes nobody anything.

Doubtless, Stone would have worked towards this end had he lived. An indication of the state of the nation and its preparedness for this exercise is the fact that this comprehensive development programme has remained hidden from public view. To give him credit, many of his columns in the newspaper discussed these issues. Governments of Jamaica do not listen to advice, even that which they pay for. Perhaps after 13 years of further deterioration of the social fabric more persons in some command positions may be able to take on the task with more probability of success than Stone. Eight of his 11 points have to do with human and organizational capacity. One may consider them preconditions for development, not regularly found in Jamaican society.

As the Far Easterners have discovered it would be much better if local entrepreneurs do the job, otherwise the development process is halted.[5] As long as outsiders are running the enterprises, we cannot call them our own. This is what happened in the 1960s. Once the foreign companies pulled out, there were no Jamaicans left with the skills of international finance and marketing or production for a global market. It is clear that the nature of the private sector and government institutions pose serious limits. The meaning of development must include the capacity of the local institutions to generate the initiative and the management expertise to match those of the TNCs. Otherwise the result will be the creation of more dependency. The very existence of Singapore shows that there is lot of room for initiative and creativity.

Barry, Wood and Preusch continue: "Only rarely has local leadership seriously considered the possibility of breaking out of the plantation economy." The vision of the new Jamaica must transcend that. The inability or refusal of the local leadership to take the opportunities as they arise must be circumvented. It might be more generous to attribute this inability not so much to the lack of political will but to the existence of institutions that cannot recognize and exploit such opportunities. Although Don Robotham does not think highly of their efforts to create a unified society, creating the ability to exploit the circumstances is what Barbados is seriously trying to do.[6] They are well on their way to creating such institutions.

The result of the new culture

The following is the definition of the ideal Caribbean person arrived at by CARICOM heads of government in 1997.[7] Creating a programme like this could easily be the goal of a national movement.

The ideal Caribbean person should be someone who, among other things:

- is imbued with respect for human life since it is the foundation on which all the other desired values must rest;
- is emotionally secure with a high level of self-confidence and self-esteem;
- sees ethnic, religious and other diversity as a source of potential strength and richness;
- is aware of the importance of living in harmony with the environment;
- has a strong appreciation of family and kinship, values community cohesion and moral issues including responsibility for and accountability to self and community;
- has an informed respect for the cultural heritage;
- demonstrates multiple literacies, independent and critical thinking; questions the beliefs and practices of past and present and brings this to bear on the innovative application of science and technology to problem solving;
- demonstrates a positive work ethic;
- values and displays the creative imagination in its various manifestations and nurtures its development in the economic and entrepreneurial spheres in all other areas of life;
- has developed the capacity to create and take advantage of opportunities to control, improve, maintain and promote' physical, mental, social and spiritual well-being and to contribute to the health and welfare of the community and country;
- nourishes in him/herself and in others the fullest development of each person's potential without gender stereotyping and embraces differences and similarities between females and males as a source of mutual strength.

II: The Obstacles

The character of the parties

Party aims must yield place to those national
Other courses are simply not rational
They must chart a new mission
With courage and vision
And with plans realistic and functional

The first seven chapters of this volume were a *tour de force* of the current political culture and all its dysfunctions. Collectively, they demonstrate not only the workings of the culture, but also the state of mind, belief attitudes and behaviour of both the citizenry and the governments. The major obstacles here are precisely these.

The nature and character of the two major parties, particularly the JLP, has been the subject of scrutiny by a number of citizens. For reasons of space only four of them can be accommodated here.[8] One letter puts in a plug for Ossie Harding to play a more leading role. Its writer has thought of coming home himself to contest a seat but will not even consider it if Seaga remains the party leader. He credits Seaga with concepts and types of skills needed to lead in the twenty-first century. He also believes that JLP can attract energetic and expert youth by making a leadership change. The question of the comparative level of talent and expertise available to the major parties is the theme of the next article. The second writer thinks that Senator Henry-Wilson is a match for the general secretary and all three assistant secretaries of the JLP, whose senior personnel were holding office at the party's expense.[9]

Despite the special pleading in this report by Luke Douglas, the presence of Bustamante's party is one of the very things that has destroyed, and continues to destroy, any prospect of social and economic recovery for Jamaica. Its financial backers are said to be wary. Samuda does not want the central executive's decision overturned, as it would send a message giving the wrong impression of the party's determination to stick to existing structures and organizational rules.[10]

A letter from James Northover asking for the discarding of current JLP deadwood brings this subsection on the renewal of the JLP to a close. Northover believes that the information given in Dawn Ritch's article on Sunday 4 October 1998 about Seaga's choice for officers cannot be correct.

The persons who mashed up the party cannot be recycled. It should consider names like Jeremy Palmer, J.C. Hutchinson, Mike Williams, Sandra Nesbeth, Marlene Daley, Karl Samuda, Bindley Sangster and Shirley Williams. These are bright independent minded individuals who can move the party forward.[11]

This writer is in general agreement about the pressing need for change and renewal. Without this change, no economic or any other plan, except those that are welfare oriented, will ever work. The same for an unrenewed PNP, although the need has remained unrecognized. The ineptitude of the JLP is certainly part of the malaise, but a strong party, without renewal, will be just as disastrous as in the past. The single undisputed leader or one-man operator as Bustamante (1944–1955), Michael Manley (1972–1980), Seaga (1980–1989) and Patterson (1989 to present) cannot provide the organization for growth and development as did the team of 1962–1972 led by Bustamante which included Sangster, Shearer, Seaga, Lightbourne and Hill. Similarly, the team led by Norman Manley 1955–1962, consisting of Nethersole, Seiveright, Arnett and Lloyd had a much better record than any individual. The team will always outperform the individual, regardless of how talented each member is.

Today, Bustamante's party is obsolete and became so shortly after as it was formed. Both parties must be renewed to handle the challenges of the twenty-first century. Neither party has successfully handled the challenges of the latter half of the twentieth century. The PNP is as equally endangered as the JLP, but being in office has masked its collapse. Still, it is bankrupt of ideas without a clue as to how to reform itself. Finally, of the names mentioned as possible successors, many of these are not well known, even by reputation, but Mr Northover has the right idea. There is considerable doubt that he recognizes that the major candidate for discarding is the leader himself.

Constitution and system responsiveness

The task of renewing and reorganizing the political parties for the new missions ahead is a monumental one, bearing in mind the power distribution currently obtaining and the disposition of the current leaders and their vested interests. Among the major vested interests is the tremendous power which the incumbent prime minister or opposition leader has granted to him by his supporters. They too have a vested interest in maintaining the status quo. The only people who would benefit from a change are the people of Jamaica and none of our leaders, except a very few, seem to have our interests at heart. Encouragingly, signs are appearing that show that citizens do demonstrate their displeasure, by using the only means open to them, which also happen to be against the law.

Whether the chief executive is a president or a prime minister matters only to those seeking the office. It will not increase the efficiency of the civil service, the Revenue Board or JAMPRO; our schools will continue to turn out unsatisfactory graduates and our indebtedness will increase as will tourist harassment. The political culture has not been able to distinguish between trivia and real achievements.

III: The Team and its Leadership

The role of the team and its leadership
Must with care be reviewed by our readership
The result of reviewal
Must of course be renewal
To embrace us all in a new partnership

The NDM (and to a lesser extent the JLP) will not beat the PNP at the current game of political one-upmanship. The NDM's role in the long term must focus exclusively on the renewal of the political culture. The CARICOM profile above neatly states the objectives and end results of the renewal, but not the means to the desired ends. This gives a lot of flexibility to the programmes. The withdrawal of some 60 per cent of the population from the political arena gives the NDM a constituency to work on. We have argued the case to show the ill effects of our failure to understand the actual political culture that has been hampering all our efforts over the past 60 years. The NDM and the reformers must realize that the current culture is very powerful and is highly organized. There is nothing except lack of confidence to prevent the organization of the silent majority. It amounts to a truism to state that the majority is silent, because it is unorganized.

In this connection, this writer's most optimistic wish will be fulfilled if the current volume were to have the impact of providing the necessary catalyst of getting the uncommitted to commit themselves to the reform process. The big question is whether the various citizens' groups and civic organizations, including the Consumers' League, the Jamaicans for Justice, the NDM, the New Beginning, the UPJ and the church can look beyond their narrow interests and come together to promote a programme of national redemption. Will there be an inspirational mission or vision to lead the way? The various groups need to recognize that significant change will not come from the isolated focus on narrow interests. All must realize that they have a single common enemy. The Jamaicans for

Justice must understand that their particular problems have the common provenance as those of the Consumers' League.

Party prospects and the political culture: the twenty-first century

The following citations show, from time to time, that some thought has been given to the desirability of the various political parties coming together to create a government of national unity. The citations raise issues beyond the immediate one of leadership and show some awareness that the parties must be radically changed to meet the needs of the future. Thus Ritch believes that the JLP is still a going concern. Her commentary on the unexpected performance of JLP councillors at the local government election is quite upbeat. The results apparently justify the defiance of the party leadership. They won 56 seats when the party hierarchy did not expect more than 26. The result has been credited to Mike Henry.[12] Hope continues to spring eternal in the human breast in spite of half a century of disappointment. The visionary Winston Seymour calls on the JLP, PNP and NDM to unite in the interests of the country. The government cannot be entrusted to men who are against business, progress and capital. The PNP will be in power as long as Seaga leads the JLP. He should therefore resign.[13]

Both these citations deal with the urgent necessity for a renewal and reorganization process. Each case notes the ego of one individual standing in the way. It is not likely that he will take advice to exclude wimps, lackeys and yes-men. On the question of unity between the three parties, under certain circumstances it would be disastrous, if they all persisted with the stultifying and obsolete culture.

Dr Alfred Sangster has been learning quickly about the way our political culture works and that its pernicious influence goes far beyond the reach of CAFFE and electoral reports. He goes beyond the immediate issues of changes in the leadership of one or both parties to examine the fundamental character of the party system. His article is a direct challenge to the political culture. He wants definitive answers to the core question of whether or not the election results reflect the collective will of the people. If not, and he seems to have assumed this answer; the challenge therefore is for people of goodwill, with the political parties taking the lead, to start changing the political culture. The burning issues are the continued existence of the garrison communities, victimization of outsiders, the assignment of contracts to activists and the relationships of both parts of the opposition, NDM and JLP, each rejecting the other. He spots the weaknesses of the Jamaican Westminster model, those not noticed in the more orthodox examination of studies like Mills'.[14]

Dr Sangster is looking into the hard core of the political culture and all citizens should be grateful that he definitely does not like what he sees. His questions stir up the muddy waters containing some fundamental issues. For example, he leads one to ask what is the collective will and whether it can be ever demonstrated inside the current political culture. The citizens of goodwill will have to act alone, since the political parties are not likely to take the lead in the reform process, unless under tremendous pressure. The commercial culture also needs reform, from trader mentality to entrepreneur mentality. The struggle of the citizens of goodwill is an illustration of reason versus Power, with Power being the more likely to win out.

The role of leadership

A few comments from an interview with Bruce Golding, can usefully open a discussion on the role of leadership.[15] These remarks are illustrative:

> The new president needs space. So my own role will be somewhat muted, but perhaps just as assiduous as before ... having left the JLP and its association with old style tribal politics, one has to understand that it is not an easy process for me to say ... you are not to be seen with the PNP or JLP, because they are not practising what we stand for, they are as tribalistic as the politics I walked away from ... believing that by simply changing the government, the treatment of the fundamental problems will change in any fundamental way. And that won't happen ... The truth is that politicians get away with immaturity because the Jamaican people are prepared to tolerate it. If the people were really indignant about that type of behaviour, politicians could not afford to keep it that way.

The last part of the comment raises the issue of whether we can change the attitude of the people into accepting a style of leadership based on function instead of on charisma and personality. Modern thinking on leadership recognizes that it is both a process and a property. As a property it is an integral part of the leader's personality. Emphasis here is placed on who the leader is and what he personally does. This is the thought behind the demand for a benevolent dictator to solve our economic and other social problems. At the same time, these same persons are repulsed by a Lee Kuan Yew, whom they describe as being a dictator. What escapes these thinkers is the importance of the other aspect of leadership, that of its being a process. The essence of this approach is that the leader is evaluated not on who he is (charisma) or his personal contribution to the effort (work habits), but solely on what he inspires his people to do and how well he organizes and facilitates their so doing. Such a leader has trust in his people: his aim is to remove any feeling of dependency.

The dynamics of change and renewal

The approach favoured by Maurice St Pierre uses a period of Jamaica's history to illustrate the dynamics of leadership emergence. His review of the 1938 disturbances in Jamaica discusses some of the dynamic factors that operate in a situation of change and renewal. With respect to the leadership dimension, the oppressed themselves at first played the leadership role. The lower classes are forced to question the legitimacy of the structure of power and to use violence to disarrange the structure. The achievement of legitimacy for the group is a key aspect of the leadership role. The role of the leader is to "define the ends of group existence, design an enterprise distinctively adapted to these ends, and see that the design becomes a living reality".

Two dynamics operate here. First, leadership based on political violence will fail in the long run. Secondly, in a colonial situation, informal leadership as provided by the masses must be formalized. Bustamante and Norman Manley were acceptable under the criteria, while St William Grant was not. In any case, St Pierre believes that 1938 was reformist, not revolutionary violence, not intended to overturn the structure, but to gain certain concessions from it.[16]

St Pierre delivers an intriguing perspective, which might explain the slight feeling of discomfort among the establishment, when faced with the prospect of a totally black prime minister. The colonial authorities had legitimized Bustamante and Manley, both from the top layer of the social strata and who were light skinned as well. A genuine people's reform movement was absorbed by middle class leaders and turned to their own purposes. We are thus grateful to St Pierre for throwing light on what could be one of the problems with reform movements from below.

In view of what we shall be recommending in due course, it is ironic that the two-party system has been generally regarded as one of the distinctive contributions to the development of the Caribbean. That might be true, even if we discount the first choice of our leaders by the colonial office. Gordon Lewis, however, notes the virtual monopoly enjoyed by the two-party system and its ability to keep other parties out of existence and that Jamaica has been paying a heavy price for this monopoly.[17] Today both the major political parties and the political culture, which has engendered and sustained them, are in dire need of renewal. The mission of the old political culture was to maintain the status quo as long as possible

and to look after the residual interests of the British and the new imperi-
alists, the Americans. The interests of the Jamaican people were brushed
aside as irrelevant. Of course, after some 60 years of deprivation, the People
are striking back. Since they have not been represented in Parliament, they
are now taking to the streets.

Public disquiet about the evolution of the two-party system has spilled
over into a controversy in the JLP. On the surface it revolves around the
continued presence of Mr Seaga as the absolute and undisputed leader of
the party. Since no one man, however all powerful, can run an organization successfully, this principle of undisputed leadership is one of the first
things that must be sacrificed by the renewed party if the country is to
make any material progress.

It is not mere coincidence that the best period of economic growth in
Jamaica took place at a time (the 1960s) when the leadership of the JLP
was disputed or perhaps only shared. Bustamante, Sangster, Shearer,
Lightbourne, Hill and Seaga himself contributed a wealth of ideas and
acted to restrain the wilder and less realistic actions of their colleagues.
Every successful economy in the world boasts that kind of shared leadership, even if the top man is the only one known to the outside world, and
is a formal dictator. The Chinese knew just how dysfunctional one-man
rule can be when they took the opportunity of the death of Chairman
Mao to denounce the personality cult. The United States has this shared
leadership built into its cabinet practice almost from the beginning.

Economists in explaining the 1960s, of course, will point to the
favourableness of the world economy then and the expansion of the bauxite industry as well as the capital inflows attendant on the policy of
industrialization by invitation as the cause of such growth. One must
wonder if the 29 years of negative growth since 1972 was accompanied by
a similar slump in the world economy. What is certain is that the 29 years
were marked in Jamaica by one-man, and not shared leadership.

The task of renewal of the political culture must fall first of all upon
the young Turks most of whom have more recently been inducted into
the political parties, before they become absorbed by the existing culture.
Offhand, we could mention persons like Delroy Chuck, David Panton,
Andrew Holness, Audley Shaw, Mike Henry and Pearnel Charles of the
JLP. They run the risk of being branded traitors by the leader of their
party and ostracized like Bruce Golding and the Gangs of Five and Eleven
as we have seen in the past.

A far more vital question is how the ordinary citizens of Jamaica can
contribute to the process of political renewal. The first requirement

would be to understand the history and culture of the political system and how it has affected them in the past and how it will continue to affect them in the future. Given the levels of illiteracy prevailing in the society, this in itself appears almost a non-starter. Perhaps a group of dedicated citizens could start a political education campaign upon the nature of our political system – not just the superficial, third form Civics model, but of real issues such as the nature of a political party, whether it is a private or a public organization and whether society can continue to grant it a near monopoly upon political office at the highest level. The current system encourages the participation not of men and women of talent but of flatterers and hangers-on, and discourages present or potential critics.

A discussion of what might become the perspective of the governing political party, the PNP, is appropriate here. Recent reports have indicated that the general secretary of the PNP, Senator Maxine Henry-Wilson, has been looking seriously into some of the fundamental questions included above (chapter 7).[18] In the event that they prove to be genuine reflections of the movers and shakers of the PNP, it will represent one of the most significant changes since party politics came to Jamaica. If these become the official stance of the PNP and if that party as government puts into place the necessary culture and infrastructure to support these aims, then we will be well on our way to the First World! Apparently the good lady does not yet realize that the achievement of these objectives would mean the total abandonment of the entire political culture which the governments of Jamaica (note the plural) have created and exploited over the past 60 years. She does not seem to realize also that neither the PNP nor JLP as currently constituted can deliver on these promises because the current political culture makes it impossible for them to deliver. On the other hand, she might be extremely well informed as to the implications of the change, but has decided to sacrifice the current culture.

Using the power of organization

In illustrating the dependency syndrome at work and the failure of fairly autonomous citizens to demonstrate the level of innovation and enterprise, one may begin with some of the thoughts of Professor Norman Girvan. In an article published in 1979, Girvan laid out the six constituents of a technological capability which would be based on the linkages and interchanges between them.[19] Unfortunately, in each case the culture has tended to force each constituent into relative isolation from one another. The six constituents may be roughly described as follows:

- the research and development institutions like UWI, UTECH and SRC;
- the productive systems, such as the manufacturing and processing plants;
- the educational system, especially the technical schools and colleges, culminating in UWI and UTECH;
- the specialist workshops and facilities;
- the engineering and consultancy firms; and
- the policy makers in the government.

Twenty-two years afterwards, there have only been token movements in the integration of the 'Girvan 6'. Just recently, the UWI and the SRC agreed to collaborate on research. The Prime Minister, UWI Principal Hall and Dean McMorris recently opened new science buildings and strong sentiments were shared by all participants that Jamaica must harness technology. An agreement is signed to facilitate collaborative research between UWI and SRC.[20] The interlinks and interchanges between those two research institutions (group one) and the other five constituents have not been the subject, to our knowledge, of any collaborative working arrangements.

A wall of suspicion has emerged between the UWI and the productive systems. Both sides still contribute to the standoff because of deep ideological divisions intensified by the excesses of rhetoric during the socialist 1970s and 1990s – not that things improved much during the eighties. This fact, more than all, confirms my belief that the limiting factors to the development of Jamaica are not economic at all, but behavioural. Until the walls of suspicion and distrust that surround the six constituents are replaced by free and open communication and understanding, Jamaica and the Caribbean will continue to miss out on opportunities.

Even while well-deserved attention is paid to the fortunes and improvements of any single institution, the realization has not seemed to creep into the decision makers that the key to national development and their securing a place in the new dispensation is by collaboration. Even warnings by Caribbean prime ministers that their contributions to the maintenance of the UWI might be cut unless some changes occur, are ignored. In Jamaica, at least, UTECH seems prepared to accept the challenge.[21] Its aim, according to its president, is to become a first class regional institution. Admirable as this may be, it still needs to be integrated into the developmental system. Isolation from the other components of the technological capability will not secure it a guaranteed place in the future.

Several citations point to the potential for the use of technology and knowledge in the various fields of endeavour, particularly in agro-industry. As far as this writer can judge from the figures for export and the widening adverse balance of trade, the potentials have remained thus so far. The good news is that recognition of the role to be played by the applications of technology is gaining ground. Paul Geddes, lecturer at the Northern Caribbean University, formerly West Indies College repeats the case for technology in the development process in Jamaica and tells of the advantages to be gained and what it has achieved in the developed world.[22] Martin Henry thinks that the announcement by the prime ministers and the provision of money are meaningful steps in the enhancement of science and technology for economic development. It is not smooth sailing, however. Although the prime minister has cited it as an example of the prowess of science and technology, the mid-island project, with a capacity for producing 20,000 pounds per day of dehydrated fruit, has not exported single pound of fruit. There is little institutional support, despite the personal initiative of frustrated scientists and farmers. They have been hampered by bureaucratic obstacles in the importation of vital equipment. Henry adds that there are lots more projects at the research and development, but not at the implementation phase.[23]

These reports of support by the highest institutions in the land are encouraging. What is not so encouraging is Henry's comment that the plant had yet (May 1998) to export its first pounds of fruit since its establishment. Obviously all the links between the constituents of a technological culture have not been put into place. These depend upon the introduction of organizational systems, structures and strategies and all the requisite systems, based on mutual communication and shared values. Although the possibility exists for a strong research unity between UWI, UTECH, NCU, SRC and others, one fears that parochialism and individualism, the products of the political culture, may inhibit real cooperation.

IV: Psychological and Behavioural Realities

Behavioural change must be made
For foundations of growth to be laid
Application of merit
Helps the meek to inherit
If we're pleased not to crawl in the shade!

The nature of the task

The recent flurry of letters and articles pro and con the survival of Anancy in the literature to which children are exposed revives the controversy over what influences the subsequent behaviour of the child. The persistence of the folk-hero has been alleged, among other things, to have caused adverse effects on the minds of many.[24] Pat Roxborough labels Anancy a 'CARICOM Misfit' and asks plaintively, "Is there anything we have been doing in the past twenty-five years that may have helped to produce so many children and young people who display such indisciplined behaviour? To what extent have we taught our young people that there are consequences to their actions?"

Pauline Bain whose letter, quoted by Roxborough, ignited the most recent flurry, explains that her call was made in the context of the need to revive the teaching of moral and spiritual education in our schools. She admits that there have been many responses to her remarks about Anancy. The nature and intensity of the responses suggest that the principles derived from Anancy stories are deeply embedded in the unconscious part of our psyche.

Despite the indignation of letter-writers on the subject, Anancy was not the cause of the attitude. Anancy is merely an embodiment of the skills needed to survive in environments made more hostile by the comparative economic neglect endured by the country over the past 50 or so years. That is why it is buried so deeply in the psyche. Anancy helped to smooth out the injustices of a formerly slave society and make them a little more tolerable. He will go quietly when he is no longer needed. Those who want to ban Anancy must first change the social conditions that gave rise to his existence.

Preparing the *People*: pull factors in behavioural change

In bringing about any change in the political culture, one must bear in mind that citizens are both the originators and the targets of the change. The change has to be one of behaviour. We place high hopes on education, but will be disappointed to discover that education alone has absolutely no impact on behavioural change. Socialization and learning have a greater impact on behaviour. The facts are that the lifestyles and examples of our leaders, official or community, tend to negate all the positive values we try to inculcate in the formal system. The system itself must provide a steady stream of positive influences to reinforce those we try to disseminate in the formal education system.

The achievements of the Far East in their own economic growth and development are so stupendous that economists of other countries simply tot up the figures that substantiate the achievement without bothering to think just how these results came about. They give an explanation of sorts in terms of the movement of capital and investment and the policies that were used to attract capital. They might tell you that the governments, by and large (they did have some financial crises), made consistently good decisions and managed the processes well, but they cannot tell you *why* they made these consistently good decisions and *how* they ensured that the quality of management needed would be supplied, motivated and controlled.

In the case of Singapore, Henry Rowen and his colleagues have amassed the evidence to suggest that the combination of skilled workforces, competent management and an uncorrupted political system did not come about by chance.[25] They were created by the masterful mind of Lee Kuan Yew, using the only raw materials, the People, that nature had provided. *That choice is and was available to every developing country.* Those countries that choose otherwise, like Jamaica, and suffer hard times, have only themselves to blame.

Keith Panton argues that the possession of a highly skilled workforce, including management, is an asset which the balance sheet does not highlight.[26] Many organizations tend to take their people for granted. To the highly successful former manager of ALCAN Works in Jamaica, this is a fatal mistake. Panton's experience and that of the Department of Management Studies of the Mona Campus of the UWI show that with a careful plan and the cooperation of the individuals concerned it is possible to create high quality individuals with the ordinary people as your raw materials. Since 1986 the department has created from its own students some 20 lecturers with PhDs and respectable teaching and research experience – some of it world class.

Following on the work of Fred Nunes, Panton traces the development of the Jamaican worker through the phases of slave (1640–1840), peasant (1840–1940) and worker (1940 to present), showing the changing social and environmental conditions. He suggests that the two reversals of the working relationship, from worker in organization to free agency and back to worker in organization have had an unsettling impact. To Panton, these illustrate the influence of social environment and organizational culture upon the individual.

He also comments upon the phenomenon of the migrant Jamaicans being more productive and creative than the stay-at-homes, and wonders what the work ethic has to do with this observation. He also recognizes some positive trends arising out of developments in industrial relations, the practices of some organizations like MPM, HEART, Women's Construction Collective, Hanes Printables, and ALCAN Jamaica Company, his own company, under features like corporate values, communications, meetings, safety considerations and so on.

These comments give strong support for the thesis of the vital role played by the relations of people and their effects on productivity, profitability and the maintenance of the organization. Economists in their drive to make their vocation more scientific (meaning more mathematical) and less people oriented, have made the whole exercise less meaningful or useful. Massive investments in education, socialization and learning of their citizens are keys to the economic success of the Far Eastern economies. They also ensured that merit, not political considerations, was the only criterion for appointing these highly educated people to positions of authority and service. Jamaica failed not because it did not attract investments of this magnitude, but it used them for welfare and short-term show projects, and for short-term electoral purposes instead of true investments. The most neglected area was bringing the ordinary people into the mainstream of development.

The warning of the UWI Principal that we face a radically different twenty-first century workplace underlines the poignancy of the situation since many major actors on the stage have not yet emerged from the nineteenth. The changes in the relationships between staff and organization will create fundamental challenges to be faced.[27] Organizational success will be related to the quality and quantity of investment in employees, who will be called on for "imagination, flexibility and commitment to results". These new values are likely to replace "obedience, diligence, loyalty and protection" of the old bureaucratic dispensation.

The scope of the work

Tony Hart hints at the scope of the work in this letter:

> . . . having travelled the same road with a similar vision for a new and different political order where accountability, justice and education were passionate causes and the diffusion of confrontational and tribalized politics was an important part of our agenda ...[28]

At this point the normal solution would be to call for a massive public education campaign, until one realizes that education does not change behaviour. The team must understand that it will take it about 25 to 30 years to become effective. It must replace the current political tribalism with a programme of national aims and objectives. It must consider leadership not just as a property of an individual, but must focus on the interaction and the relationship between leader and led.

Purging the mind: the scale of the reform process

The biggest change needed in Jamaica is a change of our mental and psychological state. The state of denial is rampant among many of us who refuse to open our eyes to what is going on around us. If we do wake up, we tend to look for someone to blame. If the politicians make a mess of things, then it is our fault for accepting the minimal performance they promise and not holding them to something higher. In Bob Marley's words, the time is well overdue for emancipating ourselves from mental slavery. We must embrace the vision of Marcus Garvey and reverse the betrayal. It is vital to know the truth of our development, or rather, the lack thereof. Historical research is needed into the motives, opportunities and options available at different times in our history. We need to trace the relationships between cause and effect and support them with sound theory and sounder observation. Even after we do all this, the question still remains of whether a brainwashed people will accept that these things have been done to them.

A feature of our political culture is our tendency to resort to violence, even in the matter of the election of a PNP area representative. The allegation that the voters' list was faulty has not been proven, but something triggered off the violence. Barry, Wood and Preusch, though not in connection with this incident, note the tendency to resort to violence, but cannot see its purpose. They think it is a sort of mindless, undirected violence, not aimed at the state, but against their own class, against those who merely compete with them for scarce resources. To them the whole thing is somewhat vague and they keep asking just what is the violence directed at.[29]

Barry, Wood and Preusch, correctly interpret Bishop's attack on five-second democracy and the absence of a year-round vehicle for popular power. But Bishop's attempts to remedy this resulted in continuous democracy for only a part of the nation. The solution appears worse than the problem, as some persons are permanently deprived of even the five seconds. One may comment that such institutions are not effective or lasting because they operate outside of the prevailing culture and cannot serve its needs, even for institutional survival. They operate within hostile native environments. As to the inter-class violence, we think that no American can appreciate what it means to those in the depressed areas to be known to have backed the losing party. This fact is a matter of literal life or death.

The *People's* role in cultural reform

The silent majority is also the unorganized majority: that is why they are silent. Political stability may be a necessary, but not a sufficient condition for development. Only wealth creation, by the people themselves, can solve the problem of distribution of income and permanent relief from poverty. Espeut believes that there is a conspiracy afoot to make this kind of permanent relief next to impossible.[30] The chaos in Jamaica is an example of what happens when the entire country is poor and indebted. It does take cash, earned not borrowed, to care.

As we have mentioned, probably ad nauseam, the blocking of roads is interpreted as a sign that the communication path between and the people and their so-called representative is missing or faulty. The usual protest is against the deplorable state of the roads and poor representation by parish councillor and the inconveniences it brings. The people insist that the poor road conditions are the result of a lack of representation by the councillor, that they are tired of him and he should be removed as soon as possible.[31]

In spite of the evident partisan bias by MP Chuck, he too maintains that the citizens have a right to protest. He notes that the national stress of summer, economic hardship, lack of water, police abuses and bureaucratic delays provide countless occasions for legitimate protests. These provide emotional relief; and the belief that those who play by the rules get shafted encourages a dramatic and demanding approach. He supports a free speech amendment similar to the one in the American constitution and proposes that a caring government should learn from the protests and demonstrations of citizens.[32]

One may comment that these are welcome and timely words, but their implementation into policy depend too much upon the personality of the leadership of the government. Neither Mr Patterson nor Mr Seaga will listen, unless they have a political point to make. MP Chuck must join in the process of institutional reform, to guarantee this government awareness, regardless of the personality of the incumbent leader. A foolproof system, like giving back its power to parliament, must be designed and that activity cannot be left to the whims of the incumbent. Governments must have mechanism to sense when they are given a powerful signal from a protest.

V: Organization, Strategies and Tactics

Organizational strategies and tactics
Do not call for advanced mathematics
They depend on a plan
From a creative man
Or a woman who knows some statistics!

As a first step, the team should seek consensus on a set of national goals and priorities, such as those set out in the first section of this chapter. Occasional utterances by government and opposition sometimes suggest that this is part of their agenda, but the history of the political culture over the past 50 years has consistently demonstrated that their major priority is to hold office, and every other consideration has been sacrificed for this aim. The enunciation of national priorities cannot be left to the political parties. One needs to have a complete reversal of the normal practice, to one where the people present their leaders with a statement of goals and priorities and base the election campaign not upon what the parties concede for their own survival and benefit, but on what the people want.

Success in the reform of the political culture requires some interventions into the way the political process operates. A practical first step is to intervene in the process of political campaigning. Currently, political campaigning is based on mass demonstrations, rallies with much colour and pageantry, and motorcades that have the effect of intimidating the opposition. These have led, in the past, to criminal actions when the people, emotionally charged after a rally, have stormed the neighbourhoods of the opposition and carried out acts of mayhem and murder.

Community and civic groups like the various Chambers of Commerce which dot the island could take the initiative to change that by having a different type of campaign meeting. This writer suggests that these groups use their powers of persuasion to encourage rival candidates at the constituency level to conduct most of their campaigning indoors or in enclosed premises, in conditions where the entire audience is seated. This arrangement would facilitate a focus on the issues. The technology is available whereby a few cordless microphones can be scattered throughout the audience and the members of the public encouraged to ask questions of the candidates and their colleagues. This would force the candidates to become familiar with the issues themselves, in order the answer the queries of the citizens.

One might go a bit further by inviting the rival candidates to appear periodically, if not always, on the same platform. A moderator would control proceedings and the candidates would be limited to an opening and a closing statement of not more than ten minutes or so. The rest of the meeting will be question time and the moderator must not permit political oratory in support of one or the other candidate. This would put an end to the mindless harangues that currently pass for campaign speeches.

The nature of constitutional reform

A good example of a product that the people do not need, but will get anyway, is the constitutional reform making Jamaica into a republic. The people will get it because it is something that the system can deliver. The problem with constitutional reform is that to the public in general it matters little that some changes are made, since they will not affect the people anyway. The current proposals by the majority parties of giving the country a choice between an executive and a ceremonial president represent one such change. Real power will remain out of the hands of the people's representatives, the Members of Parliament.

Constitutional changes that will benefit the people are not going to be proposed by any major party if it is going to reduce the power of the executive by one iota. In any case, the stripping of the power of parliament occurred over some 55 years, since 1944, without the benefit of any constitutional change whatsoever. No change in the constitution is likely to restore the power of parliament, if they had any in the first place. The people's constitution had been wrested away from them without a struggle.

This being the truth of the matter, the observance of the forms of constitutional reform is a pointless exercise of going through the form and ignoring the substance. The editor of the *Daily Observer* reports that the constitutional reform process is going on with the acceptance by the House of the committee report. Three party positions are declared in the summary of the document. The JLP proposes a ceremonial president, the PNP wants to a republic with an executive president, while the NDM wants an American style separation of powers with separate power bases for legislature, president and court. The editor expects that the government will not skew the choice towards its preference and sets out its desiderata for a public education campaign.[33]

As any student of the political culture would conclude, the major parties are behind the cosmetic changes, since it would mean business as usual, with the people, as usual, being left out as they have been since 1944. Secondly, the wishes of editor will not come true, as there is too much power at stake. It would mean a serious diminution of the power of the party leader if country went the NDM way. In any case, the proposed constitutional reform without concurrent political cultural reform will be disastrous and extinguish the urge for further reform, by misleading people into believing that the process has been completed. If the news media campaign actively for the best choice, they will incur the wrath of both the government and the major opposition.

One writer believes that the numbers game will make nonsense of the whole exercise anyway. Kevin Johnson declares confidently that the "Jamaican parliament cannot function as a body which controls the government for a simple reason". He then gives details of the numbers game, pointing out that there are more representatives in government (cabinet and the full establishment) than in the House in Jamaica.[34] Britain has over 600 House Members while the government has no more than 60. There are no backbenchers in Jamaica (with the possible exception of Ronnie Thwaites). My informants tell me that there are regular complaints in England about the domination of the cabinet. These suggest that some members recognize the erosion of their powers as MPs. Without the possibility that some backbenchers might rebel and vote against the government, there would be no necessity for the institution of the parliamentary whip.

Unlike in Jamaica, the British government cannot take the support of the House for granted. Here the Members of the House belong heart and soul to the party, or more accurately, the party leader. This is one of the fundamental questions raised by Sangster and others, but is taken for granted within our political culture. Do the MPs represent the people or the party? The answers given by the people of mob rule and role of informal leaders in the garrison constituencies and the self-emancipation via football suggest one answer. Simply put, the MPs are not in control of the parliamentary process.

Bovell Barnes is not surprised at the action of the major parties in the constitutional reform exercise.[35] He believes, as we do, that an important right of the people is about to be taken away without consultation. He thinks that the 1962 constitution was drafted when elite groups, political and legal, took over the process and saturated it with their own special interests and values, permitting no involvement of ordinary Jamaicans. The current exercise needs a multi-pointed programme to ensure the people's participation.

Innovation and institutional response

George Beckford, although conceding that the fortunes of the developed world are closely related to the misfortunes of the Third World, stresses that external relations alone do not account for persistent underdevelopment. The internal pattern of economic, social and political organization should be analysed to uncover those factors that constrain development in plantation economies. Orthodox economists place heavy reliance on studies of other, more advanced, societies. Insufficient recognition is given to the fact that the institutional environment of undeveloped countries differs in fundamental ways from that of the more advanced countries.[36]

Among the preconditions for development, Beckford includes a highly motivated population willing and able to make the sacrifices involved and the appropriate institutional arrangements that provide the necessary incentives and reward for effort. In addition, economists concerned with problems of development are becoming increasingly aware of the limitations of a single discipline approach. Economics alone cannot explain the development process, and the need for political economy is asserting itself. The serious analyst must widen his disciplinary focus by drawing on history, sociology, anthropology, and geography.

Even while acknowledging the support of an eminent economist for our own approach, we are struck with a horrendous thought. If Beckford's work has had so little impact, how about ours? He supports the internal response theory, emphasizing the importance of not ignoring the environmental variables of the target population. He supports also the idea that the preconditions for development lie in the commitment and motivation of a whole people and would doubtless note the fulfilment of this precondition in the case of Singapore. One may compare John Rapley's features of a developmental state, where the People figure as pawns in a Power play. If one wants to understand what happened over the last half a century in Jamaica, one must adopt a broad interdisciplinary reach. Ours covers not only those disciplines but also law, organizational behaviour, management theory and education.

The issue of technical feasibility touches on the question of whether the skills, knowledge and other factors on which to base our strategy exist in the society. The latest figures published on our illiteracy rate put the figure at 24 per cent overall, about a quarter of the population. By any measure one generally assumes that the undergraduate population of a university would represent the cream of the literate members of the society. This writer has been teaching in the largest and most popular department at the UWI for the last 18 years and he still has grave doubts about the quality of the input.

Innovation and decentralization

Further points of light emerge in the increasing willingness of the people of Jamaica to undertake responsibility for their own psychological growth and economic development. The decentralization of their efforts and their group and community approach are other hopeful signs. Here the spotlight falls on Hanover and Manchester. In Hanover, the local authorities have taken the responsibility for lobbying for a Foreshore Road to alleviate traffic congestion and to enhance the tourism product. Mandeville in Manchester remains a viable and futuristic business community. Led by the Manchester Chamber of Commerce, it is creating an image by repainting and refurbishing and widening and lighting of roads. By remaining relatively crime free, it attracts a high percentage of returning residents.[37, 38]

The Hanover initiative has limited social aims and is not in the scale or scope of Manchester. The Hanoverians are a pressure group at the moment, but when they get no response from government, they may become entrepreneurs. In Mandeville, fast food outlets hardly count as overseas investment, but they do brighten up the place and may act as models for local businessmen.

Afterword: building a nation, shaping a society

This writer makes no apology for borrowing ideas, words and phrases from others, as long as they are appropriate. Historical antecedents show that all human progress has been as a result of the appropriation by some groups of the innovations and discoveries of others. It therefore pains me to find out that many of my fellow countrymen, and these might include many of my friends from the rest of the Anglophone Caribbean, appear to be aiming for a spurious self-sufficiency. Neither Japan, nor Europe, nor Asia, nor Latin America nor the United States nor Canada made such a mistake.

Incidentally, the phrase in this heading is borrowed from Rex Nettleford, in his foreword to *A Caribbean Reader in Development*.[39] The phrase poses a challenge to us, asking whether in the last 60 years or so we have built a nation and shaped a society.

Have we done so? Not by a long chalk. Our society possesses no firm economic basis, no democracy, but is marked by a division of the People, the arrogance of Power, alienation, crime, savagery and cruelty to animals, children, adults, the mentally ill, and the street people. We are getting the reputation of a drug-riddled and murderous society. All the ills we suffer from are the consequences of features that were designed into the system, deliberately or by default. We, the citizens of Jamaica, must redesign the system to get them out again. There is no other choice.

We had hoped to create a new nation
But our path so far has led to damnation
Though our future's unclear
We'll proceed without fear
Make our country our new decoration!

Notes

1. 'Realistic', "JLP Old Wood" (letter), *Daily Observer* (Thursday 23 July 1998), p 8.
2. Erica Virtue, "Reconstruction Time, Say Opposition Parties" (report), *Daily Gleaner* (Friday 23 October 1998).
3. John Butterworth, "Time for JLP to Renew Itself" (letter), *Daily Gleaner* (Thursday 22 October 1998), p A5.
4. Stone, in Davis, 27, p 141. Stone, 148, presents the general background.
5. Stevenson, 143. See also Tom Barry et al., 5, and West Indian Commission, 159.
6. Don Robotham, 132, p 14.
7. Pat Roxborough, "Anancy – a CARICOM Misfit" (article), *Daily Gleaner* (Thursday 26 April 2000), p D11. She is quoting from a CARICOM Heads of Government agreement.
8. R.D. Reid, "The JLP and Change" (letter), *Daily Gleaner* (Friday 23 October 1998), p A5.
9. Thomas Laidlaw, "No Wonder the PNP Outsmarts the JLP" (article), *Daily Observer* (Monday 29 June 1998), p 7.
10. Luke Douglas, "Stop Mash up Busta Party!" (report), *Daily Gleaner* (Tuesday 21 July 1998), p A1.
11. James Northover, "Discard the JLP Deadwood" (letter), *Daily Gleaner* (Saturday 17 October 1998), p A5.
12. Dawn Ritch, "Day Not Yet Done for the JLP" (article) *Sunday Gleaner* (20 September 1998), p 9A.
13. Winston Seymour, "A Vision of Unity" (article), *Daily Observer* (Thursday 18 June 1998), p 7.
14. Alfred Sangster, "The CAFFE and Carter Reports" (article), *Daily Gleaner* (Monday 4 May 1998), p A8.
15. Bruce Golding, "I'll Remain with the NDM" (interview with Erica Virtue), *Sunday Gleaner* (8 April 2000), p 8A.
16. Maurice St Pierre, 154, p 171.
17. Gordon Lewis, 78, pp 183–184.
18. Dorothy Campbell, "Inner Cities Neglected – Henry-Wilson" (report), *Daily Observer* (Saturday 26 September 1998), p 3.
19. Norman Girvan, 38, pp 19–20.
20. "National Progress Linked to Science and Technology" (report), *Daily Gleaner* (Thursday 16 July 1998), p A3.
21. "UTECH Changing and Improving, Says Davis" (report), *Daily Observer* (Monday 23 March 1998), p 3.
22. Paul Geddes, "Importance of Research and Development" (letter), *Daily Gleaner* (Tuesday 24 March 1998), p A8. See chapter 6, #73.
23. Martin Henry, "Good News for Science, Technology" (article), *Daily Gleaner* (Thursday 21 May 1998), p A4.
24. Lindsay Moncrieffe (letter), *Sunday Gleaner* (8 April 2001), p 10A. The reference to Roxborough is given at endnote #7 to this chapter.

Roxborough opens her article with a reference to Pauline Bain's remarks to a joint conference of Caribbean Union of Teachers and the Jamaica Teachers Association held in March 2001.

25. Rowen (ed), 133.

26. Keith S Panton, 112, p 1. This work is based, without acknowledgement, on Nunes, 106.

27. "UWI Principal - Radically Different 21st Century Workplace" (report), *Daily Gleaner* (Monday 30 March 1998), p C12.

28. Tony Hart, "Never Give Up" (letter), *Sunday Gleaner* (8 April 2000), p 10A.

29. Tom Barry, 5, p 8. For a contrary view, see Horace Levy, 70.

30. Peter Espeut "The Worst is Yet to Come" (article), *Daily Gleaner* (Wednesday 7 October 1998), p A4.

31. "Protesters Block Road in PM's Constituency' (report), *Daily Observer* (Thursday 25 June 1998), p 5.

32. Delroy Chuck, "The Right to Protest" (article), *Daily Gleaner* (Wednesday 20 May 1998), p A4.

33. "Constitutional Reform: Let the People Decide" (editorial), *Daily Observer* (Tuesday 4 August 1998), p 6.

34. Kevin Johnson, "Separation of Powers and Reality" (letter), *Daily Gleaner* (Thursday 24 March 1998), p A5.

35. Bovell Barnes, "Shaping the People's Constitution" (article), *Daily Observer* (Wednesday 29 April 1998), p 7.

36. George Beckford, 6, p xvii. See also John Rapley, 126, p 125.

37. Dale McNish, "Hanover Forms Development Committee" (report), *Daily Gleaner* (Wednesday 8 April 1998), p A10.

38. "Mandeville Poised for Economic Growth" (report), *Daily Gleaner* (Wednesday 6 May 1998), p C12. Judith Wedderburn, (ed), 159, p 1.

Books and Articles Cited

1.   Abedin, Najmul. 1986. "The Ombudsman in the Caribbean: an Overview". *Caribbean Finance and Management* 2, no. 1 (Summer): 29–40.
2.   Alleyne, Mervyn. 1988. *Roots of Jamaican Culture*. London: Pluto Press.
3.   Anderson, Patricia. 1987. *Minibus Ride*. Univ. of the West Indies, Mona: ISER.
4.   Barrow, Christine. 1996. *Family in the Caribbean: Themes and Perspectives*. Kingston and Oxford: Ian Randle Publishers and James Currey Publishers.
5.   Barry, Tom, Beth Wood, and Deb Preusch. 1984. *The Other Side of Paradise*. New York: The Grove Press.
6.   Beckford, George L. 1972. *Persistent Poverty: Underdevelopment in Plantation Economies of the Third World*. New York, London, Toronto: Oxford University Press.
7.   Beckford, George L., and Michael Witter. 1980. *Small Garden, Bitter Weed: Struggle and Change in Jamaica*. London: Maroon Publishing House.
8.   Bernal, Richard. 1988. "The Great Depression, Colonial Policy and Industrialization in Jamaica". *Social and Economic Studies* 37, nos.1&2: 2.
9.   Bertram, Arnold, 1995. *P. J. Patterson: a Mission to Perform*. Kingston: AB Associates.
10. Best, Lloyd. 1968. "Outlines of a Model of Pure Plantation Economy". *Social and Economic Studies* 17, no. 3 (September): 283–326.
11. Blackman, Courtney. 1982. *The Practice of Persuasion*. Bridgetown: Cedar Press.
12. Brodber, Erna, and Dorian Powell. 1990. *Street Foods of Kingston*. Univ. of the West Indies, Mona: Inst. of Social & Economic Research.
13. Brodber, Erna. 1975. "Yards in the City of Kingston". Working Paper Series. Univ. of the West Indies, Mona: Inst. of Social & Economic Research.
14. Brodber, Erna. 1974. "The Abandonment of Children in Jamaica". (Working Paper Series). Univ. of the West Indies, Mona: ISER.
15. Brown, G. Arthur. 1992. "Patterns of Development and Attendant Consequences for Jamaica and the Caribbean". Kingston: Grace, Kennedy Foundation.
16. Brown, Lynette, and Elsie LeFranc. 1997. "Work Ethics, Work Attitudes and Entrepreneurship in the African-Caribbean Community". In *Institutional Aspects of West Indian Development* (Critical Issues in Caribbean Development, no. 3), ed. Edwin Jones et al. Kingston: Ian Randle Publishers and ISER.

17. Bryan, Patrick E. 1990. *Philanthropy and Social Welfare in Jamaica.* Univ. of the West Indies, Mona: ISER.

18. Cameron, Desmond. 1985. "The Manntract Principle and Planning in Public Enterprise". *Caribbean Finance and Management* 1, no. 2 (Summer): 18.

19. Campbell, Carl, and Patrick Bryan (various years). *Caribbean Social History Project.* (Handbook). Univ. of the West Indies: Department of History.

20. Carter, Kenneth. 1997. *Why Workers Won't Work.* London: Macmillan Education Ltd.

21. Chuck, Delroy. 1986. *Understanding Crime.* Kingston: Delroy Chuck.

22. Clark, Rodney. 1979. *The Japanese Company.* New Haven and London: Yale University Press.

23. Clarke, Edith. 1957. *My Mother Who Fathered Me: a Study of the Families in Three Communities in Jamaica.* London: Allen and Unwin.

24. Council of Voluntary Social Services (CVSS). 1987. "A Handbook of the Social Services in Jamaica". Kingston: CVSS.

25. Davies, Omar, Yacob Fisshea, and Claremont Kirton. 1980. "Small-Scale Non-Farm Enterprises in Jamaica". *Social and Economic Studies* 29, no. 1 (March): 1.

26. Davies, Omar. 1986. "An Analysis of the Management of the Jamaican Economy: 1972–1985". *Social and Economic Studies* 35, no. 1: 30.

27. Davies, Omar, ed. 1986. *The State in Caribbean Society.* Monograph Series, no. 2. Univ. of the West Indies: Department of Economics.
    A. Introductory Note by Rex Nettleford, p 1.
    B. Trevor M.A. Farrell, "The Caribbean State and its Role in Economic Management", p 6.
    C. Dwight Venner, "The State in The Caribbean with Special Reference to a Mini-Economy", p 34.
    D. Dwight Nelson, "Comments on Venner", p 56.
    E. C. Y. Thomas, "The Authoritarian State in Caribbean Society", p 62.
    F. Carl Stone, "Democracy and the State: the Case of Jamaica", p 90.

28. Demas, William G. 1997. *West Indian Development and the Deepening and Widening of the Caribbean Community.* Critical Issues in Caribbean Development, no.1. Kingston: Ian Randle Publishers; Univ. of the West Indies, Mona: Inst. of Social & Economic Research.

29. Drucker, Peter. 1988. "The Coming of the New Organization". *Harvard Business Review* (Jan-Feb).

30. Eaton, George. 1975. *Alexander Bustamante and Modern Jamaica.* Kingston: Kingston Publishers.

31. Emmanuel, Patrick A. M. 1993. *Governance and Democracy in the Commonwealth Caribbean.* Univ. of the West Indies, Cave Hill: Inst. of Social & Economic Research.

32. Evans, Hyacinth. 1989. "Perspectives on the Socialization of the Working Class Child". *Social and Economic Studies* 38, no. 3 (September): 177–204.

33. Farrell, Terrence, and Arthur Lewis. 1980. "The Case for Caribbean Industrialization". *Social and Economic Studies.* (Special Issue in honour of Sir William Arthur Lewis) 29, no. 4 (December): 52.

34. Fayol, Henri. 1949. *General and Industrial Management.* Translated by Constance Storrs. London: Sir Isaac Pitman & Sons.

35. Fiedler, Fred E., Martin M. Chemers, and Linda Mahar. 1976. *Improving Leadership Behaviour: a Leader Match Concept.* NY: John Wiley and Sons, Inc.

36. Galbraith, John Kenneth. 1979. *The Nature of Mass Poverty.* Cambridge: Harvard University Press.

37. Girvan, D.T.M. 1993. *Working Together for Development.* Edited by Norman Girvan. Kingston: Institute of Jamaica Publications.

38. Girvan, Norman. 1979. "Approach to Technology Policy Studies". *Social and Economic Studies* 28, no. 1: 1.

39. Girvan, Norman, ed. 1997. *Poverty, Empowerment and Social Development in the Caribbean.* Univ. of the West Indies, Mona: Canoe Press.
    A. Norman Girvan, "Introduction: Report on the Caribbean Symposium on Social Development".
    B. Clive Y. Thomas, "The Inter-relationship between Economic and Social Development".
    C. Marjorie Newman-Williams and Fabio Sabatini, "Child-centred Development and Social Progress in the Caribbean".
    D. Kirk Meighoo, Donneth Crooks and Norman Girvan, "Empowerment and Social Development: Theory and Practice".
    E. Ralph Henry and Alicia Mondesire, "Poverty Alleviation and Reduction Programmes: the Commonwealth Caribbean Experience".

40. Girvan, Norman, and George Beckford, eds. 1989. *Development in Suspense, Selected Papers and Proceedings of the First Conference of Caribbean Economists.* Kingston: Friedrich Ebert Stiftung and Association of Caribbean Economists, UWI.
    A. Editor's "Introduction".
    B. Keynote Address by Alister McIntyre, "The International Economic Situation: Elements for a Policy Agenda".

41. Government of Barbados. 1998-2000. "Protocol Three for the Implementation of a Social Partnership". Govt. of Barbados.

42. Government of Jamaica. 1996. "Freedom of Information: A Door to Open Government" (June).

43. Government of Jamaica. 1996. "National Industrial Policy: Growth and Prosperity – the Way Forward."

44. Gray, Obika. 1994. "Discovering the Social Power of the Poor". *Social and Economic Studies* 43, no. 3: 169–189.

45. Hammer, Michael, and James Champy. 1993. *Re-engineering the Corporation*. NY: Harper Business.

46. Harriott, Anthony. 2000. *Police and Crime Control in Jamaica*. Barbados, Jamaica & Trinidad: Univ. of the West Indies Press.

47. Harris, Donald. 1997. *Jamaica's Export Economy, Toward a Strategy of Export-led Growth*. Critical Issues in Caribbean Development, no.5. Kingston: Ian Randle Publishers.

48. Harris, Thomas. 1973. *I'm OK, You're OK: a Practical Guide to Transactional Analysis*. London: Pan Books.

49. Hart, Richard. 1985. *Slaves Who Abolished Slavery*. Vol 2, *Blacks in Rebellion*. Kingston: Inst. of Social & Economic Research.

50. Headley, Bernard. 1994. *The Jamaican Crime Scene*. Mandeville: Eureka Press Ltd.

51. Henry, C. Michael. 1987. "Economic Growth and Economic Development: a Distinction Without a Difference". *Social and Economic Studies* 36, no. 4.

52. Henry, Paget, and Carl Stone. 1983. *The Newer Caribbean: Decolonisation, Democracy and Development*. Philadelphia: Institute for the Study of Human Issues.

53. Henry, Ralph M. 1989. "Knowledge and Economic Transformation: a Commonwealth Caribbean Perspective". *Caribbean Finance and Management* 4 (May).

54. Hofstede, Geert. 1990. "Motivation, Leadership and Organizational Development: Do American Theories Apply Abroad?" In *Organization Theory*, ed. D. S. Pugh. London: Penguin Books.

55. Huff, Daryl. 1984. *How to Lie With Statistics*. London: Penguin Books.

56. James, Vasciana. n.d. "Jamaica's National Industrial Policy: Development Strategy and Economic Performance". Research Paper.

57. Jefferson, Owen. 1972. *The Postwar Economic Development of Jamaica*. Kingston: ISER.

58. Jones, Edwin. 1981. "Class and Administrative Development Doctrines in Jamaica". *Social and Economic Studies* 30, no. 3 (September): 1.

59. Jones, Edwin. 1987. *Coalitions of the Oppressed*. Univ. of the West Indies, Mona: Inst. of Social & Economic Research.

60. Jones, Edwin, ed. 1997. *Institutional Aspects of West Indian Development*. Critical Issues in Caribbean Development, no. 3. Kingston: Ian Randle Publishers; Univ. of the West Indies, Mona: Inst. of Social & Economic Research.
    A. "Strategies and Their Operationalisation", p 21.
    B. Lynette Brown and Elsie LeFranc, "Work Ethics, Work Attitudes and Entrepreneurship   in the African-Caribbean Community".

61. Jones, Edwin. 1978. "The Political Uses of Commissions of Enquiry". *Social and Economic Studies* 27, no. 3 (September): 284.

62. Jones, Edwin. 1992. *Development Administration: Jamaican Adaptations.* Kingston: CARICOM Publishers.

63. Kanter, Rosabeth Moss. 1990. "Power Failure in the Management Circuit". In *Organization Theory*, ed. Derek Pugh. London: Penguin.

64. Kaufman, Michael. 1988. "Democracy and Social Transformation in Jamaica". *Social and Economic Studies* 37, no. 3.

65. Knight, Franklyn W. 1990. *The Caribbean: the Genesis of a Fragmented Nationalism.* Oxford: Oxford University Press.

66. Kristol, Irving. 1978. *Two Cheers for Capitalism.* NY: The New American Library.

67. Lall, Sanjaya. 1996. *Learning from the Asian Tigers: Studies in Technology and Industrial Policy.* London: Macmillan Press Ltd.

68. Lalta, Stanley, and Marie Freckleton. 1993. *Caribbean Economic Development: the First Generation.* Kingston: Ian Randle Publishers.

69. Lee Kuan Yew. 1998. *The Singapore Story: the Memoirs of Lee Kuan Yew.* Singapore: Times Editions.

70. Lee Kuan Yew. 2000. *From Third World to First: the Singapore Story.* NY: Harper Collins.

71. LeFranc, Elsie, ed. 1994. *Consequences of Structural Adjustment.* Univ. of the West Indies: Canoe Press.

72. Leo-Rhynie, Elsa. 1993. *The Jamaican Family: Continuity and Change.* Kingston: Grace, Kennedy Foundation.

73. Levy, Horace. 1996. "They Cry Respect: Urban Violence and Poverty in Jamaica". Kingston: UWI Centre for Population, Community and Social Change.

74. Lewin, Kurt. 1951. *Field Theory in Social Science.* NY: Harper and Row.

75. Lewis, W. Arthur. 1955. *A Theory of Economic Growth.* London: Allen and Unwin.

76. Lewis, W. Arthur. 1977. *Labour in the West Indies.* London: New Beacon Books.

77. Lewis, Gordon. 1968. *The Growth of the Modern West Indies.* NY: Monthly Review Press.

78. Lewis, Gordon. 1983. *Main Currents in Caribbean Thought.* Baltimore and London: Johns Hopkins University Press.

79. Lewis, Rupert. 1987. *Marcus Garvey: Anticolonial Champion.* London: Karia Press.

80. Lindo, Locksley I. 1997. *Caribbean Organizations.* Kingston: Locksley Lindo.

81. Lynn, Jonathan, and Anthony Jay. 1981. *The Complete Yes Minister.* London: BBC Publications.

82. McBain, Helen. 1987. "The Impact of the Bauxite/Alumina MNC's on Rural Jamaica: Constraints on the Development of Small Farmers". *Social and Economic Studies* 36, no. 1 (March): 137-170.

83. McClelland, David, and David Burnham. 1992. "Power is the Great Motivator". In *Management and Motivation*, ed. Victor Vroom and Edward L Deci. London: Penguin.

84. Manley, Michael. 1974. *The Politics of Change: a Jamaican Testament.* London: André Deutsch.

85. Manley, Michael. 1982. *Struggle in the Periphery.* Third World Media Ltd in association with Writers and Readers Publishing Cooperative Society Ltd.

86. Manley, Michael. 1986. *The Search for Solutions.* Toronto: Maple House Publishing Co.

87. Maslow, Abraham H. A. 1943. "Theory of Human Motivation". *Psychological Review* (July): 370–396.

88. Mendes, Margaret. 1985. "Professional Manpower: Is Overseas Recruitment the Solution or the Problem?" *Caribbean Finance and Management* 1, no. 2 (Winter): 37.

89. Mendes, Margaret. 1994. *Perspectives on Cooperatives.* Kingston: CFM Publications.

90. Miller, Errol. 1990. *Jamaican Society and High Schooling.* Univ. of the West Indies, Mona: Inst. of Social & Economic Research.

91. Miller, Errol, ed. 1991. *Education and Society in the Commonwealth Caribbean.* Univ. of the West Indies, Mona: Inst. of Social & Economic Research.

92. Miller, Errol. 1994. *The Marginalization of the Black Male.* 2nd ed. Univ. of the West Indies: Canoe Press.

93. Mills, Gladstone E. 1997. *Westminster Style Democracy: the Jamaican Experience.* Kingston: Grace, Kennedy Foundation.

94. Mills, Gladstone E. 1994. *Grist for the Mills.* Kingston: Ian Randle Publishers.

95. Mills, Gladstone E., and Paul D. Robertson. 1974. "Attitudes and Behaviour of the Senior Civil Service in Jamaica". *Social and Economic Studies* 23, no. 2 (June): 311–343.

96. Mitchelmore, Michael, and Naomi Clarke. 1993. "Gender, Nutrition and School Achievement in Jamaica". *Social and Economic Studies* 42, nos. 2 & 3 (June and September)

97. Morissey, Michael. 1983. "Country Preferences of School Children in Seven Caribbean Territories". *Caribbean Quarterly* 29, nos. 3 & 4: 1.

98. Munroe, Trevor. 1978. *The Politics of Constitutional Decolonisation:Jamaica 1944–1962.* Univ. of the West Indies, Mona: ISER; London: Allen and Unwin.

99. Naisbitt, John. 1995. *Megatrends Asia*. London: Nicholas Brealey.
100. Naisbitt, John, and Patricia Aburdene. 1985. *Reinventing the Corporation*. NY: Warner Books.
101. Nettleford, Rex. 1970. *Mirror, Mirror: Identity, Race and Protest in Jamaica*. Kingston: Collins Sangster.
102. Nettleford, Rex. 1971. *Manley and the New Jamaica*. London: Longman Caribbean.
103. Nettleford, Rex, ed. 1989. *Jamaica in Independence: Essays on the Early Years*. Kingston: Heinemann Caribbean; London: James Currey.
     A. Omar Davis and Michael Witter, "The Development of the Jamaican Economy Since Independence", pp 75 – 101.
     B. Edwin Jones and Gladstone Mills, "The Institutional Framework of Government", pp 105–129.
104. Nettleford, Rex. 1993. *Inward Stretch, Outward Reach: a Voice from the Caribbean*. London: Macmillan.
105. Nunes, Frederick. 1976. "The Nonsense of Neutrality". *Social and Economic Studies* 25, no. 4 (December): 347.
106. Nunes, Frederick. 1986 "Culture, Motivation and Organizational Performance". *Asset* 5, no. 2: 3–16.
107. Nurse, Lawrence. 1993. "Work and Workplace Relations in the Commonwealth Caribbean". *Social and Economic Studies* 42, nos. 2 & 3: 1.
108. Odle, Maurice. 1979. "Technology Leasing: Guyana and Trinidad". *Social and Economic Studies* 28, no. 1: 1.
109. Orane, Douglas. 1999. *The Orane Report: the Findings of a Task Force to Reduce Waste in the Public Sector*. Kingston: Jamaica Observer.
110. Orwell, George. 1945. *Animal Farm*. London: Penguin Books.
111. Panton, David. 1993. *Michael Manley: the Great Transformation*. Kingston: Kingston Publishers Ltd.
112. Panton, Keith S. 1990. "Manager's Perspective: Productivity through People – the Jamaican Experience". *Caribbean Finance and Management* 6, nos. 1 & 2 (Summer/Winter): 1.
113. Panton, Keith S. 1994. *Leadership and Citizenship in Post Independence Jamaica: Whither the Partnership?* Kingston: Grace, Kennedy Foundation.
114. Parkinson, C. Northcote. 1981. *The Law*. London: Penguin
115. Pascale, Richard T., and Anthony G. Athos. 1981. *The Art of Japanese Management*. London: Penguin Group.
116. Patterson, H. Orlando. 1965. *The Children of Sisyphus*. Boston: Houghton Mifflin.
117. Patterson, H. Orlando. 1969. *The Sociology of Slavery*. Rutherford, NJ: Fairleigh Dickinson University Press.
118. Persaud, Wilberne H. 1987. "Justifying a National Airline: the Case of Air Jamaica". *Caribbean Finance and Management* 3, no. 1 (Summer): 1.

119. Peters, Thomas, and Robert Waterman. 1984. *In Search of Excellence*. NY: Warner Books.

120. Plunkett, Warren R., and Raymond F. Attner. 1997. *Management: Meeting and Exceeding Consumer Expectations*. Cincinnati, Ohio: South Western College Publishing.

121. Powell, Dorian, and Erna Brodber. 1990. *Street Foods of Kingston*. Univ. of the West Indies, Mona: Inst. of Social & Economic Research.

122. Priestly, Margaret. *Administrative Reform Enquiries*. Kingston: Administrative Staff College.

123. Pugh, Derek, et al. 1990. *Organization Theory*. London: Penguin.

124. Punnett, Betty Jane 1986. "Management Approaches from North America: Can they be used in Caribbean Countries?" *Caribbean Finance and Management* 2, no. 2 (winter): 24 ff.

125. Quah, John T. S. 1990. *In Search of Singapore's National Values*. Singapore: Times Academic Press.

126. Rapley, John. 1996. *Understanding Development: Theory and Practice in the Third World*. Boulder, Colorado: Lynne Riener Publishers Ltd.

127. Radzinowicz, Leon, and J. King. 1979. *The Growth of Crime*. London: Penguin.

128. Richardson, Mary. 1982. "Socialization and Identity". *Social and Economic Studies* 31, no. 2 (June): 1.

129. Richardson, Mary. 1983. "Out of Many, One People: Aspiration or Reality? An Examination of the Attitudes to the Various Racial and Ethnic Groups within the Jamaican Society". *Social and Economic Studies* 32, no. 3 (September): 143.

130. Richardson, Mary. 1991. "'Fear of Success' and Jamaican Adolescents". *Social and Economic Studies* 40, no. 2 (June): 63–82.

131. Robinson, John W. 1994. "Lessons from the Structural Adjustment Process in Jamaica". *Social and Economic Studies* 43, no. 4 (December): 87.

132. Robotham, Don. 1998. *Vision and Voluntarism*. Kingston: Grace, Kennedy Foundation.

133. Rowen, Henry S, ed. 1998. *Behind East Asian Growth*. London and New York: Routledge.

134. Satchell, Veront. 1990. *From Plots to Plantations: Land Transactions in Jamaica 1866 to 1900*. Univ. of the West Indies, Mona: Inst. of Social & Economic Research.

135. Sayle, Elsie. 1994. *CVSS: the First Fifty Years*. Kingston: Kingston Publishers Ltd.

136. Seabrook, Jeremy. 1967. *The Unprivileged*. Harmondsworth, Middlesex: Penguin Books.

137. Sealy, Theodore. 1991. *Sealy's Caribbean Leaders*. Kingston: Eagle Merchant Bank (in association with Kingston Publishers).

138. Simey, T. S. 1946. *Welfare and Planning in the West Indies.* London: n.p.
139. Singham, Archie. 1968. *The Hero and the Crowd in a Colonial Polity.* New Haven:Yale University Press.
140. Shakespeare,William. 1992. *Julius Caesar.* Cambridge School Shakespeare Series, ed. Tim Seward. London: Cambridge Univ. Press.
141. Smith, M. G. 1989. *Poverty in Jamaica.* Univ. of the West Indies, Mona: Inst. of Social & Economic Research.
142. Smith, M. G., Roy Augier, and Rex Nettleford. 1961. *Report on the Rastafari Movement in Kingston.* Univ. of the West Indies, Mona: Inst. of Social & Economic Research.
143. Stevenson, Harold W. 1998. "Human Capital, How the East excels". In *Behind East Asian Growth,* ed. Henry S Rowen. London and New York: Routledge.
144. Stone, Carl. 1986. *Power in the Caribbean Basin.* Philadelphia: Institute for the Study of Human Issues.
145. Stone, Carl. 1989. *Politics Versus Economics.* Kingston: Heineman Caribbean (Publishers) Ltd.
146. Stone, Carl. 1983. "Patterns of Insertion into the World Economy: Historical and Contemporary Options". *Social and Economic Studies* 32, no. 3 (September): 299–304
147. Stone, Carl. 1985. *Class, State and Democracy in Jamaica.* Kingston: Blackett Publishers.
148. Stone, Carl. 1980. *Democracy and Clientelism in Jamaica.* New Brunswick, NJ: Transaction Books.
149. Stone, Carl. 1986. "Crime in Jamaica: Causes and Effects on the Economy". *Caribbean Finance and Management* 2, no. 2 (Winter).
150. Stone, Carl. 1989. "Rethinking Development". *Caribbean Finance and Management* 5, no. 2 (Winter).
151. Stone, Carl. 1982. *Work Attitudes Survey: Report to the Jamaican Government.* Brown's Town: Earle Publishers.
152. Stone, Carl. 1995. *Carl Stone Speaks on People, Politics and Development.* n.p.
153. Stone, Carl. 1994. *The Stone Columns: the Last Year's Work.* Edited by Rosemarie Stone. Kingston: Sangster's Book Stores.
154. St Pierre, Maurice. 1978. "The 1938 Jamaica Disturbances: a Portrait of Mass Reaction against Colonialism". *Social and Economic Studies* 27, no. 2 (June): 171.
155. Thomas, Clive Y. 1997. "The Inter-relationship between Economic and Social Development". In *Poverty, Empowerment and Social Development in The Caribbean,* ed. Norman Girvan. Univ. of the West Indies Press, Mona: Canoe Press.
156. Toffler, Alvin. 1985. *The Adaptive Corporation.* NY: McGraw-Hill.

157. Weber, Max. 1930. *The Protestant Ethic and the Spirit of Capitalism*. NY: Harper Collins Academic. Reprint 1992, London and New York: Routledge.

158. Weber, Max. 1947. *The Theory of Social and Economic Organizations*. Translated by A. M. Henderson and Talcott Parsons. Fair Lawn, NJ: Oxford University Press.

159. Wedderburn, Judith, ed. 1986. *A Caribbean Reader in Development*. Kingston: Friedrich Ebert Stiftung.

160. West Indian Commission. 1992. *Time for Action*. Black Rock, Barbados: West Indian Commission.

161. Wint, Alvin. 1997. *Managing toward International Competitiveness*. Kingston: Ian Randle Publishers.

162. Wright, Ashton. 1994. *No Trophies Raise*. Kingston: Ashton Wright.

Author and Subject Index

Afro-Jamaican
  adopt Western culture?, 14
Alleyne
  aesthetics of culture, 14
ancient China
  Mandarins, men of learning, 8
attitudes and values
  acceptance of corruption, 128
  creating norms and standards,
    131
  creation of corporate values, 217
  impact on public behaviour, 123
  preconditions for development
    See Cultural influences
  tokenism and corruption, 128
attitudes and values formation
  the process of perception, 106

Barry, Tom, 4
BCG investment opportunities
  cash cow, star, question mark and
    dog, 159
Beckford, George, 38, 52, 191, 223
  Persistent Poverty, 30
Bustamante, Alexander, 23, 24, 40,
  45, 48, 53, 54, 70, 73, 133, 174,
  206, 211
  welfare patronage regime, 162

CAFFE
  influence on political culture, 209
Cargill, Morris 32, 75, 142, 154,
  164. See slap happy reproduction, 8
CARICOM, 50, 92, 98, 101, 162,
  181, 197, 198, 205, 208, 216
  ideal Caribbean person, 205
  the Caribbean Century, 197
  the Creative Imagination, 197
Carter, Kenneth
  Why Workers Won't Work, 105

Civil Service
  nature and role in development,
    80
colonial system
  hostility to ordinary people, 46
Constitution
  evolution of practices, 186
  impotence of Parliament, 186, 187
  letter vs spirit, 186
  meaningless reform to Republic,
    221, 222
  Representation of Party (Leader)
    Act, 192
  vote of no confidence, 185
  Westminster-Whitehall heritage,
    19
Contractor General
  lack of parliamentary support, 189
Council of Voluntary Social Services
  139; charitable orgainzations, 49
  assistance to poor, 145
creation of wealth
  George Beckford, Persistent
    Poverty, 52
  low or no priortiy from govern-
    ments, 34
crisis in Guyana (C Y Thomas)
  permanent, periodic, general
    crises, 62
cultural influences
  achievement motivation, 117
  attitudes and values, 13, 117
  community and institutions, 120
  conditioning by the church, 119
  core national values, 123
  corporate values and culture, 120
  fear of success syndrome, 117
  growth of violent crime, 121
  Hofstede's dimensions of national
    culture, 116
  illiteracy, 36

Jamaican family patterns, 117
occupational identity, 36
socialization at the workplace, 120
socialization by the school, 118
the role of Anancy, 216

Davies, Omar, 3
death of capitalism and socialism, 5
democracy
    corruption of elections, 20
    justice and elections, 20
dependency syndrome
    myth of 'the lazy Jamaican', 129
development
    creation of high quality individuals,
        217
    theory and practice (Rapley), 168
development projects
    feasibility and social soundness, 47
development with people
    management expertise and initia-
        tive, 193
    people's voluntary involvement,
        60
    towards income equality, 161
development without people
    Rapley, John, 47

economic development
    corruption and ideology as
        barriers, 73
    dismal economic performance, 18
    fallout of slavery and colonialism, 18
    First World aspirations, 43
    human ingenuity, innovation,
        creativity, 5
    incrementalism, 45
    internal response theory, 24, 35
    motivation and commitment, 224
    not same as economic growth, 87
    political economy, 2
    popular attitudes towards, 54
    pre, co and post conditions, 160
    preconditions – aims and objec-
        tives, 163, 167

preconditions – education, 163
profit maximizing entrepreneur, 35
quality of life considerations, 93
rising tide analogy, 89
role of functional literacy, 51
role of private sector in, 89
role of state intervention, 87
role of technology and knowledge,
    214
role of trauma in, 12
social structure as intervening
    variable, 54
technical feasibility, 224
the brain drain, 171
theories of development, 88
trade versus aid, 91
traditional vs modern practice, 13
type, desire, feasibility, commit-
    ment, 12
economic growth
    enrichment of the People, 172
    international bragging stakes, 31
    not same as economic develop-
        ment, 28, 29, 30
    quality of life considerations, 31
    the financial sector, 30
    welfare, distribution and patronage
        orientation, 87
economic problems
    no economic causes, 3
education
    cost versus value, 130
Edu-tech 2000 and Smart Partner-
    ships, 99
Emergence of National Society,
    Jamaica, 40
emerging national society
    aims and objectives, 44

Farrell, Trevor
    review of Caribbean performance,
        98
financial sector
    nature and role in development,
        82

Garvey, Marcus, 40, 45, 48, 53,
    57, 192, 219
Girvan, Norman 24, 39, 62, 97,
    107, 160, 213
Grace, Kennedy lectures
    Mills, Taylor, Leo Rhynie,
        Panton, 18, 19

Horace
    laugh while telling truth!, 103
    not bound to swear, 2
housing and squatting
    long term solutions, 142
Huff, Daryl
    How to Lie with Statistics, 102

ideal Caribbean economy
    trade orientation, market diversifi-
        cation, 43
image and appearance
    edifice complex, 103
    Government by Announcement,
        102
    state of denial, 100
institutional collapse
    organizational paralysis, 17
    searching appraisal, 19
institutional failure
    intention/implementation gap, 62
    tapping Jamaican talent, 49
institutions for development
    fitness for task, 167
interests of Empire
    design of Jamaican constitution, 41
internal response theory, 4, 24, 35,
    224
    Robert Lightbourne, 53
    vs. world economic conditions, 35
investment in people
    trust and confidence building, 62

Jamaican government
    policy and administrative capabil-
        ity, 204
Jamaican social structure, 40, 54

Jamaicans for Justice, 196, 198, 208
    administrative reform, 198, 199
Jefferson, Owen 34, 35, 87, 95, 108
Jones and Mills, 3
justice, system of
    contempt for the citizen, 106
    ombudsman, the 104, 105
    people and the state, 105
    selective rule enforcement, 126
    sense of injustice and unease, 107

Kitchen Cabinet, Theory of the, 94, 95

leadership, 4, 15, 23, 24, 25, 46,
    69, 80, 111, 114, 142, 152, 162,
    175, 202, 204, 206, 209, 210,
    211, 212, 220,
    193, 195
    arrogance and aristocratic
        behaviour, 26
    as a process, 23
    as a property, 23
    by divine right, 25
    committed, passionate and en-
        lightened, 15
    constraints on leadership, 27
    dynamics of change and renewal,
        211
    group dynamics, 24
    hierarchical party rituals, 55
    outstanding Jamaican leaders, 23
    role in development, 22, 29
    role under challenge, 24
    shared leadership. See Kitchen
        Cabinet
    supportive leadership theory, 94, 95
    undisputed leadership effects, 25,
        207, 212
    undisputed leadership theory, 24
Lee Kuan Yew, 4, 6, 7, 8, 12, 16, 21,
    28, 35, 87, 89, 97, 154, 158, 169,
    174, 178, 185, 210, 217
    refusal of prescribed role, 4
Lewin's behavioural change phases
    unfreezing, moving, refreezing, 154

Lewis, Gordon, 7, 13, 39, 40, 50, 53, 66, 69
Lewis, Sir Arthur, 7

Manley, Michael, 4, 23, 33, 35, 39 42, 47, 61, 65, 70, 73, 75, 79, 81, 114, 132, 134, 158, 175, 184, 208
Manley, Norman, 23, 40, 50, 53, 64, 70, 133, 134, 185, 207, 211
Marley, Bob
mental slavery emancipation, 219
Miller's Theory of Place
constraints on behaviour, 125
impact on black entrepreneurship, 55
impact on socialization process, 123
Monroe Doctrine
USA imperialist policies, 42
Moyne report
Jamaican hopes rely on Jamaican efforts, 50
Myth of 'the lazy Jamaican'
justifying exclusion. *See* dependency syndrome

Naipaul, Vidia
Mimic Men; Biswas, 10
national development
building a nation/shaping a society, 225
consensus on goals and priorities, 220, 221
role of public sector in, 80
role of the state in, 72
national motto
aspiration or reality?, 112, 113
Nettleford, Rex, 3, 15, 41, 70, 140, 225
building an nation/shaping a society, 41
Manley's vision of new Jamaica, 44
norms and standards
impact on public behaviour, 124

renewal of community, 130
renewal of professional, 133
renewal of traditional, 131

ombudsman, 104, 105
description of duties, 105
undermined by parliamentary weakness, 190

Patterson, P. J., 13, 23, 25, 57, 70, 96, 112, 126, 151, 162, 171, 192, 207, 220
perception process, 9
anecdotes and stories, 9
projection, 9
plantation system
persistent underdevelopment, 191
rejection and replacement, 44
political culture
authority of area don, 108
changes in behaviour, 216
changing the culture, 189
characteristics of Jamaican political culture, 69, 70, 71
choice of candidates for House, 187
confounding positive values, 132
contempt for citizen, 20, 47
definition of (by Carl Stone), 72
division vs unity of nation, 14
electoral system corruption, 66, 82
evolution of party system, 67
impact on black entrepreneurs, 55
impact on development tools, 167
impact on national development, 191
institutional flexibility and learning, 71
lacking accountability and truthfulness, 25, 33
merit vs incompetence, 172
nature and character of JLP and PNP, 206
nature and role of political parties, 64, 206

no admission or correction of
mistakes, 51
no rights for ordinary people, 77
political vs economic rationality, 174
privilege and patronage, 26, 31, 37
process of change and renewal,
202, 207, 211
PSOJ as pressure group, 171
reform of campaigning process,
221
replacing political tribalism, 218
role of silent majority, 208, 219
shape of new political culture, 201
short-term electoral prospects, 56
visionary and inspiring leadership,
52
welfare vs achievement, 48
welfare/handout/comfort syndrome, 26, 35
political parties
government of national unity, 209
talent and expertise available, 206
political regimes
form vs substance, 21
poverty, 14, 31, 33, 44, 46, 49,
52, 68, 86, 97, 118, 121, 122,
123, 125, 129, 138, 140, 142,
144, 146, 150, 152, 154, 156,
158, 159, 160, 162, 163, 164,
173, 191 197, 199, 201,
219
alleviation by reclassification, 154
ascent from, 141
creation of wealth only solution,
141, 157
housing and squatting, 142, 143
lack of wealth generating structures, 143
outcome of government policy,
156
streak of fatalism, 140
structures that reinforce, 139, 150
poverty: dynamics of
breaking the cycle, 152
intergenerational socialization, 152

poverty: theories of
C Y Thomas's typology of poverty, 150
Galbraith's equilibrium of poverty,
150
Lindo's behavioural theory, 153
national response to threats, opportunities, 157
Power and *People*, 1, 2, 5, 6, 14, 192
domination of political parties,
64
interaction between, 14
interplay between, 4
medieval morality play, 2
power in organization
efficiency and effectiveness, 76
private sector
as dependent, 179
as engine of growth, 78, 179, 180
entrepreneurial or white knight
version, 178, 182
entrepreneurial vs mercantile, 96
low level of professionalism and
motivation, 79
the Marxist version, 178
motivation and perception, 179
notion of Jamaican private sector,
180
the real one – the ordinary
people, 177
theory of the private sector, 176
privilege and patronage
political connections, 42
Protestant Ethic and Spirit of Capitalism, 112
PSOJ
political pressure group, 183
rift with JCC, 183
survival and pressure group, 180

quality of life
high rates of suicide, 46
higher order needs. *See* economic
growth, development
social power vs education, 146

renegotiation of terms
  Moses Committee, Manley Bauxite Award, Barbados Protocol,
  5
Rodney, Walter, 4
role of males in society
  Marginalization of the Black Male,
  70

Sangster, Donald, 23, 24
scandals covered up
  National Investment Bank of
  Jamaica, 11
Seaga, Edward, 14, 22, 23, 24, 67,
  79, 81, 107, 162, 170, 171, 173,
  174, 179, 183, 202, 206, 207,
  209, 212, 220
  structural adjustment, 175
  structural adjustment of economy,
  79
Shakespeare, William
  The fault, dear Brutus, 4
Shearer, Hugh 23
Singapore, 4, 5, 6, 7, 8, 9, 10, 11,
  12, 13, 14, 15, 18, 21, 28, 31,
  35, 40, 44, 49, 53, 54, 60, 69,
  81, 87, 89, 93, 99, 111, 123,
  131, 148, 152, 169, 175, 185,
  191, 195, 199, 204, 217, 224
  style of development, feasibility, 10
  the reluctant model, 13
  Third World to First, 6, 174
solutions as problems
  illegal vending and tourism harassment, 144
state
  agent of social transformation,
  168
  critical aspects of role abandoned,
  193
  state and market imperfections,
  168

the developmental state (Rapley),
  176
Stone, Carl, 4, 38, 50, 54, 68, 72,
  79, 81, 88, 99, 112, 114, 122
  Work Attitudes Survey, 112
symptoms, treating the
  problems and solutions, 155
systems approach or systems theory
  creation of public opinion, 113
  formal vs informal systems, 185
  government as a system, 26
  single course thinking, 27

technological capability
  Girvan's six constituents, 213
tourism prospects
  saturation and diversion theories,
  145, 156

wealth creation, 11, 40, 49, 52, 90,
  91, 92, 93, 97, 98, 107, 131,
  162, 164, 172, 193, 201, 219
  debt used for speculative ventures,
  179
  incomeless society policy, 29
  participation of the people, 173,
  174
  preconditions for growth and
  development, 94
  production waves, 11
  welfare as substitute, 138
welfare orientation, 30, 31, 32, 40,
  53, 143, 163, 174, 201, 203, 207
  impact on productivity, 174
Westminster/Whitehall system
  colonial model of government,
  185
  functions and outcomes, 72
  unresponsive to Jamaican needs,
  66
Williams, Eric, 4
Witter, Michael, 3